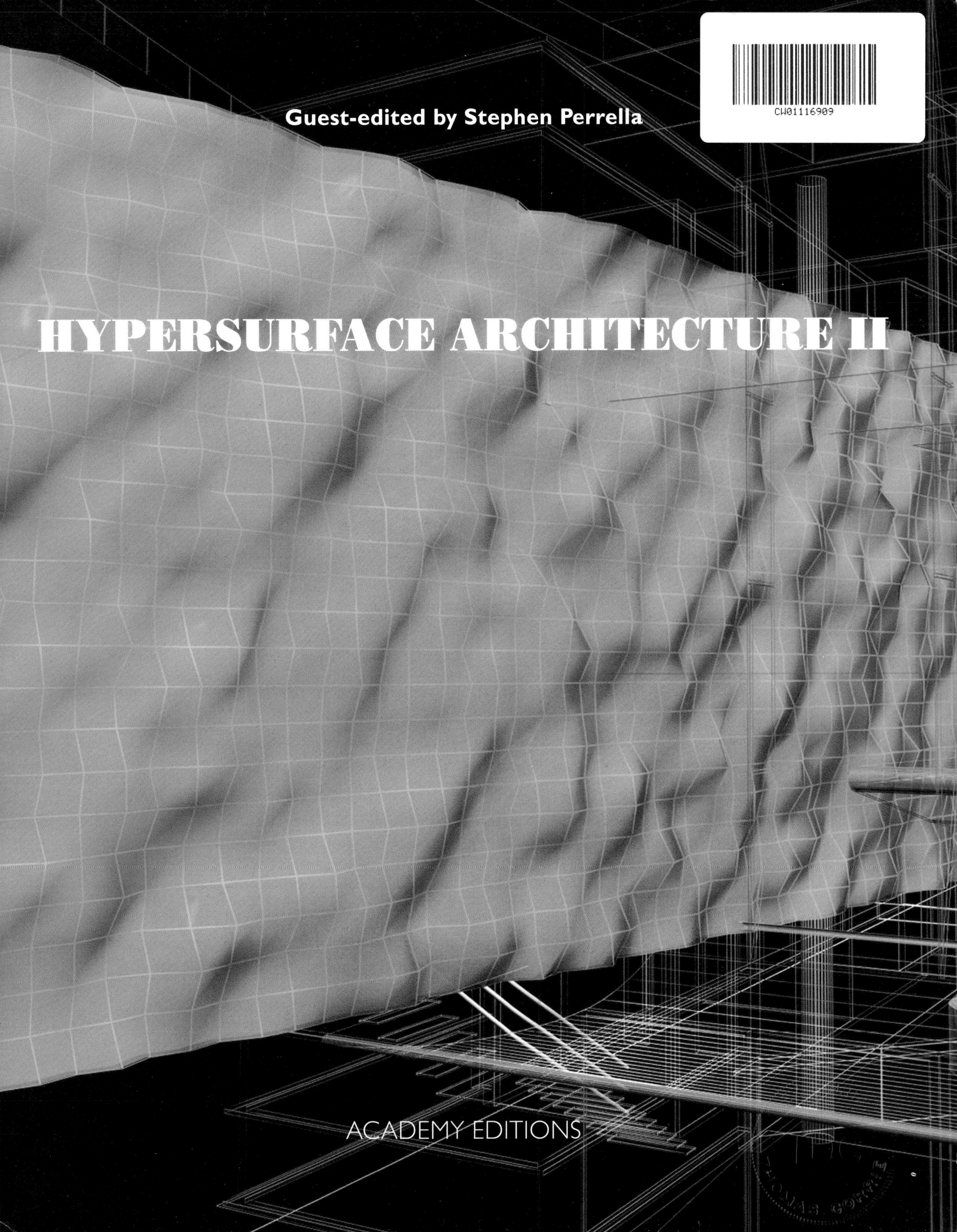

Guest-edited by Stephen Perrella

HYPERSURFACE ARCHITECTURE II

ACADEMY EDITIONS

editor Maggie Toy
managing editor Helen Castle
production Mariangela Palazzi-Williams
advertisement sales Jackie Sibley - Tel: 01243 843272

design Mario Bettella and Andrea Bettella/Artmedia

consultants Catherine Cooke, Terry Farrell, Kenneth Frampton, Charles Jencks, Heinrich Klotz, Leon Krier, Robert Maxwell, Demetri Porphyrios, Kenneth Powell, Colin Rowe, Derek Walker

EDITORIAL OFFICES 4th Floor, International House
Ealing Broadway Centre, London, W5 5DB
Tel: 0181 326 3800 Fax: 0181 326 3801

SUBSCRIPTION OFFICES:
UK John Wiley & Sons, Ltd
Journals Administration Department
1 Oldlands Way, Bognor Regis
West Sussex, PO22 9SA
Tel: 01243 843282 Fax: 01243 843232
e-mail: cs-journals@wiley.co.uk

USA AND CANADA John Wiley & Sons, Inc.
Journals Administration Department
605 Third Avenue, New York, NY 10158
Tel: + 1 212 850 6645 Fax: + 1 212 850 6021
cable jonwile telex: 12-7063
e-mail: subinfo@wiley.com

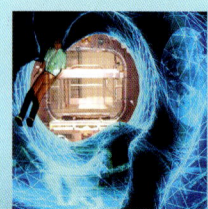

Photo Credits All material is courtesy of the authors and architects unless otherwise stated. Attempts have been made to locate the source of all images to obtain full reproduction rights, but in the very few cases where this process has failed to find the copyright holder, our apologies are offered. Cover: Kas Oosterhuis, Trans_Ports 2001. Photographic credits: p1 courtesy Mark Goulthorpe; pp6-7 courtesy Stephen Perrella: p8 © Cameron Robbins; p15 courtesy Relational Architecture, photos: Jorg Mohr; p18 courtesy Relational Architecture, photo: Dietmar Tollerind; p20: courtesy FTL happold; p22 courtesy Stephen Perrella and Rebecca Carpenter; p24 © Steven Holl Architects; p27 and p30 © Herzog & Meuron; pp33-37 courtesy Haresh Lalvani; pp38-49 courtesy Kurt Kulas, Associate of Broadcasting at WB Doner; p50 © Terry Rosenberg; p51 © Stephen Perrella and Terry Rosenberg; pp52-59 courtesy Nox; pp60-5 courtesy Mark Goulthorpe-Decoi; pp66-71 © Bernard Cache, photos: Patrick Renaud and Marie Combes; p77 courtesy Diller+Scofidio; pp78-83 courtesy Mark Burry; pp84-9 Kas Oosterhuis; p90-3 © ARS, NY and DACS, London 1999, photos: Steven Sloman, pp98-9 courtesy of the Royal National Theatre Press Office, photo: E Valette; pp100-1 Thea van den Heuvel; p102 (tl) courtesy Alison Brooks; p102 (br) courtesy of ABA, photo: C Kircherer; p103 (cl) courtesy ABA, photo: G Dagon; pp104-6 courtesy ABA; p109 (t) © Royal Commission on the Ancient and Historical Monuments of Scotland; p109 (b) © Scottish Media Newspapers Ltd; p112 courtesy Zvi Hecker.

First published in Great Britain by Academy Editions
a division of
JOHN WILEY & SONS
Baffins Lane, Chichester, West Sussex PO19 1UD

ISBN 0-471-99871-0
ISSN 0003-8504

Architectural Design vol 69 9-10/1999 Profile 141

Copyright © 1999 John Wiley & Sons, Ltd. All rights reserved. No part of this publication may be reproduced or transmitted in any form or by any means, electronic or mechanical, including photocopying, recording or any information storage or retrieval system without permission in writing from the Publishers. Neither the Editor nor John Wiley & Sons, Ltd hold themselves responsible for the opinions expressed by writers of articles or letters in this magazine. Copyright of articles and illustrations may belong to individual writers or artists. The Editor will give careful consideration to unsolicited articles, photographs and drawings; please enclose a stamped addressed envelope for their return (if required). Payment for material appearing in AD is not normally made except by prior arrangement. All reasonable care will be taken of material in the possession of AD and agents and printers, but they regret that they cannot be held responsible for any loss or damage.

ANNUAL SUBSCRIPTION RATES 1999: UK £135.00 (institutional rate), £90.00 (personal rate); Outside UK US$225.00 (institutional rate), $145.00 (personal rate). AD is published six times a year. Prices are for six issues and include postage and handling charges. Periodicals postage paid at Jamaica, NY 11431. Air freight and mailing in the USA by Publications Expediting Services Inc, 200 Meacham Ave, Elmont, Long Island, NY 11003.

SINGLE ISSUES: UK £18.99; Outside UK $29.95. Order two or more titles and postage is free. For orders of one title please add £2.00/$5.00. To receive order by air please add £5.50/$10.00.

All prices are subject to change without notice.

POSTMASTER: send address changes to AD, c/o Publications Expediting Services Inc, 200 Meacham Ave, Elmont, Long Island, NY 11003.

Printed in Italy

contents

50 Henry Wojdyla
Terry Rosenberg - Generatrix

51 Terry Rosenberg, Stephen Perrella and Henry Wojdyla
Hypersurface Analysis of 'Cool World'

52 Nox
Off the Road/103.8 MHZ
V2 Lab (Part of V2 Engine)
Deepsurface - The Unvisual Image

60 Mark Goulthorpe - Decoi
Aegis Hyposurface

66 Bernard Cache
Objectile

72 Marcos Novak
Eversion

77 Diller + Scofidio with Paul Lewis
Jump Cuts

78 Mark Burry
Paramorph

84 Kas Oosterhuis
Space Station Module
Trans_Ports 2001

90 Frank Stella

94 Biographies

4 Maggie Toy
Editorial

5 Stephen Perrella
Electronic Baroque

8 Pia Ednie-Brown
Falling into the Surface

12 Brian Massumi
Strange Horizon

20 Rebecca Carpenter
Force Affect

26 Giovanna Borradori
Against the Technological Interpretation of Virtuality

32 Haresh Lalvani
Meta Architecture

38 Stephen Perrella
Commercial Value and Hypersurface

40 Greg Seigworth
Protegulum

48 Charlie Watson
Cool World

AD Plus

97 Howard Watson
Beyond Expression?

100 Helen Castle
Organic Ablutions

102 Practice Profile
ABA

107 Helen Castle
Shaping a Generation

108 Miles Glendinning
Private Lives, Public Lives

110 Book Reviews

112 Site Lines
Circular Thoughts

EDITORIAL
MAGGIE TOY

Since Architectural Design published 'Hypersurface Architecture I', over a year ago, there has been a wealth of innovations and new explorations. The first edition clearly presented an analysis of contemporary culture that identified two simultaneous and interpenetrating trends. On the one hand there was the confines of avant-garde architecture and on the other there were the practices of everyday commerce. 'Hypersurface Architecture II' demonstrates the convergence of these two forces that radicalises form and deterritorialises subjectivity and investigates further the way in which effects emerge within and around architecture. For this second issue, Stephen Perrella has once again collected together an impressive array of designers, innovators and projects that demonstrate the expanding field of hypersurface theory. The continuing need to stretch the boundaries of architecture in every direction is being satisfied with this relatively new exploration. The existence and possibilities that begin with the computer, and its expansive opportunities, are being explored by many. The direction taken by Perrella and others included in this issue shows a potential new way forward for architects, perhaps a solution for many who are looking for positive methods by which to fully utilise the techniques open to them.

Rebecca Carpenter discusses the ideas of events in architecture and how the construction of space can be the result of topological transformations. Architecture ceases to be a backdrop for actions, becoming an action itself. This helps define the properties of the subject. Brian Massumi continues his argument from the first issue, as well as opening a different argument in discussing the sense in the paperless studio and the growing familiarity with technology. He spotlights what is rotten on the shelf of spatial-awareness theory and suggests a way forward and around these issues. Massumi defines and illustrates the many discussions and terms created by hypersurface theory and presents them in an exciting and graspable language. He also explains the complexities of the synaesthetes and perceivers contribution to the ideas behind the notions demonstrated, leaving the reader reeling with intrigue. Giovanna Borradori draws against the technological interpretation of virtuality explaining that in architecture as in philosophy the representationalist approach entails a conception of the new as foreseeable possibility whereas by contrast, from a perspectivist angle, novelty corresponds to the actualisation of virtual presences: presences virtually contained in the real, but not yet actualised. Nietzschean interpretations are used to assist this comprehensive analysis. As in the last issue, the brilliant work of Marcus Novak draws in the observer with the imagination of the imagery and with the philosophies that aid their creation, which are equally as hypnotic. The brilliance of this combination clearly demonstrates that he is one of the world leaders in this field. The work of Nox Architecture, the group, consolidates this by showing the development made in realising this architecture, quelling earlier arguments that the ritual and the real are by nature conflicting. Their schemes for domestic and traffic barring, as well as a laboratory, display and inspirational medley of imaginary and reality. Decoi architects were not included in the previous edition, but their contribution here, ëAegis Hyposurfaceí, adds yet another component to this complex area by exploring the shifts in architectural production from a psychological perspective. The trauma of the ongoing cultural adaptation of society to an electronic environment is analysed, placing emphasis on the positive environment that can evolve. Their project work displays an inventive use of the computer environment. Haresh Lalvani discusses meta-Architecture and the manipulation of morphologically structured information, via algorithms and genetic codes. Lalvani suggests a method by which the architect could be liberated from the building process as an artificial genetic code enables growth, adaptation, evolution and replication of buildings, permitting architecture to design itself. Perhaps this is the future of the collaborative use of computers within architectural design.

Overall this issue shows that this new movement has established itself as a new force within architecture and investigation, breaking new boundaries and hatching new ideas and directions. As the refining of digital construction and manufacturing systems means that much which had previously remained conjective or ritual can be built, those such as Lalvaniand his fellow exponents continue to project themselves forwards to a future that will fully grasp the potential that fast developing technologies present.

STEPHEN PERRELLA
ELECTRONIC BAROQUE
Hypersurface II: Autopoeisis

'Our perceptions give us the plan of our eventual action on things much more than that of things themselves. The outlines we find in objects simply mark what we can attain and modify in them. The lines we see traced through matter are just the paths on which we are called to move. Outlines and paths have declared themselves in the measure and proportion that consciousness has prepared for action on unorganised matter – that is to say, in the measure and proportion that intelligence has been formed.'

Henri Bergson[1]

What's a hypersurface?[2]

The projects produced out of the general thesis of hypersurface architecture entail new relations and affects between media (inclusive of both print and the electronic) and topological surfaces in architecture. As stated in the first issue of 'Hypersurface Architecture', published last year, experimentation a decade ago with computer workstations using animation software, revealed uncanny possibilities for the relations between form and image. Any form whatsoever could be textured with any image – whatsoever. It seemed imminent that a widespread use of this new technology would unleash a new dimension of effects because there is realm of potential relations between image and form. Currently and historically, however, the relations between image and form are superposed schizophrenically.

An analysis of the built environment reveals a systematic deployment of commercial images connected and controlled by the interests of consumer capitalism leading to a system of representation. The media image is a logic that has little to do with architecture and the way architecture thinks about itself. On the other hand architecture as a discipline has varying schools of thought on how architectural form is an image, but for the most part, architecture is about form. Over the last decade or so, the electronic era is transforming these two polarities: image and form, each from within its own context. While new technology is taking media into an unbounded zone we know as cyberspace, architectural form is also coming to question its Cartesian foundations. These two simultaneous trends, what may be called 'hyper' (media) and 'surface' (topological architecture), have not yet been considered in relation to one another. This is because each calls the other into question. If each dimension, image and form comes with its own disciplinary logic, for example two-D and three-D, then when each questions the other, neither two-D or three-D are adequate concepts to explain the new interdynamic. This is why hypersurfaces may be important to many of the new effects that we are seeing today, as the unravelling of the world of the image enmeshes with the unfolding of form into the image. When I least expect it, I notice minor, sporadic developments of hypersurface in precise surroundings in variegated contexts. It subtly slips into everyday life and is hardly perceptible. One almost has to work backwards to see from where hypersurfaces are being initiated, but it seems to be enlivened by the implosion of three-dimensional action, fuelled by the density of commercialism, (the onrush of consumerism-as-force) coupled with the connections, lightning-like, between things.

For instance, the other day when I went looking to purchase a camera, a film shop that I ventured into had one specific camera announcing a new advanced film system. Being a bit fussy, I made them explain the significance of this film as opposed to going with a digital camera. The shop owner enthusiastically brought out a large glossy image that was fairly impressive in its clarity and depth. He said it had to do with a three-dimensionality within the chemical make-up of the film. Quietly stunned, I noted this prime example of how, in everyday consumerism, and with the incessant march of the development of technology, hypersurfaces unfold. This seemingly minor evolvement of the three-D within the realm of two-D imaging establishes a new layer of connective dimensional infrastructure and is how hypersurfaces are filling out the middle. What is really remarkable about the example though, is that it was in the chemistry. In retrospect, it seems foolish to argue for any kind of foundationalism in the face of this phenomenal infilling, especially since it seems so difficult to make anything meaningful in architecture today. It is not surprising also, that I find examples and developments contributing to ways of working with hypersurfaces among a selection of our colleagues's work. What I value in their work are the careful progressions they are making in finding ways to make this new 'withinness' more vigorous, more engaging.

It strikes me too, that if I am rigorous about this infilling of the middle, that there might be enough 'flesh' in what was once a dialectical void for there to be another way for us to begin considering how things become meaningful. In other words, if all modes of connections are being made, in multiplicate contexts within our world, then at a certain point, there might be a logic of connections superseding the mostly polarised logics that currently exist. An almost mundane example would be the links between sites within the worldwide Web, where amid the density of content and language, exists this immense web of connectivity. The associative drift (surfing) that occurs as a result becomes a way of being on the web. But because this emergence-of-connection occurs on many different levels, what may be most significant for architecture might be what occurs between the realms of media and of materiality.

So, without sounding too apocalyptic or even delirious, it seems to me that what may be building-up within this in-between zone that we have been calling hypersurface, is a more direct interface between thought and matter. Could it be, that we are working here to describe minute transitions leading to a switch-over point, whereby new relations between media and matter change the possibilities for thought? If so, then consider the detrimental role that architecture will play in that. Martin Heidegger

Stephen Perrella with Tony Wong and Ed Keller, Studio AEM, Institute of Electronic Clothing, *1990*

Marquee at 1500 Broadway in Times Square. Photo by S. Perrella, 1999

Stephen Perrella, The Virtual Corporation, *1993*

once called language the 'House of Being'. That describes 'Being' nicely, but it rather privileges an immaterial realm. So today we might ask, what is the 'House of Being' if the material house is infused and interfaced with language?

Why is the world of the sign so disassociated from the world of materiality? How is it that these two realms run parallel to each other, having little actual relation, yet creates what is essentially our built surround? Is it that everywhere we look there is this division, or is it in our way of looking that constitutes it? Can we approach this another way?

With varying degrees of inhabitability, a hypersurface is the envelopment of exchanges between human agency and matter. Hypersurface is a zone of exchange between consciousness (language or text) and levels of the inorganic. Hypersurface requires reciprocal relations where exchanges are the operative principle. These exchanges are intensities stemming from multiple planes of imminence. Considering that the gene and the bit are not yet and may never be unified, we must settle for relations between these two worlds, and there are all manner of relations. There are innumerable ways of considering the interweavings between media and matter but the predominant logics are dialectically and dualistically divided, something deeply written into cultural habit.

What can be made of these divisions? Are they harmless or are they denigrating? Where to begin in asking this question? Answer: in the middle, middle-out. What middle, middle of what? Answer: any place is already the middle, the middle is always already presupposed in the framing of the question. How to work from the middle-out? Answer: focus on the issue of relations and forget the frame, remember there is no originating point to the middle to adhere to or give reference. This is to speak of a plane of imminence. A surface whereby effects are completely determined through systems of exchange.

Hypersurface is the word we are using to describe any set of relationships that behave as systems of exchange. A system of exchange that when physically constituted as the present is the presupposition of one set of points or the dynamic deformation of the space of one set of points into the adjacent set of points in the production of the new. The presupposition of the set of points is not simply a construction of successive points but the coexistence of the two. The coexistence of the two means that both stretch out alongside each other disassociated but always in combination when they emerge into the present. We can write pairs of points that describe this dynamic; past–present, image–form, two-D/three-D, memory/matter and so forth. Animation offers the potential to actualise these constructions as the present by stopping time in a two-D frame, yet it also offers the potential to experience the surplus space of its transformation, the literal coexistence of differential geometries as movement, like image and form.

This is the geometry of topological transformation where all the complexity of the coexistence of relations is held within the singular flatness of a vertical plane, a plane loaded with excess experience, overly abstract and abundant with information. We can pull-out, pop-out, leave-out, splice out, but the moment we do we are not describing hypersurface any more we are talking about a static figure, definable in relation to, but not the fullness of the shared figure. Hypersurface is after the shared figure, the set of relations in their coexistence, the excess and the experience of this excess.

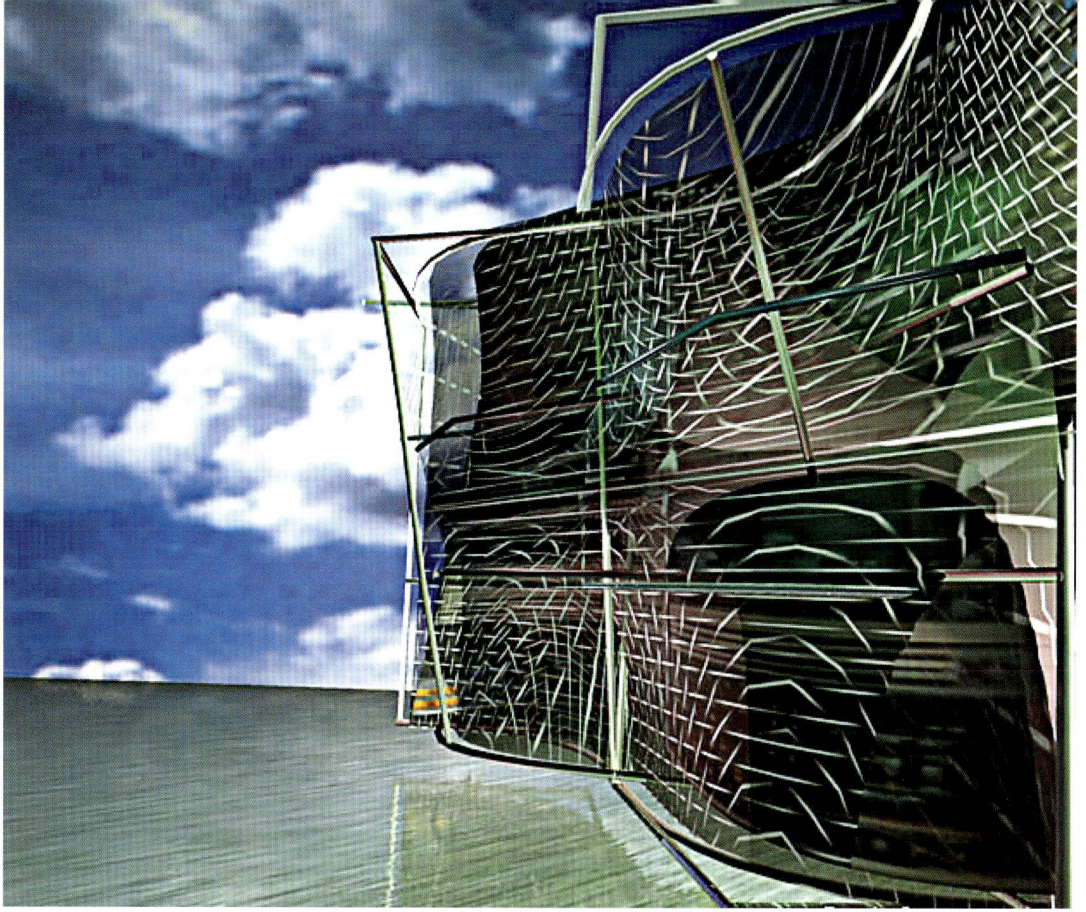

Stephen Perrella, Us, 1998

Notes
1 *Creative Evolution*, Arthur Mitchell (trans), Dover Publications (Mineola, New York), p188.
2 Quoted from a check-out clerk at a local foodstore upon reading the company name on my credit card.

References
Beckmann, John (ed), *The Virtual Dimension: Architecture, Representation, and Crash Culture*, Princeton Architectural Press (New York) 1998 (see my essay, 'Socius Fluxus').
Braidotti, *Rose Patterns of Dissonance: A Study of Women in Contemporary Philosophy*, Routledge (London and New York), 1991.
DeLanda, Manuel, 'Non Organic Life', ZONE Incorporations.
Dienst, Richard, *Still Life in Real Time: Theory after Television*, Duke University Press (Durham and London), 1994. See chapter two on 'Image/Machine/Image: Marx and Metaphor in Television Theory' is very good on Marx and 'machinery' 'value,' and 'circulation'. The last chapter 'Ineluctable Modalities of the Televisual' is on Deleuze and Guattari.
du Gay, Paul (ed), *Production of Culture/Cultures of Production*, Series: Culture, Media and Identities, vol 4, SAGE Ltd. Published in association with The Open University, 1997.
Hartz Michael and Gilles Deleuze, *An Apprenticeship in Philosophy*, Univ. of Minnesota Press (Minneapolis), 1993 (see last chapter 'Parallelism').
Holland, Eugene, *Deleuze and Guattari's Anti-Oedipus: Introduction to Schizoanalysis*, Routledge (London and New York), 1999.
Lazzarato, Maurizio, 'Immaterial Labor', Paolo Virno and Michael Hardt (eds), *A Potential Politics: Radical Thought in Italy*, Theory Out of Bounds Series, vol 12, University of Minnesota Press (Minneapolis, London).
Levy, Pierre, *Becoming Virtual: Reality in the Digital Age*, translated from the French by Robert Bononno, Plenum Press (New York),1998.
Jameson, Frederic, 'Marxism and Dualism in Deleuze', edited by Ian Buchanan, *A Deleuzian Century?* South Atlantic Quarterly 96:3, Summer 1997. This is useful for an understanding of 'axiomatic' and flux/flow and code.
Massumi, Brian, *A User's Guide to Capitalism and Schizophrenia: Deviations from Deleuze and Guattari*, The MIT Press (Cambridge, Mass), 1992.
Morse, Margaret, *Virtualities: Television, Media Art, and Cyberculture*, Theories of Contemporary Culture, Univ Press, 1998.
Riley, Terrence (ed), 'The Un-Private House', catalogue to the exhibition at The Museum of Modern Art, 1999.
Rodowick, DN *Gilles Deleuze's Time Machine*, Duke University Press (Durham and London), 1997.

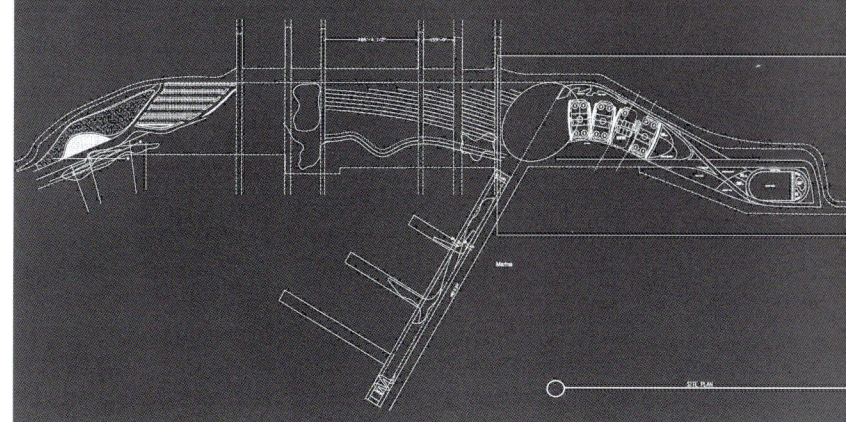

Stephen Perrella with Louis Wein, Henry Wojdyla, Dennis Pang, Paul Cumming and Frank Scicchitano of Ellerbe Beckett, Staten Island Homeport Redesign/HarbourFest, 1998-99

ACKNOWLEDGEMENTS
I am grateful for the continued encouragement and support of Bernard Tschumi and the Columbia University GSAP. The kind efforts of Karen Ocaña who translated the Bernard Cache's text is greatly appreciated. I thank Louis Wein for his efforts in the Staten Island homeport project, toward actualizing hypersurface architecture. And to Sara Foster of Rhythm & Hues for her extraordinary concerns and effort in helping out with our Mazda, Cool World collaboration. To Rebecca Carpenter for her belief in my ideas. Rebecca, this issue is dedicated to you. To Ciro Asperti, Clair Cipriani for their friendship and undying support. To Daniel Pavlovits, Henry Wojdyla, Dennis Pang and Paul Cumming for their service as assistants and for their energetic investments in my theoretical project. To Stelarc for his interest in future collaborations. To Jose Sanchez for his assistance with computers. To Susan Sanders, Greg Siegworth and Leonard Ragouzeos and Pia Ednie-Brown for their interest and support in my recent lectures that helped to clarify my ideas. And most recently, thanks to Lori Andreozi, for her ability to help take hypersurface theory into the marketplace.
Stephen Perrella

PIA EDNIE-BROWN
FALLING INTO THE SURFACE
Towards a Materiality of Affect

Hypersurfacing becomes a matter of provoking an amplification of barely perceptible movements such that the actual surface bears an even more pronounced expression of these conditions of emergence. It is important that the virtuality is felt. Some kind of stimulus is required to open up architectural processes across an expanded, sensitised field.

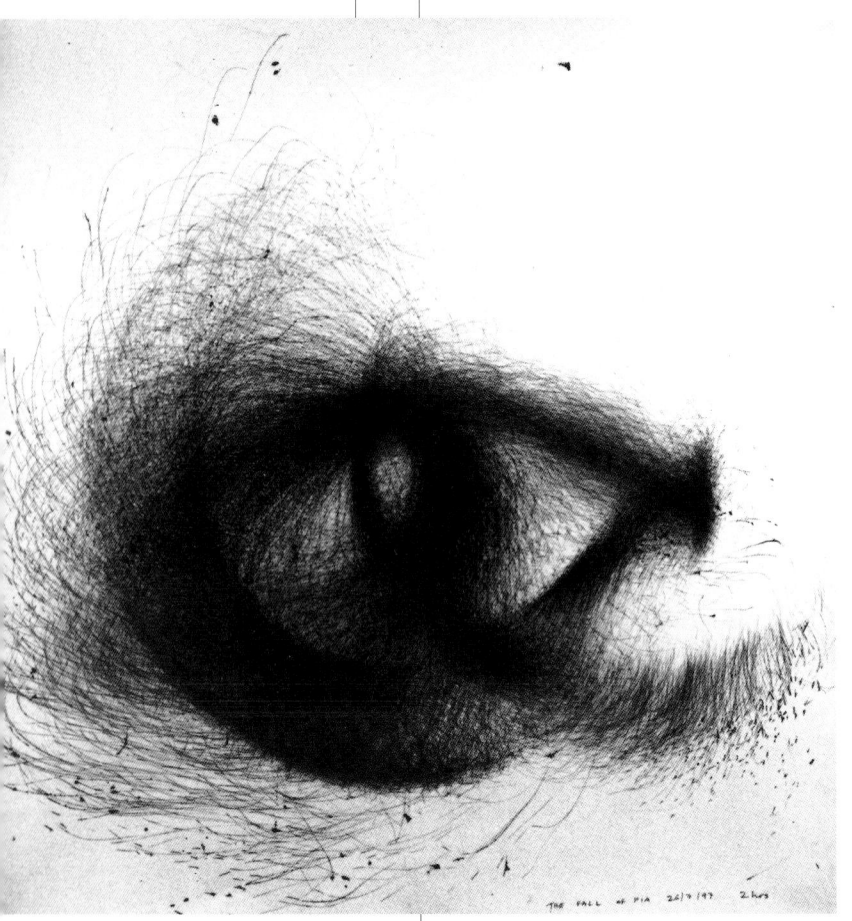

Cameron Robbins, The Fall of Pia, *1997*

Motionless on the surface, in its very depth it lives and vibrates.[1]

The discipline of architecture is constantly concerned with the effectual nature of its processes of production. It struggles with the co-ordination of the variegated and complex field of forces that come into play in the creation of a building. Ultimately, the imperative is to sustain its effective consequentiality. The security of its stature and relevance has relied on a maintenance of belief in the significance of form. Architectural history presents a catalogue of renovations and additions to the structure of its rhetoric of authority. The shifts driving the processes of history's architectural undertakings have pivoted on the import of form.

Lately, the 'virtual' has risen to the surface of architectural discourse through the reverberative tremor of prevailing cultural desires. The term is often used as convenient, attractive packaging aimed at consumptive desires for increased mobility while, paradoxically, keeping mobility contained and vacuum packed. In a climate of cultural production that invests explicit movement with sovereign value, the insistent stasis of buildings has been absurdly claimed to signal the imminent obsolescence of architecture. The foundations of authority upon which architecture has curated itself have begun to crack.

The challenge of how design processes could be re-articulated to address active engagements with the virtual has become a source of experimentation. Reactionary efforts towards re-valuation have at times evoked the Emperor in his (virtual) new clothes: sensational, but forgetting actual sensation. The opportunities presented to contemporary architecture are not to be found in a subservience to illusions of this kind. Rather, they lie in the manner with which the operations of architectural practices realign their affiliation with the concrete actuality of buildings as an engagement with the virtual.

Brian Massumi, in his text 'Sensing the Virtual, Building the Insensible',[2] asks the question: 'what philosophy can or might enter into a symbiosis with architectures engaging with the virtual . . . ?', calling up 'radical' or 'superior' empiricism as the answer. He goes on to suggest that, 'For architecture, the effect of such a symbiosis is a willingness to bring into even more pronounced expression its processual dimensions.'[3] Design and construction processes are always insinuated in the building itself. As that which steers their formation, they are never *not* expressed – even if unconsciously. It is the 'willingness' and the 'even more pronounced' of Massumi's suggestion that become the imperatives. This essay attempts to articulate modalities through which these imperatives may be addressed.

The manner in which radical empiricism expresses the virtual *within* lived experience, as always insinuated in actual events, imbricates it with the actuality and solidity of buildings. This holds great potential for the development of architectural practices in that the conceits produced by dichotomous logic can be productively redressed. Where there can be no actuality without the virtual, stasis no longer points to a death (of architecture) but to an invigoration of the zone of potential that plays around the concrete. This impacts directly upon the limits and dimensions of processuality, as it involves a shift in the arrangements with which the modalities of practice can engage with the virtual. Contrary to a placement of events according to a division between supposedly exclusive terms – form and social praxis, for example – there is a more subtle intertwinement, which, in as much as it still presents a division, has itself been realigned. As Philip Goodchild writes: 'The fundamental division is no longer that between the subjective and the objective, the mental and the material, artifice and nature, but between spontaneity and receptivity: the power to affect and the power to be affected'.[4] This shift invigorates the potentiality of the relationships themselves.

Within these folded realignments, Massumi's suggestion can be seen to have simultaneous relevance to both processes of design and experiential processes involved in the 'completed' building itself. This fundamental issue of radical empiricism challenges architectural discourse, which has a blithe tendency to regard anything after the closure of construction and prior to an appearance in the pages of a historical text to be outside the interest and authority of the discipline. This gap in disciplinary attention has arisen in tandem with the hold maintained by subjectivity on questions of experience. In humanist models of subjectivity, the subject, the perceiver, holds the balance of power (to affect and be affected). The building (or object) falls into a realm of unspeakable action in that it cannot be contained by authoritative moulds. Radical empiricism invites an effort both to acknowledge and to realign these otherwise silent but nevertheless inscriptive affects. Significantly, the restructuring of relationships with which this effort is undertaken is set up so that acknowledgments of the virtual do not fall back into the insistent banality of disciplinary authority. The task is to release life (the virtual) wherever it may be trapped.

Radical empiricism calls up this challenge through a vastly expanded notion of subjectivity that invites architecture to stretch out and test its processual limits. Félix Guattari set out the extended limits of this refigured subjectivity in his final book, *Chaosmosis: An Ethico-Aesthetic Paradigm*, in which he writes:

> How are the new fields of the possible going to be fitted out? How are sounds and forms going to be arranged so that the subjectivity adjacent to them remains in movement, and really alive?[5]

Embedded within this passage is a radical (empirical) twist. The problem is not subjective uncertainty but how subjectivity is kept alive; how significance can be released from the classical moulds of objectivity. Objectivity is merely fixed subjectivity: the subjective forced still. The life of subjectivity is not simply in the shifts of an interpretative field, but the operations of a set of engagements, a 'machinic assemblage'. Here, the subjective is not 'originated' in an individual, rather, it is produced through the transitory assemblages of a vast array of impersonal forces.

These assemblages crystallise or precipitate through a twist onto a surface that expresses the textures of perception. In turning to touch, to make sense of this tactility, these emergent, textural signs are contracted into tools of action. The act of contraction divides this information into distinct modalities whereupon perception emerges and reconverges as geometrical, reasonable forms of appearance. Subjectivity moves about these contractions and dilations of the processes of surfacing. Designing arrangements that may actively keep subjectivity alive falls back on setting out the conditions or parameters of processes that are themselves open and mobile.

Forming Habits

Architectural practice has a tendency to establish the visualisation of form as the primary condition enabling processes of design. Form, as an exercise in itself, untied from the specificities of durational presence (matter), is linked to the status of geometry as an idealised phenomenon. Geometrical laws appear as universal truths cut free from temporality and the affective dimensions of historicity. An equilateral triangle was the same for Pythagoras as it is for us today. As an idea, geometry arrives as an already-made, an unchanging set of truths that simply exist, apparently prior to and separate from perception. In the work of French philosopher Henri Bergson, there is an effort to turn back upon the conditions within which geometry emerges. Geometry and form are thereby rendered as contingent, undermining their claim to universality. As Bergson writes: 'the universe is not made, but is being made continually'.[6]

Perception of space and form is defined by what Bergson calls a 'virtual geometry'. In *Creative Evolution* he explains:

> You cannot present this space to yourself without introducing, in the same act, a virtual geometry which will, of itself, degrade itself into logic . . . space cannot be given without positing also logic and geometry, which are along the course of the movement of which pure spatial intuition is the goal.[7]

Form, arrived at through logical interpolations upon virtual geometries, becomes a habit secreted from memory: empirical information accumulates in mnemonic refrains and inscribes itself through patterns of perception. Pure form, on the other hand, as an idealised, static geometry, violates memory through a suppression of its power to affect; it is a ready-made set of laws of dry and seemingly autonomous consistency. These laws are so consistent that they insist on being (true) and defy the transformative impulse of becoming. Bergson suggests that consciousness must 'detach itself from the *already-made* and attach itself to the *being-made*'[8] in order for it to engage with the principles of its emergence. Already-made laws tend to restrain the perceived from flowing out of strictly delimited moulds, and train it to abrogate the shifts that rustle across the surface of perception. They maintain an impeccable garden in which new life is already tame, and unplanned emergence is outlawed.

When architects design primarily through the manipulation of form, they tend to assume the already-made of form itself. Particular forms will emerge, but will lose potential dimensions of mobility in the process. This is no less the case in the movements of morphing computer animations than in orthogonal extrusions of floor plans. How might architectural practice turn back and attach itself to the being-made of form? How can form affect and be affected by movements not already contained within the parameters of a form-driven process? This requires a departure from processual habits, venturing instead into a sensitised field.

Becoming Sensitive

The operations of this sensitised field can be usefully illustrated by Massumi's account of warm water:

> If heat is increased at a certain rate, a threshold is reached at which order spontaneously arises out of chaos. The liquid differentiates. Certain regions turn in on themselves, 'nucleate', form fluid boundaries. Whirlpools form: convection currents. These vortices appear because the liquid is under another constraint besides the command to regain equilibrium through thermodiffusion. That second constraint is gravity . . . In the process, the liquid became 'sensitive'. The effect of gravity on a liquid at rest is normally negligible, but in its agitated state, the liquid suddenly 'perceived' it and was transformed.[9]

Here, the process of becoming sensitive involves the awareness or perception of an otherwise relatively latent presence. The vortices swirl the liquid into a moment of intensive order so that the entire body of water becomes highly co-ordinated and 'any chance disturbance that might occur in one area will immediately be "felt" everywhere'.[10] A set of relations are at once articulated, and this is what the idea of pure form seeks to obliterate: namely, the conditions of its emergence.

Think of a moment in which instability arises. Say, for instance, you teeter and fall – or almost fall. The experience is one in which the sensation of gravity lurches forward as an amplified presence. This can be completely overwhelming – as if an invisible hand has thrown you. Commonsense falls apart as the senses fall together into the realm of sensation. You become integrated and dispersed across a singularly co-ordinated gesture. The limits of the subject become uncertain. Subjectivity becomes sensitive.

Typically, gravity is the habitually ensconced forgotten of the upright world. Deeply implicated in the formation of all our habits, gravity is a critical dimension in the processes and organisation of perception. According to Buckminster Fuller, 'Gravity is the inside outness of energy-as-matter: the integrity of Universe'.[11] It is the vital pulse. Things fall, but the fall is one into potentiality as much as a falling down to the ground. A fall into the surface is a leap of potentiality. It entails both the rise and fall of affect. A willingness to fall is an openness to the power to affect and be affected. The categories of the animate (life) and the inanimate (matter) necessarily fall into one another. As Bergson writes:

> The vision we have of the material world is that of a weight which falls: no image drawn from matter, properly so called, will ever give us the idea of the weight rising. But this conclusion will come home to us with greater force if we press nearer to the concrete reality, and if we consider, no longer only matter in general, but, within this matter, living bodies.[12]

The passing of 'living bodies' through matter can be as simple as heat through water. 'Living' is not simply an attribute of organisms, for it subsists in all matter. Living becomes a virtual reality. The life that passes is the reality of change. Both water and heat, in falling into one another, are mutually affected. The event of becoming sensitive is an intensification in the power of change. Something extra is perceived. This extra dimension was always there, but not yet *explicitly* active, not yet becoming explicit, in the changes occurring in the system.

Design processes that become sensitive have the potential to make far more explicit processual dimensions. Where process itself is open to the perception of otherwise implicit dimensions, it becomes capable of 'even more pronounced expression of its processual dimensions'.

Hypersurfacing

Rearticulating classical divisions of architectural design is at the basis of Stephen Perrella's Hypersurface theory: 'Hypersurfaces are an interweaving and subsequent unlocking of culturally instituted dualities.'[13] In attempting to situate the development of this theory in relation to the imperatives investigated here, the hypersurface can be twisted into a roaming verb so as to encounter the potentiality of its actions. It becomes a useful expression of the becoming explicit of extra-dimensionality.

'Surface', in common parlance, is generally understood as the exterior boundary of things, the outer skin of any object. In this sense, surfaces are actual, material, textural entities that are the most directly *felt* aspects of the world. They are that which we directly encounter. The surface is also taken to be something that conceals: 'it was not what it appeared to be on the surface'. It is when things surface that they become evident; they appear out of a previously concealed latency. Surfacing is an action of becoming explicit, of becoming experientially apparent in a movement from virtuality to actuality – of becoming expressed across the limits of perception. Surfacing is the process of becoming perceptible and actual.

To be 'hyper' is to be overexcited, super-stimulated, excessive, on edge. This state of intensity is a mode of over-being: an excess of being in that the processes of becoming exceed constraints to existence. Things foam at the edges. The 'hyper', when conjoined with 'surface', turns up the volume on emergence: it is a becoming more than simply explicit, an 'even more pronounced expression [of] its processual dimensions'. Between the explicit act and the myriad of potential acts, consciousness[14] finds its emanative expression. Hypersurfacing unleashes the surface into bearing witness to an even more pronounced expression of the conditions of emergence. Hypersurfacing is an act of falling into the surface.

Fallibility: Tending Towards a Materiality of Affect

In a moment of intensive rupture, such as falling, the body twists open into an extra-dimensionality, attaining an extensivity than renders both the 'self' and the object highly contingent. A release from absolute valuations of self and objecthood is implicit in the imperative of willingness, as Massumi suggests. Engagements with the virtual are amplified with a porousness across which an active folding out and infolding can become operational. Through a willingness to fall open, the play of the dice throw[15] is admitted into the dimensions of processuality. Chance events can enact their regenerative impulse. The release from the primacy of the human subject, fundamental to the efforts of radical empiricism, enables the potentiality of an event as an arrangement of connectibilty. As Massumi writes:

> What is virtual is the connect*ibility*: potential (the reality of change). It cannot be overemphasised that the virtual is less the connection than its -ibility.[16]

The 'fall into the surface' is not exclusively a falling *down*, it is an opening out into the readiness for change, into a sensitivity to potentiality. This leads to the articulation of a tendency that I will call fall*ibility*; an admittance of errant ways. Fallibility becomes an imperative of 'willingness'.

A useful model for the arrangement of processes that address this imperative can be found in the wind-drawing machine of artist Cameron Robbins, which performs through mechanisms driven by the speed and direction of the air. Working within certain tendencies and patterns, all the drawings produced by this simple machine express the specificity of their duration. Each has its own enigmatic quality. The action of the mechanism is such that the ink tends to be marked out more or less within a circular outer limit. 'More or less' because the machine is sensitive enough for chance to cut in; for the intensities of forces to throw the pen into paroxysms of leaping that extend beyond the provisional limits of its less intensified paths; for rain to splatter and spread the ink; for things to go 'wrong' so that the unexpected will emerge.

No attempt is made to control the environment in which the act of production takes place: rather than enveloping the process with an authorial container, the processual engagements are granted a spontaneous dimensionality of life. That which is designed is the mechanism of perception: the in-built receptivity that renders explicit the forces within which perception endures. The process of production is open and sensitive to the specificities and complexities of its duration. That which is made explicit is the interplay of affects in the lived experience of the mechanism 'out for a walk'.[17]

The prevailing trend in architectural practice is to establish a processual relationship in which intended or at least partly preconceived formal outcomes direct the paths of production. Within the wind-drawing process this relationship becomes inverted. The process of production, within mutable limits, governs the formal outcome. In turn, form itself takes on an expanded ontology. As an expression of affects at play in the process of formation, form takes on its own materiality. Materiality is no longer subservient to the desires of a designated form.

This more expansive, durational notion of form can thereby be understood as the materiality of affect. As much as this materiality is of insistent virtuality, it is implicit to the actual. Form gathers an extra-dimension of expression. The vast array of impersonal forces productive of subjectivity actualises into a consistency expressive of manifold duration. Rather than form being enmeshed with humanist models of perception, it is gathered through the engagement of potentiality.

Design experimentations aiming for engagements with the virtual might depart from their current impasse of nostalgia should they turn their processual arrangements away from form and the movement of form, and instead toward processes that are themselves open and mobile. This does not mean designing morphic architecture. Rather, it involves a willingness to break out of self-perpetuating habits. Through modes of fallibility, experiments can expand their processual dimensions and propel them into even more pronounced expressions. What then may emerge are buildings that emanate in a materiality of affect.

A Final Admission (A Falling Open)
Art does not reproduce the visible; rather, it makes visible.[18]
Subsisting throughout these words is a particular event, of a certain extra-dimensional quality, which took place in 1997. It is both the connectibility of this text and the fallibilty that underwrites it.

Cameron Robbins accompanied myself and the students of a design studio I conducted at RMIT on a trip to the southernmost shoreline of Australia. It was a site of wind-driven intensity. Shortly after arrival, Cameron set the machine into action and we walked around the cape. At one stage, we reached a fence. In a clumsy attempt to climb over, I fell. In the moment of losing balance, it felt as if I was pushed; as if a strong, invisible hand had loomed up from behind and thrown me. In falling I lost myself; any sense of 'I' was dissolved in a far greater impulsion. My surroundings collapsed; exteriority became articulated only as an antinomy of stasis. Time stretched and dissolved into an expanded flight of perplexity. It wasn't until after hitting the ground that I managed to gather a clear comprehension of the event: I had fallen. Sitting up, I faced an audience of shocked faces, their anaemic hue registering the gash in my chin. My body had become the machine through which gravity made its extra mark. Cameron and the students went back to the machine to see what had been produced. They discovered that part of the mechanism had been blown over in our absence. The drawing itself was somewhat unusual (the machine having been altered with its fall), strangely resembling an eye. Musing on the apparent simultaneity of falls, Cameron titled it *The Fall of Pia*: an exfoliation off the scaly surface of authoritarian certainty. The coincidence of the falls and the uncanny appearance of the eye produced a palpable sense of some virtual form – a becoming explicit of a materiality of affect – designed in partnership perhaps with 'Dionysus snickering at fate as he steals an extra turn'.[19]

It would be easy to think of the fall in terms of genetically coded clumsiness. Instead, for reasons of an uncertain nature, I'm inclined to see it as a pure event of fallibility.

Notes
Thanks to Ned Rossiter for his generous and invaluable contributions to this text, and to Robyn Barnacle, Brent Allpress, Peter Morse and Stephen Perrella.
1 Henri Bergson, *Matter and Memory*, Margaret Paul and W Scott Plamer (trans.), Zone Books (New York), 1991, p204.
2 Brian Massumi, 'Sensing the Virtual, Building the Insensible', *AD: Hypersurface Architecture*, vol 68, no 5/6. Academy Editions (London), 1998, pp22–3.
3 Ibid, p23.
4 Philip Goodchild, *Deleuze and Guattari: An Introduction to the Politics of Desire*, Sage Publications (London), 1996, p27.
5 Félix Guattari, *Chaosmosis: An Ethico-Aesthetic Paradigm*, Paul Bains and Julian Pefanis (trans.), Power Institute (Sydney), 1995, p133.
6 Bergson, *Creative Evolution*, trans Arthur Mitchell, Dover Publications (New York),1998, p241.
7 Ibid, p212.
8 Ibid, p237.
9 Massumi, *A User's Guide to Capitalism and Schizophrenia: Deviations from Deleuze and Guattari*, MIT Press (Cambridge, Massachussetts), 1992, pp59–60.
10 Ibid, p61.
11 Buckminster Fuller, *Synergetics. Explorations in the Geometry of Thinking*, MacMillan (New York), 1979, p306.
12 Bergson, *Creative Evolution*, op cit, p245.
13 Stephen Perella, 'Hypersurface Theory: Architecture><Culture', *AD*, op cit, p7.
14 Bergson states, 'consciousness is the light that plays around the zone of possible actions or potential activity which surrounds the action really performed by the living being. It signifies hesitation or choice', *Creative Evolution*, op cit, p144.
15 'Every moment in life is a step in a random walk. Uncannily familiar as the shore may seem, looking back reveals no Eden of interiority and self-similarlity, no snowflake state to regain. Ahead lies nothing with the plain reliability of solid ground. You can never predict where the subatomic particle will appear, or what will flash across the synapse (the pure instantaneous event). Once thrown, however, the dice are destiny. God as a drunken gambler. Dionysus snickering at fate as he steals an extra turn.' Massumi, *A User's Guide*, op cit, p23.
16 Massumi, 'Sensing the Virtual', op cit, p23.
17 'A schizophrenic out for a walk is a better model than a neurotic lying on the analyst's couch. A breath of fresh air, a relationship with the outside world.' Gilles Deleuze and Félix Guattari, *Anti-Oedipus: Capitalism and Schizophrenia*, Robert Hurley, Mark Seem and Helen R Lane (trans.), University of Minnesota Press (Minneapolis), 1994, p2.
18 Paul Klee, 'Creative Credo' (1920), in *The Inward Vision: Watercolours, Drawings and Writings by Paul Klee*, trans Norbert Guterman, Abrams (New York), 1959, p5.
19 See note 16.

BRIAN MASSUMI
STRANGE HORIZON
Buildings, Biograms and The Body Topologic

Computer-assisted topological design technique in architecture is no longer a novelty. With the required software and hardware becoming more accessible, paperless studios and offices are less the exceptions they once were. With growing familiarity have come inklings of discontent. There is a common drift to many of the reactions voiced at lectures, conferences, and in the classroom. It seems to be widely held opinion that the abstractness of digital space of topology contradicts the spatial reality of bodies and buildings. 'Since we do not live in non-Euclidean space', the objection goes, 'why are you foisting mutant geometries on us that fail to correspond to anything real? Topological architecture is just too abstract. It can't connect to the body as we experience it. Besides, you can animate architectural design practice as much as you like, but you still end up with a building that isn't going anywhere. It's all a sham. Design techniques based on continuity and movement rather than static form betray themselves in the fixity of their final product. If you're so stuck on continuity, where's the continuity between your process and its product? It's all very pretty, but why should we, your public – livers-in and passers-by of your buildings – why should we care?'

But what if *the space of the body is really abstract?* What if the body is inseparable from dimensions of lived abstractness that cannot be conceptualised in terms other than the topological? The objections that topological architecture is too abstract and does not connect at all with the body would dissipate. Conversely, the question of how precisely the process continues in the product would become all the more pressing. Topological architecture would need to do more than it has up to now to develop a response. After all, its very effectiveness as a design method is in the balance. The answer may well disappoint partisan of concreteness incarnate. It may turn out that computer-assisted topological design technique has inadequately addressed the question of its end-effectiveness because *it is not yet abstract enough* to be a fitting match for the abstract resources of 'concrete' experience.

The Argument from Orientation
It is with some chagrin that I confess to having sat contentedly in my temporary office at the Canadian Centre for Architecture, for no less than two months, looking at the wrong street out of the window. I was looking east onto rue St-Marc, when in fact I was looking north onto rue Baille. I am sad to report that there is no resemblance between the two scenes. Something seriously disorienting was happening in the time it took me to get from the side entry of the building to the door of my office. But that's only the half of it. The seriously disorienting thing that was happening as I snaked my way through the corridors overpowered the evidence of my eyes. It was completely overriding the clear-as-day visual cues available to me from the window of my office. The sudden realisation that my north was everyone else's east was jarring. True, I hadn't paid much attention to the scene. But it wasn't only this. When it hit me, I had the strangest sensation of my misplaced image of the buildings morphing, not entirely smoothly, into the corrected scene. My disorientation wasn't a simple lack of attention. I had been positively (if a bit vaguely and absent-mindedly) seeing a scene that wasn't there. It took a moment's effort to replace what positively hadn't been there with what plainly was. When you actively see something that isn't there, there's only one thing you can call it: a hallucination. It was a worry.

Thinking about it, I realised that I could make my way to and from my office to the exit without error, but if I'd been asked to sketch scenes from the corridors or to map the route, I couldn't have done it with any accuracy. I had precious little memory of the way, yet I navigated it flawlessly. Correction: I had precious little *visual* memory of the way. I must have been navigating on autopilot, using some form of basically nonvisual memory. If I put myself mentally through the paces of exiting, instead of seeing passing scenes, I felt twists and turns coming one after the other with variable speed. I was going on a bodily memory of my movements: one of contorsion and rhythm rather than visible form. There is in fact a sixth sense directly attuned to the movement of the body: proprioception. It involves specialised sensors in the muscles and joints. Proprioception is a self-referential sense in that what it most directly registers are displacements of the parts of the body relative to each other. Vision is an exo-referential sense, registering distances from the eye.

It appears I had been operating on two separate systems of reference: a predominantly proprioceptive system of self-reference for the tunnel-like bowels of the building, and a predominantly visual system of reference for the vistas outside. The two systems were not calibrated to each other. Or they hadn't been, until my moment of hallucinatory truth before the window. Their respective spaces of orientation had been noncommunicating, like qualitatively different monads of experience. The idea that this is not as unusual a situation as my initial concern had suggested came to me in the subway on the way home. If you've ever ridden a subway, it's likely that you've had a similarly jarring experience when surfacing at street level.[1]

That must be it. The paucity of visual cues in tunnel-like places such as corridors and subways requires a back-up system to take over from the usual way of orienting: using visible forms grouped into fixed configurations to make what psychologists call 'cognitive maps'. I had a happy ride, until I thought about how I'd got where I was. My memory of getting from the exit of the building to the subway stop just moments before was virtually blank. Not quite (not again!): twists and turns in rhythm. Yes, again, I had been on autopilot. I had gotten to the train by habit and it was evidently my proprioceptive system of reference that seemed to be the habitual one, window or tunnel, vista or no vista. Clear visual images of forms in mapped configurations now seemed the exception. Landmarks I remembered – sporadically – rising into the light from rhythms of movement, as from an unseen ground of orientation, in flux.

Close your eyes and try to make your way to the fridge. Your visual memory of the rooms and the configurations of the furniture will start to fade within seconds. But chances are, you'll 'intuitively' find your way to the food with relatively little difficulty. Especially if you're hungry. If you think about it, we all go about most of our everyday lives on habitual auto-pilot, driven by half-conscious tendencies that gently gnaw at us like mild urban hungers. Orienting is more like intuitively homing in on the food with your eyes closed than it is like reading a map.

Something is rotten on the shelf of spatial-experience theory. Cognitive maps, built on the visual basis of generic three-dimensional forms in Euclidean geometric configurations, aren't all they're advertised to be. As a general explanation of orientation, they're past their use-by date. The way we orient is more like a tropism (tendency plus habit) than a cognition (visual form plus configuration).

Research in spatial orientation has been stumbling in the same direction. Recent studies assumed the traditional cognitive model, based on 'reading' visual cues embedded in the forms and configurations of objects. It was found, however, that the emptier the space, the better the brain's ability to orient. The conclusion was that humans orient more by the 'shape of the space' than by the visual characteristics of what's in it.[2] But what is the shape of empty space? Indeterminate – except for the rhythm of movement through it, in its twistings and turnings. The studies were suggesting that the proprioceptive self-referential system – the referencing of movement to its own variations – was more dependable, more fundamental to our spatial experience, than the exo-referential visual-cue system. Self-referential orientation is called 'dead reckoning', after the nautical term.[3] It is known to be the basis of many animals' ability to orient. It is a key element, for example, in the well-known feats of navigation achieved by homing pigeons. Its role in human orientation has significant implications for our understanding of space because it inverts the relationship of position to movement. Movement is no longer indexed to position. Rather, position emerges from movement, from a relation of movement to itself. Philosophically, this is no small shift.

It takes little reflection to realise that visual landmarks play a major role in our ability to orient. Landmarks stand out, singularly. Most of us would be capable of pasting them together into a visual map. But to do that, you have to stop and think about it. It takes effort – an effort that interferes with the actual movement of orientation. Cognitive mapping takes over where orientation stops.

The way landmarks function in the actual course of orientation is very different from reading a map. They're what you habitually head towards or away from. They trigger headings. Vectors. Landmarks are like magnetic poles that vectorise the space of orientation. A landmark is a minimal visual cue functioning to polarise movement's relation to itself in a way that allows us habitually to flow with preferential heading. The vectorial structuring effected by landmarks gives the space of orientation a qualitative dimension, expressed in tropistic preference. The cognitive model assumes that visual cues are somehow used to calculate distances, as if our brains were computers, preprogrammed in inches and feet. Isn't it more plausible that our bodies are habituated in steps? And that steps relate more directly to other steps than they do to conventional feet? The computational fiction is a natural outgrowth of the assumption that we effectively move through and live in a static, metric or quantitative, Euclidean space. I for one don't count my way around town. A qualitative space of moving, step-by-step self-reference accords better with my navigationally competent (if at times cognitively challenged) sense of where I am.

Landmarks rise up visibly from a nonvisual sea of self-related movement. They refer more directly to the self-referencing of the movements surrounding them than to each other. Fundamentally, each landmark stands alone with its associated coursings. What they mark most directly is a monad of relation, a patch of motion referencing its own self-variations (the multiple headings it carries). Landmarks and their associated patches of qualitative relation can be pasted together to form a map – but only with an additional effort that must first interrupt the actual course of orientation. It is in a second moment, in an added operation, that the quantifiable cognitive product is fed back into the space of movement. This can indeed increase the flexibility and precision of a body's orienting. But it remains true that cognitive mapping is secondarily applied to the experience of space, or the space of experience. This makes it an overcoding – a certain way in which experience folds back on itself. It is very uncommon, a limit-case rarely attained, that we carry within our heads a full and acccurate map of our environment. We wouldn't have to carry maps on paper if we had them in our brains. No matter how consciously overcoding we like to be, our mappings are riddled with proprioceptive holes, threatening at any moment to capsize the cognitive model (like the empty areas filled with sea-monsters on medieval maps). No matter how expert or encompassing our cognitive mapping becomes, the monstrous sea of proprioceptive dead reckoning is more encompassing still. We are ever awash in it.

The very notion of cognitive overcoding implies that we orient with two systems of reference used together. The contradiction between them is apparent. Pragmatically, they co-function. Visual cues and cognitive mappings function as storage devices, allowing us more ready reaccess to less habituated proprioceptive patches. They also serve as useful correctives, when we find ourselves hallucinating buildings that positively aren't there. The reverse is also true: proprioceptive orienting can act as a corrective to visual awareness. When we are momentarily lost, the buildings in front of us are in plain view. They may be strangely familiar, but we still can't place ourselves. Oddly, the first thing people typically do when they realise they're lost and start trying to reorient is to look away from the scene in front of them, even rolling their eyes skyward. We figure out where we are by putting the plain-as-day visual image back in the proper proprioceptive sea-patch. To do that, we have to interrupt vision, in the same way that visual awareness interrupts proprioception. The alarmingly physical sense we feel when we realise we're lost is a bodily registering of the disjunction between the visual and the proprioceptive. Place arises from a dynamic of interference and accord between sense-dimensions.

Our orienting abilities, then, combine the resources of two different dimensions of experience. The places we plainly see as we go about our daily lives are products of a co-operation between two sense systems. A synaesthetic system of cross-referencing supplements a systemic duality, exo-referential and self-referential, positional and moving, Euclidean and self-varyingly monadic. Synaesthetic co-operation links these dimensions to each other, always locally – specifically, where we are lost. Cross-sense referencing forms a third hinge-dimension of experience. This 'lost' dimension of experience is where vision's conscious forms-in-configuration feed back into the vectorial tendency-plus-habit of proprioception, and where proprioception feeds forward into vision.

Where we go to find ourselves when we're lost is where the senses fold into and out of each. We always find ourselves in this fold in experience.

An aside: If the positioned sights we plainly see always result from synaesthetic interference and accord, was there really a difference in nature between the sight I positively saw that wasn't there out of my window, and the one with which I laboriously replaced it? Weren't they just two sides of the same coin: the interference side and the accord side? If every effectively placed experience is a synaesthetic production, it becomes difficult to maintain that there is a difference in nature between hallucination and perception. Isn't it just a pragmatic difference, simply between cross-referenced and not cross-referenced? It would stand to reason that there would be a kind of continental drift naturally affecting proprioceptive experience patches due to their self-referential, monadic operation. Their mode of *reality* demands it. Isn't getting lost, even seeing things that aren't there, just a momentary grounding in an impractical dimension of reality? It is the encompassing reality of what we really experience in a spatial way that gets lost if we try to narrow our understanding of space down to vision in its exo-referential single-sense functioning and the associated Euclidean geometry of form-in-configuration. In Euclidean vision, where we always find ourselves is what gets lost.

Look at things from the proprioceptive side. Its elements are twists and turns, each of which is already defined relationally, or differentially (by the joint nature of the proprioceptors), before entering into relation with each other. That makes the relation entered into among elements a double differentiation. The elements fuse into a rhythm. The multiplicity of constituents fuses into a unity of movement. The resulting patch is a self-varying monad of motion: a dynamic form figuring only vectors. Although effective, the dynamic form is neither accurate nor fully visualisable. It is operatively vague; a vector space not containable in metric space. It is a qualitative space of variation referenced only to its own movement, running on autopilot. It is not a space of measure. To get a static, measurable, accurately positioned visual form, you have to stop the movement. This capsizes the relation between movement and position. Now position arises out of movement. Static form is extracted from dynamic space, as a quantitative limitation of it. Anexact vector space feeds its self-variational results into the limitative conditions of quantitative, Euclidean space, populated placidly by traditional geometric forms plottable into configurations.

Doesn't this sound familiar? Doesn't the proprioceptive experience-patch sound a lot like a topological figure in the flesh? Doesn't the way it all shapes up sound very like the way Greg Lynn describes computer-assisted design – starting with differential parameters that automatically combine to govern unities/continuities of self-varying movement, ending only when the programme stops running, leaving a Euclidean form as a static witness to its arrested dynamism?[4] Doesn't topological design method digitally repeat what our bodies do noncomputationally as we make our way to and from our work stations? Then, when we watch the programme run, aren't we doing it again, slumped before the screen? Are we not, though immobile, repeating our body's ability to extract form from movement? When we stare, barely seeing, into the screen, haven't we entered a 'lost' body-dimension of abstract orientation not so terribly different from the one we go to when we roll up our eyes and find ourselves in the fold?

The proprioceptive dimension of experience was described as one of two experiential dimensions. But the two were also described as folding into each other. That folding of the Euclidean and non-Euclidean into and out of each other is itself understandable only in topological terms. This hinge-dimension between quantitative and qualitative space is itself a topological figure – to the second degree, since topology already figures in it. It is a topological hyperfigure. The non-Euclidean – qualitative and dynamic – is more encompassing than the Euclidean – quantitative and static – by virtue of this double featuring. Simply, to put the two together, you have to make a move between them. You have to fold experience back on itself. You have to twist one of its dimensions into the other and cross-reference them both to that operation. This means that all orientation, all spatialisation, is operatively encompassed by topological movement – from which it derives in the first nonplace.

The space of experience is really, literally, physically a topological hyperspace of transformation.

Note on Terminology

'Topology' and 'non-Euclidean' are not synonyms. Although most topologies are non-Euclidean, there are Euclidean topologies.[5] A Möbius strip or a Klein bottle are Euclidean figures, of one and two dimensions respectively. The distinction that is most relevant here is between topological transformation and static geometric figure: between the process of arriving at a form through continuous deformation, and the determinate form arrived at when the process stops. An infinite number of static figures may be extracted from a single topological transformation. The transformation is a kind of superfigure that is defined not by invariant formal properties, but by continuity of transformation. For example, a torus and a coffee cup belong to the same topological figure because one can be deformed into the other without cutting. Anything left standing when the deformation is stopped at any moment, in its passage through any point in-between, also belongs to their shared figure. The overall topological figure is continuous and multiple. As a transformation, it is defined by vectors rather than co-ordinate points. A vector is transpositional: a moving through points. Because of its vectorial nature, the geometry of the topological superfigure cannot be separated from its duration. The figure is what runs through an infinity of static figures. It is not itself determinate, but determinable. Each static figure stands for its determination, but does not exhaust it. The overall figure exceeds any of its discrete stations, and even all of them taken together as an infinite set. This is because between any two points in Euclidean space, no matter how close, lies another definable point. The transformation joining the points in the same superfigure always falls between Euclidean points. It recedes, continuously, into the between.[6] The topological superfigure in itself is the surplus passing through between Euclidean spatial coordinates. Logically, it is not sequential, even though it is oriented (vectorial). It is recessively transitional. In this essay, the word 'non-Euclidean' is used as a convenient shorthand for a space of this kind: one that cannot be separated from its duration due to a transitional excess of movement. 'Non-Euclidean' is a good enough nontechnical term for dynamic or durational 'spaces' that do not fit into the classical Euclidean (actually Cartesian) intuition of space as a triple-axis co-ordinate-box containing things. In this view, widely thought to correspond with our everyday experience, time is an independent variable adding a fourth, formally distinct, dimension to the traditional three of space. Topologically speaking, space and time are dependent variables. They are not formally distinguishable. They cannot be separated from each other without stopping

Relational Architecture, *which most of the following images belong to, refers to large-scale interactive installations that create opportunities for buildings to decline their established roles in their particular social performance. The interventions are not 'site-specific' but rather 'relationship-specific', as the public is an actor of the ephemeral transformation. Based on dissimulation and insinuation, relational architecture pieces dematerialise the environment and amplify participants to an urban scale. Contact:* rafael@csi.com

LEFT: Positioning Fear, Relational Architecture 3 - Transformed the Landeszeughaus arsenal in Graz, Austria. *A teleabsence interface projected shadows of passers-by onto the building. Using tracking systems, the shadows were automatically focused and generated sounds. A real-time IRC discussion about fear, involving 30 artists and theorists from 17 countries, was projected inside the shadows. Project web site:* http://xarch.tu-graz.ac.at/home/rafael/fear
Credits: Rafael Lozano-Hemmer (concept, visuals), Will Bauer (audio, programming), Robert Rotman and Conroy Badger (programming), Nell Tenhaaf (IRC moderator).

RIGHT: Piel Capaz, a technological coffin for vampire buildings. *A virtual reality installation that visualises resting sites for emblematic buildings that are not allowed to have a natural death. The participant's motion controls the point of view in the projected environments on the wall and on the floor.*
Credits: Emilio Lopez-Galiacho (concept, visuals), Rafael Lozano-Hemmer and Will Bauer (interaction).

the process and changing its nature (Euclideanising it). The relation of the dimensions of space to that of time is one of mutual inclusion. This mutual inclusion, and the strange logical and especially experiential effects associated with it, is what is termed a 'hyperfigure' or 'hyperspace' for the purposes of this text. It may be noted in passing that even a Euclidean topological figure may generate a surplus effect, although in a more static vein. A Möbius strip is a one-dimensional figure whose twisting creates a two-dimensional effect. A Klein bottle is a two-dimensional figure whose folding in on itself creates a three-dimensional effect. The 'effects' are real, but not part of the formal definition of the figure. They are in the figure as it is really experienced, adding another quality to it, precisely in the way it stands out from its formal limits. They are extra-formal, stand-out or pop-out effects. The word 'hyperspace' may also be applied to experiential surplus-dimension effects of this kind, whatever the geometry. Experience itself may be defined as a hyper-dimensional reality: as the 'being' of the excess of effect over any determinate spatial configuration. As the following argument from synaesthesia asserts, the 'shape' of experience can be considered to be a one-sided topological figure: an abstract (recessive/pop-out) 'surface' for the reception, storage and reaccess of qualitative hyper-effectivity that can only be approached head on.

The Argument from Synaesthesia
The hinging of the proprioceptive to the visual in the movement of orientation is a synaesthetic interfusion. It is not the only one. Each side, for example, enters into its own synaesthetic fusion with the tactile: a determinate, positioned sight is a potential touch; the tropism of proprioceptive twisting and turning is assisted by past and potential bumps, and the tactile feedback from the soles of our feet. There are many other synaesthetic conjunctions, involving all the senses in various combinations, including smell and hearing. Clinical synaesthesia is when a hinge-dimension of experience, usually lost to active awareness in the sea-change to adulthood, retains the ability to manifest itself perceptually. In synaesthesia, other-sense dimensions become visible, as when sounds are seen as colours. This is not vision as it is thought of cognitively. It is more like other-sense operations at the hinge with vision, registered from its point of view. Synaesthetic forms are dynamic. They are not mirrored in thought; they are literal perceptions. They are not reflected upon; they are experienced as events. Synaesthetes who gain a measure of willful control over them still perceive them as occurrences in the world, not contents of their heads. They describe summoning them into perception, then moving toward or around them. Synaesthetic forms can be usefully recombined with an experience of movement. They serve as memory aids and orientation devices. Since they work by calling forth a real movement-experience, they retain a privileged connection to proprioception. This is not cue-based, form-and-configuration vision. Although synaesthetic forms are often called 'maps', they are less cartographic in the traditional sense than 'diagrammatic' in the sense now entering architectural discourse.[7] They are lived diagrams based on already lived experience, revived to orient further experience. Lived and relived: *biograms* might be a better word for them than 'diagrams'.

It is worth paying close attention to how synaesthetes describe their 'maps'. The biograms are usually perceived as occupying the otherwise empty and dimensionless plane between the eyes and objects in the world. This liminal nonplace has been characterised as 'peri-personal'. It lies at the border of what we think of as internal, personal space and external, public space. The appearance of the biogram is borderline in time as well. It is accompanied by a feeling of 'portentous' *déjà vu*: an already-past, pregnant with futurity, in present perception.[8] This makes experiencing the biograms, in the words of one synaesthete dubbed MP in the literature, like 'seeing time in space' – a good way of describing an event. They have a feeling of thickness or depth, like a 'flexible moving third dimension'. But the depth-likeness is vague enough that they can still be compared to diaphanous 'slides' projected on an invisible screen. They retain a surface character. The 'maps' MP draws at the researcher's request do not satisfy her. Her biograms are not plainly visible forms. They are more-than visual. They are event-perceptions combining senses, tenses and dimensions on a single surface. Since they are not themselves visual representations, they cannot be accurately represented in mono-sense visual form. Oddly, although they appear in front and in the midst of things, the biograms are to MP, 'larger than my visual range, like looking at the horizon'. They are geometrically strange: a foreground-surround, like a trick centre twisting into an all-encompassing periphery. They are uncontainable either in the present moment or in Euclidean space, which they instead encompass. Strange horizon.

Since they are determinately positioned neither in time nor space, their presence can only be considered a mode of abstraction. They are real – really perceived and mnemonically useful – abstract surfaces of perception. Since they continue indefinitely, in order to bring up certain regions the synaesthete has to move around, into, or away from them. She doesn't *actually* walk, of course. The movement, though really perceived and mnemonically useful, does not measurably take place in Euclidean space. It is an *intensive* movement, occuring in place (as at a workstation, or with rolled-up eyes) – or more accurately out-placed, in the event. This is an abstract movement on an abstract surface.

The synesthete uses her biograms, for example, to keep track of birthdays. On the birthday biogram, each region stores a conjunction between a date, a name, and a colour. When she has to recall a birthday, she will use the colour as a landmark, and when she approaches the right coloured region, the name and date will appear. The shape and sound of the letters and numbers are stored in the colours, diaphanously merged into them as in a dissolve, or like strands 'woven together' in a patch of fabric. They are accessed by a reverse dissolve that is like 'pulling out threads'. Shape, sound and language: of a fabric with colour.

MP has a unique biogram for everything she needs to remember. The biograms are 'not connected in any way'. They are like separate monads of abstract lived experience. Except that in their strange twisting between foreground and horizon, each loops back at a certain point into darkness. Each biogram arcs in multicoloured mnemonic glory from a sea of shadow. What lies in the darkness at the end of the rainbows? The answer comes without the slightest hesitation: 'other people's minds'.[9]

Biograms cannot be described without resorting to topology: centres folding into peripheries and out again, arcs, weaves, knots and unthreadings. Face it. You are always facing it. Wherever you are, whoever you are, whatever day or year it is, the biogram is in front of you. The synaesthetic form of experience is faced, in something like the sense in which writing is handed.[10] Except that a left has a right, and this front doesn't have a back (yet it still has shadow?). This means a biogram is a one-sided topological surface – really, strangely, usefully.[11] This is not a metaphor. If there is a metaphor in play, isn't it rather the mathematical representation that is the metaphor for the biogram? The biogram is a literal, graphically diaphanous event-perception. It is what is portented when you remember seeing time in space.

Synesthesia is considered the norm for infantile perception. The theory is that it becomes so habitual as to fall out of perception in the 'normal' course of growing up. It is thought to persist as a nonconscious underpinning of all subsequent perception, as if the objects and scenes we see are all 'threads' pulled by habit from a biogrammatic fabric of existence.[12] Synesthetes are 'normal' people who are abnormally aware of their habits of perception. 'Normality' is when the biogram recedes to the background of vision. Biograms are always in operation. It is just a question of whether or not their operations are remarked.

For all perceivers, the biogram is the mode of being of the intersensory hinge-dimension. Its strange, one-sided topology is the general plane of cross-reference not only for sights, sounds, touches, tastes, smells, proprioceptions; it is also the general plane of cross-reference for numbers, letters, words, even units of grammar. On that plane, the learned forms that are usually thought of as restricted to a 'higher' cultural plane re-become perceptions. Practice becomes perception. The cognitive model has it that 'higher' forms are associative compounds built up from smaller sights and sounds as from elementary building blocks. But the workings of synaesthetic biograms shows that the higher forms feed back to the 'lower' perceptual level. They enter the general dissolve, on a level with the elementary, fused into the surface, interwoven components of the fabric of life. This makes it impossible to apply to 'raw' experience distinctions such as 'higher' and 'lower', 'perceptual' and 'cognitive', or even 'natural' and 'cultural'. There is no 'raw' experience. Every experience takes place in the already taken place of higher and lower, where they join for the future. Every experience is a portentous *déjà vu* at a hinge.

The relevant distinction is between involuntary and elicited. Or rather: this is the relevant connection. Biograms are described as having an odd status: they are 'involuntary *and* elicited'.[13] They retain the surprise of the *déjà vu* even for clinical synaesthetes who can summon them forth and consciously navigate them for future heading. Eliciting with future heading is not the same as willing. Biograms remain their own creatures even for proficient synaesthetes. They maintain a peri-personal autonomy from psychological or cognitive containment. They cannot be entirely owned personally, since they emerge from and return to a collective darkness. But they can be tamed, induced to appear and perform feats of memory. They are less like a static image on a slide screen than a live circus act, performed in a ring that lies centre stage and encircles the tent.

Clinical synaesthetes have trained synaesthesia to perform on signal. They have perfected the trick of consciously eliciting involuntary intersense connection as a way of invoking memory. Vision is typically used as a plane of general cross-reference. It is on the abstract surface of colour that everything fuses, in a way allowing a single thread to be pulled back out as needed, before returning to the fold. All the other senses, and any and every 'higher' form, are gathered into colour, together with the three dimensions of space and time. It is as if all the dimensions of experience were compressed into vision. This is why the topology of the biogram is so strangely twisted. It is not due to any lack, say of cognitive organisation or of Euclidean accuracy. There are simply too many dimensions of reality compressed into vision. It can't hold them all in discrete, determinate, harmonious form and configuration. It buckles under the existential pressure.

The biogram is not lacking in order. It is over-organised, loaded with an excess of reality. It is deformed by experiential overfill. It is a hypersurface. Its hyperreality explains why it is so stubbornly abstract. Since it cannot concretely hold everything it carries, it stores the excess fused in abstraction, ready for useful reaccess. In other words, the hypersurface of synaesthetic experience is 'real and abstract' in precisely the way Gilles Deleuze describes the virtual: as an intense, torsional coalescence of potential individuations. 'Pulling out a thread', or decompressing a differential strand of the fusional weave of experience, involves actualising a virtuality. That is why the synaesthetic perception is always an event or performance pulling determinate form and function out of a larger vagueness, like a rabbit from a one-sided hat.

It was argued earlier that there was no essential difference between perception and hallucination, both being synaesthetic creations. The feedback of 'higher' forms and their associated functions onto the biogrammatic hypersurface expands the list. There is no fundamental difference between perception, hallucination and cognition. It was also argued that the separation between the natural and the cultural was not experientially sustainable. In view of this, is it so far-fetched to call the unseen out of which biograms arc 'other people's minds'? Not particular other people's minds, of course. The other of them all: an other of particular mindedness from which everyone's individuated perceptions, memories and cognitions emerge, and to which they return, in a twisting rhythm of appearance, and dissolve: a shared incipiency that is also a destiny. What is the other of mindedness? From what does all individual awareness arise and return? Simply: matter. Brain-and-body matter: rumbling sea for the rainbow of experience. The synaesthetic hypersurface refracts the activity of matter through many-dimensioned splendour into colour. It is the hinge-plane not only between senses, tenses and dimensions of space and time, but between matter and mindedness: the involuntary and the elicited.

Reaccessing the biogram and pulling a determinate strand of organised experience from it is to reapproach the point where the materiality of the body minds itself. It is to catch the becoming-minded of the movements of matter in the act. It is to re-perform the memorial trick of experience pulling itself rabbit-like out of the black hat of matter. This is a somewhat ontogenetic contorsion. It involves a hyperreal looping between the impersonal and the 'peri-personal'. Any personal strand is pulled out of that non-to-near-personal loop as the grande finale. After which there is nothing to do but introduce the next abstract act.

That the personal is the finale distinguishes this synaesthetic ontogenesis of experience from phenomenological approaches. For phenomenology, the personal is prefigured or 'pre-reflected' in the world in a closed loop of 'intentionality'. The act of perception or cognition is a reflection of what is already 'pre-embedded' in the world. It repeats the same structures, expressing where you already were. Every phenomenological event is like returning home.[14] This is like the *déjà vu* without the portent of the new. In the circus of synaesthesia, you never really know what act will follow. The rabbit might turn into a dove and fly away. Experience, normal or clinical, is never fully intentional. No matter how practised the act, the result remains at least as involuntary as it is elicited. Under the biogrammatic heading, the personal is not intentionally prefigured. It is rhythmically re-fused, in a way that always brings something new and unexpected into the loop. The loop is always strangely open (with just one side, how could it ever reflect itself?).

What if topological architecture could find ways of extending the 'diagrams' it designs into 'biograms' inhabiting the finished product? What if it could find ways of embedding in the materiality of buildings open invitations for portentous events of individuating *déjà vu*? Might this be a way of continuing its topological process in its product?

To do this would require somehow integrating logics of perception and experience into the modelling. Processes like habit and memory would have to be taken into account. As would the reality of intensive movement. Ways would have to be experimented with for architecturally soliciting an ongoing eliciting of emergent forms/functions at the collective hinge of perception, hallucination and cognition. Techniques would have to be found for overfilling experience. The methods would have to operate in a rigorously anexact way, respecting the positivity of the virtual's vagueness and the openness of its individual endings. Never prefiguring.

In a way, architecture could even surpass synaesthetes like MP by finding ways of building-in nonvisual hypersurfaces. There is nothing wrong with colour, light and darkness. Rainbows of experience are good. But imagine the startling effects that might be achieved by using proprioception as the general plane of cross-referencing. Imagine how positively, qualitatively moving that would be. Practices of architecture allied with experimental art, like the 'reversible destiny' architecture of Arakawa and Gins or the 'relational' architecture of Rafael Lozano-Hemmer, might have much to contribute. Technologies could be favoured that can be twisted away from addressing pre-existing forms and functions towards operating directly as technologies of emergent experience. Imagine if these were to become infrastructural to architectural engineering. What better place to start than with the much-touted 'new media', approached not only as design tools but as architectural elements as basic as walls and windows? Could architecture build on the ability of digital technologies to connect and interfuse different spheres of activity on the same operational plane, to new effect? This is a direction in which the work of Lars Spuybroek, among others, is already moving.[15]

TO BE CONTINUED . . .[16]

Displaced Emperors, Relational Architecture 2 - Intervention on the Habsburg Castle in Linz, Austria. *An* architact *interface consisted of wireless 3D trackers that calculated the direction of the participant's arm and a large projection of a human hand appearing wherever he or she was pointing. 'Touch' transformed the castle into Chapultepec Palace, the residence of the Habsburg emperors in Mexico and trigger a temporary post-colonial override consisting of a huge image of the Atzec head-dress kept at the ethnological museum in Vienna. Credits: Rafael Lozano-Hemmer (concept, visuals), Will Bauer (audio,programming), Susie Ramsay (production). Photos by Dietmar Tollerind.*

Notes

I gratefully acknowledge the assistance of the Australian Research Council and the Canadian Centre for Architecture in supporting this research.

1 Sandra Buckley analyses the differences, cultural and experiential, between ground-level movement through architectural spaces and underground movement in 'Contemporary Myths of the Asian City', in Robert Sergent and Pellegrino D'Acierno (eds), *(In)Visible Cities: From the Postmodern Metropolis to the Cities of the Future*, Monticello Press (New York), forthcoming.

2 See Russell Epstein and Nancy Kanwisher, 'A Cortical Representation of the Local Visual Environment', in *Nature*, vol 392, 9 April 1998. For a popular press account of their work on adult brain functioning during orientation tasks, see 'A Positioning Unit of Sorts in the Brain', *New York Times*, 28 April 1998, pB13: 'The experiments dovetail with work on rats and human infants showing that when they get lost, it is the shape of the space, rather than the objects in it, that are used to get reoriented'.

3 For an overview, see Ariane S Etienne, Joëlle Berlie, Joséphine Georgakopoulos and Roland Maurer, 'Role of Dead Reckoning in Navigation', in Sue Healy (ed), *Spatial Representation in Animals*, Oxford University Press (Oxford), 1998, pp54–68.

4 Greg Lynn, *Animate Form*, Princeton Architectural Press (New York), 1999; and *Folds, Bodies and Blobs: Collected Essays*, La Lettre Volée (Brussels),1998.

5 Bernard Cache provides an excellent account of the topological resources of Euclidean geometry available for architectural design in 'A Plea for Euclid', *ANY (Architecture New York)*, no 24, 1999, pp54–9. The present essay, however, diverges sharply from Cache in its assessment of the importance and usefulness of non-Euclidean conceptions.

6 'Movement in itself continues to occur elsewhere: if we serialise perception, the movement always takes place above the maximum threshold [in the super-figure's passing-through] and below the minimum threshold [recessively] in expanding or contracting intervals (microintervals) . . . Movement has an essential relation to the imperceptible; it is by nature imperceptible', Gilles Deleuze and Félix Guattari, *A Thousand Plateaus*, Brian Massumi (trans.), University of Minnesota Press (Minnesota), 1987, pp280–281. Another word for 'imperceptible' is 'abstract'.

7 Ben van Berkel and Caroline Bos (eds), *ANY (Architecture New York)*, no 23, 1998, special 'Diagram Work' issue.

8 On the peri-personal and *déjà vu*, see RE Cytowic, 'Synaesthesia: Phenomenology and Neuropsychology', in Simon Baron-Cohen and John E Harrison (eds), *Synaesthesia: Classic and Contemporary Readings*, Blackwell (Oxford),1997, pp20, 23.

9 Cytowic, *Synaesthesia: A Union of the Senses*, Springer-Verlag (New York),1989, pp217–27.

10 For diagrammatic renderings of this, see ibid, figs 7.9–7.17, pp202–9.

11 Raymond Ruyer: experience is 'a surface with just one side . . . If the sensible surface could be seen from two sides, it wouldn't be a sensation, but rather an object . . . it's an "absolute surface" relative to no point of view outside of itself: *Néo-finalisme*, PUF (Paris), 1952, pp98–9.

12 See Daphne Maurer, 'Neonatal Synaesthesia: Implications for the Processing of Speech and Faces', in Baron-Cohen and Harrison, op cit, pp224–42.

13 Cytowic, 'Synaesthesia: Phenomenology and Neuropsychology', op cit, p23.

14 The notion of intentionality is often used as a way of establishing an identity between the structure of the world and the structure of the subject in the world. The insistence on such an identity is a tacit assumption of a divide. An objective-subjective split is backhandedly enshrined in this way of thinking. A mediating instance is then required to bring the two realms back into harmony. The senses are assigned to the job. In architectural phenomenology, a building becomes a 'metaphor', 'reflecting' for the senses the identity-structure shared by the subject and the world. Architecture is called upon to express, and reinforce in concrete, that ideal fit. Its 'mission' is to concretise the 'integrity' of being-in-the-world: to close the loop. The whole process revolves around identity and an ultimately normative ideal of authenticity. The ideal is suspiciously domestic (Heidegger's 'house of being' is just around the corner). This is how Juhani Pallasmaa puts it: 'The timeless task of architecture is to create embodied existential metaphors that concretise and structure man's being in the world. Architecture reflects, materialises and eternalises ideas and images of ideal life . . . Architecture enables us . . . to settle ourselves in the world . . . Our domicile becomes integrated with our self-identity . . . Architecture is the art of reconciliation between ourselves and the world, and this mediation takes place through the senses'. The 'mental task' of architecture, Pallasmaa continues, was best formulated by Frank Lloyd Wright: 'What is needed most in architecture today is the very thing most needed in life – Integrity. Just as it is in a human being, so integrity is the deepest quality in a building . . . If we succeed, we will have done a great service to our moral nature.' It all adds up to a high-minded moralism. This is sharply at odds with any form of architectural experimentalism, whose rallying cry would not be to close the loop, but to loop-the-loop; not to ground in the 'authentic' but to dizzy with potential (remembering that position arises from intensive movement, rather than extended movement departing from pre-position). Juhani Pallasmaa, *The Eyes of the Skin: Architecture and the Senses*, Academy Editions (London), 1996, pp50–1. In the perspective of this essay, there is not an identity between the subjective and objective, or between the world and experience: there is a continuity that mutually includes each side of the divide in the same self-differentiating reality.

15 Arakawa and Madeleine Gins, *Reversible Destiny*, Guggenheim Museum (New York), 1997. Take 'reversible destiny' as 're-incipient life' (experience returning to the point of matter-minded ontogenesis). On 'relational architecture', see Rafael Lozano-Hemmer in this volume and at http://xarch.tu-graz.ac.at/filmarc/fest/fa3/fear. Take 'relational' to mean 'intensively cross-referencing disparate planes of experience'. See also Lars Spuybroek, in this publication. For an overview of his work see Spuybroek, *Deep Surface*, *NOX* (Rotterdam),1999, (exhibition catalogue, Exhedra Gallery, Hilversum). See especially 'Off the Road: 103.8 MHz', a description of a housing project and noise barrier in Eindhoven. The aim of the project is to create a 'zone of transition' (using among other devices a sound-processing feedback loop between the houses and the cars passing by on the highway) that sets up a 'resonance' between 'bits and bricks', '[air]waves and ground'. This activates the in-between as an operator of relation rather than leaving it a passive boundary. The 'zone of transition' is an airborne, abstract holding together in addition to (rather than in opposition to, or simply breaking down) the concrete holding-apart of discrete, down-to-earth divisions demanded by the need for a highway noise barrier.

16 The full text of this essay is available online at *http://www.hypersurface.net*

Nicholas Goldsmith (FTL Happold), Art on the Beach

REBECCA CARPENTER
FORCE AFFECT
An Ethics of Hypersurface

This essay investigates motion as an ethic within architecture. Three different examples are described: blobs, events-space and hypersurfaces.

It can be argued that architecture is capable of activating a set of relationships as reciprocal presuppositions in the form of time. To present this argument, I will invoke some existing ideas including those set forward by Gilles Deleuze, Félix Guattari and Brian Massumi.

We can say that architecture has the potential to express a 'virtual–actual' system. In using the term 'virtual–actual', I mean to indicate reversible intensities. That is to say, the virtual–actual pairing produces a co-resonating system. This does not mean that the virtual and the actual are simply inverse images of one another with the present occuring in the middle. Immanent here is a transformational time structure producing a topological transformation. The term 'virtual' should be understood as employed by Brian Massumi: as a nonspatial element of 'pure exteriority . . . every point of the virtual is adjacent to every point of the actual even if those points are not adjacent to each other'.[1] In other words, a system of exchange is achieved, which when physically constituted as the present, is the dynamic deformation of the space of one set of points into the adjacent set of points in the production of the *new*.

We will also draw on the terms 'form of expression' and 'form of content', as deployed by Deleuze and Guattari, and on Henri Bergson's notion of duration embodied in 'difference in kind'. In Bergson's discussion, the present is an image produced within a successive time construct set up in one's consciousness. 'Difference in kind' refers to an embodiment of time in each individual existence as a momentum towards a perfection of the space–time relationship. For Bergson, duration is set up in memory, creating a virtual co-existence of the past and present. In other words, we construct time and space through experience. Brian Massumi describes an interface of exchange between function and quality as a reciprocal presupposition: 'The term "form of expression" refers to an organisation of functions such as being an architect. The term "form of content" refers to an organisation of qualities such as brickness.'[2] The relationship between architect and brick takes place as an interface between the 'form of expression' and the 'form of content'. These relationships are presented here to describe memory and meaning as forces that are connected up in experience – for example, in the experience of making architecture. If we connect up the virtual–actual function to this idea, memory and meaning take on the form of a topological transformation, a figural diagram of flickering duration.

The potential to express the virtual–actual transformation in architecture requires that we rewind to the old architectural binary articulation: form and function. Such discrete articulations can become a conflation and inflation of the function: the actual form can constitute an incorporation of virtual functions, and actual functions can constitute a virtual experience. This conflation and inflation is really a two-point separation of form and experience. Whether we look through the discrete constitution of a form, or the abstraction of effects, we can join form and function as points on a moving curve. This transformation can be seen as an indication of their mutual blurring. In this sense, architecture can produce time.

Productive time in architecture has been introduced before in terms such as 'virtuality', 'novelty', 'transformations', 'perturbations' and a 'new pragmatism'.[3] These all suppose, in line with this argument, that architecture can integrate the structure of time by assuming its form. I am interested in the structure of time described by Gilles Deleuze as the process of becoming. In this process, the present has a plural structure. That is to say, any event has that strange plural dimension: past–future–presence. Incorporating this time structure in the construction of space is to join experience and form as a continuously transforming figure: a topological transformation where experience becomes the curve of space.[4]

Greg Lynn and Bernard Tschumi are two architects who take this approach. Each attempts, in their own way, to remove form from a static relationship to function; they reinvent form/function, idea/space, space/experience, opening up to a completely new kind of relationship. They construct what Massumi has called a 'reversible function, in the mathematical sense, a diagrammatic curve joining two points'.[5]

The methods used by these architects to construct this line should not be reduced simply to analytic integration or resistance. Lynn brings a new term to the form–function relationship. By deterritorialising two discrete areas – internal organisations (form) and external influences (function) – he produces a new term – 'blobs' – meaning a productive behavioural system of differentiation and integration. Tschumi also brings a new term to resist a dialectical notion of form and function. 'Event–space' is a concept expressing mutual resistance and heterogeneity but also accessibility.[6] We can describe these two terms, 'blobs' and 'event–space', as constructed differential relationships. However, it can be argued that the problem with both terms is that they rely on either side of the two-point structure of the function rather then the exchange between the two.

Expressing Form

We can speak about the work of Greg Lynn as existing within an ethic of movement. He calls this ethic 'anorganic vitalism'.[7] The term 'anorganic' is meant to indicate a position of differential integration, both organic and inorganic. That is, the incorporation of life science and technology into a mutual construction. This construction is an attempt to create an 'abstract machine' for producing novelty.[8] The emphasis on 'novelty' indicates an attempt to create productive time. Complex conditions create the

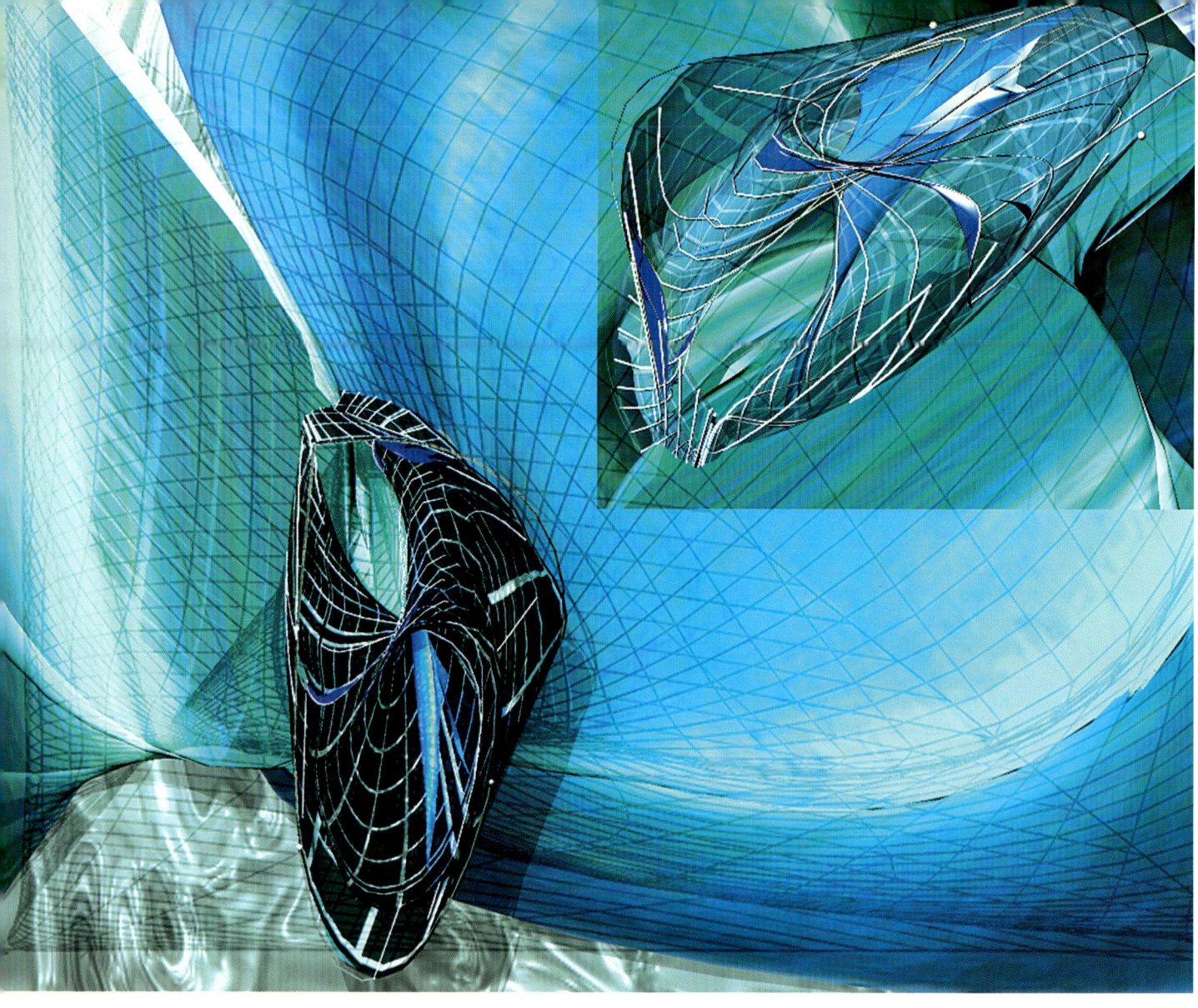

Stephen Perrella and Rebecca Carpenter,
Möbius House Study, 1998

forces determining the internal constitution of form and the external cultural influences of production. Lynn describes this 'concept of order and difference':

> Novelty, rather than some extrinsic effect, can be conceived as the catalyst of new and unforeseeable organisations that proceed from the interaction between freely differentiating systems and their incorporation of external constraints.[9]

The idea expressed by Deleuze and Guattari that language is an evolving body informs Lynn's concept of geometry. The term 'geometry' is a relative one and does not refer to a specific type of geometry; it is a general assemblage of analytic and differential geometry. D'Arcy Thompson's science of related forms and concern for the simplicity of the transformational grid inform Lynn's animate deformations. Thompson's ideas are a complex hybrid of classics, mathematics and zoology. We should note his emphasis on the diagram and Lynn's incorporation of this into his idea of form as the geometry of complexity:

> The form, then, of any portion of matter, whether it be living or dead, and the changes of form which are apparent in its movements and in its growth, may in all cases alike be described as due to the action of force. In short, the form of an object is a 'diagram of forces', in the sense, at least, that from it we can judge of or deduce the forces that are acting or have acted upon it: in this strict and particular sense, it is a diagram – in the case of a solid, of the forces which *have* been impressed upon it when its conformation was produced, together with those that enable it to retain its formation; in the case of a liquid (or of a gas) of the forces which are for the moment acting on it to restrain or balance its own inherent mobility.[10]

Lynn's notion of form can be understood to be a complexity of forces, interacting over time, that have no single 'idea' operating over them. Form is a system of internal and external forces, an incorporated behaviour over time. All form with such complex behaviour can be said to act like a 'blob'. Blobs are a set of complex behaviours. Going back into architectural theory, Lynn integrates models of complexity to form an aggregate idea about form. He incorporates a reductive approach (top down to arrive at form) and an emergent approach (bottom up to arrive at form). Complexity is seen as 'irreducible and multiple', simplicity as 'reducible and singular', hence the reductive and emergent approaches.[11] By creating an assemblage of these ideas, he generates a third idea:

> Similarly, one approach to a theory of complexity might be to develop a notion of the composite or the assemblage which is understood as neither multiple nor single, neither internally contradictory nor unified. Complexity involves the fusion of multiple and different systems into an assemblage which behaves as a singularity while remaining irreducible to any single simple organisation.[12]

Lynn's idea of complexity resolves the problematic geometry existing in these two approaches. This suggests a way of organising form based on a completely different understanding of geometry, which is diagrammatic and mobile. Isomorphic polysurfaces (blobs) are examples of an alternative geometry. They were developed within animation software to model characters and other supple forms in motion. This geometry is a freely differentiated form (a diagram for complex behaviour over time) and hence not a prescriptive geometry in the sense that it is reductive or emergent, like the previously noted models. Isomorphic polysurfaces are known as 'meta-balls' (or 'clay'), which are defined by a centre, surface area, a mass and two zones of influence (negative and positive). The form of the clay is determined by the interaction of zones of influence, that is, variables of mass, centre locations and surface areas. When forces are applied to the blobs, since they already have their own internal set of forces, the assemblage becomes a highly complex set of interactions that cannot be attributed simply to the force applied to the blob. This is a system that introduces the possibility for form to evolve within the relationship of form and function in an integrated manner.

This may not be intended to be a prescription for a 'methodology of form', but it could certainly be read as a prescription indicating that radical form produces time. The 'anorganic methodology' includes philosophy (meaning has force), life science (study of form and growth), and technology (a culturally situated method of production; a machine that is a double 'content of expression'). This 'methodology of forms' is not intended to create forms that signify a particular subject or source. Form is doubled as continuous transformation and growth, continuity and difference, in a system of forces both past and future (present). Past, because the actual form can be attributed to a system of virtual forces, and future, because the unforeseeable organisations produced by the virtual form will produce forces that affect the actual form. In this sense, the modernist separation of form and function is interrupted. Meaning, where the form signifies a subject, has been interrupted and opened up in an attempt to exclude this direction from exchanging force actualised as form.[13] It could be argued that formal constitution is the function here.

Expressing Effect
The work of Bernard Tschumi can be said to exist within an ethic of movement. This ethic can be called 'linguistic transpositions'. Architecture exists as a transposition of text through the introduction of different texts. Through interdialectics, effects are sought in architecture as an artistic narrative. The narrative is an inaccessible space moving between points – the subjective space of art. One can only access the narrative of architecture by becoming it. The exploration of the subjective space in the narrative of art is itself a new form of knowledge for architecture.

By establishing his practice in New York and Paris, Tschumi transposes the context of production as a means to access this space. Put another way, event–space is the meeting of two exclusive terms: spatial structure and dynamic movement, and this meeting can only be actualised through another event–space; architecture is in the exchange of experience:

> Take for example the buildings of Paul Andreu. We often talk about the buildings of Mies, Palladio, or van Berkel, which we have occasionally seen in person but mostly know through photographs. I've only spent a few hours in buildings by Mies but I've spent approximately a thousand times that time in Andreu's building in the last 25 years. I would even object to his point about pleasure. [Andreu has claimed that function is an 'incentive to prepare pleasure']. The greatest pleasure I had was once when I went from the taxi to the plane in two minutes in a major international airport. [He is probably referring to Charles de Gaulle Airport, Roissy] Congratulations to you; Palladio never gave me that![14]

Architecture exists as 'movement, space and event'; transformations of earlier ideas 'conceived space, perceived space, erotic space (purely subjective)'. These ideas have been moved from their original context – literature, philosophy and art – into architecture. They arrive through linguistic models to solve the problem of form and idea. Tschumi introduces a third point to subvert their duality – event–space – a concept similar to Georges Bataille's notion of deep interior experience.[15] This third point renders the duality indifferent and inaccessible. Spatial structure and dynamic movement are held apart as irreducible and mutually exclusive. They have no relationship without the abstract space of chance encounters: event–space. Event–space aims to 'maintain these contradictions in a dynamic manner, in a new relation of indifference, reciprocity and conflict'.[16] Event–space exists as movement. It is the subjective space of motion, the motion of a narrative and also the intrusion of bodies, free from the problems of consumption implicit in the dialectics. Within this context, form is not worked, event–space does the work of ensuring its noninterpretation as a signification: an unknowable potential of effects. 'Architecture ceases to be a backdrop for actions, becoming the action itself'.[17]

This system of effects introduces the possibility for effects to function against each other as a system existing outside form. The space between structure and movement keeps architecture from annihilation. It keeps chance encounters, forcing effects and resisting consumption. In this space of experience, normative descriptions of movement as geometric (you can't draw it as a form) have no real meaning. Tschumi struggles to find a word for this geometry between space and time:

> Architecture is about the meeting of mutually exclusive terms: concept and experience, virtual and real, envelope and body. That meeting takes place in an in-between, an interstitial space is ... not geometric, not merely physical. I have no name for it yet.[18]

This resistance to name indicates that the space–time connection cannot be figured; that is to say, it is not a formal analytic; it is an synthetic border of sense:

> At the border of architecture are attitudes about space, geometry and sensuality that often tell more of architecture's nature than the textbooks of architectural orthodoxy.[19]

Tschumi's resistance to formal methodology is expressed as linguistic transposition. This includes philosophy (language as a grid to be mastered through experience), art (subjective space) and culture (culturally situated between cultures). In Tschmu's case, effects are doubled as the impossible-to-grasp potentiality of dynamic movement both past and future (present). Future, because the force of virtual moving bodies can affect the actual form, and past, because the actual form and actual effect will have forces that affect virtual moving bodies. It is in this sense that the modernist separation of form and function is interrupted. Meaning, where the form signifies a subject, has been interrupted and opened up in an attempt to exclude this direction from exchanging effect actualised as event–space. It can be argued that the abstraction of effect is the function here.

Expressing Form is Effect Expressing

Topological transformations are in the form of the virtual–actual function; the experience of the space is the form of the space. In topology, a topological transformation is one in which the function of transformation is biunique and bicontinuous. A form can be deformed into another form without cutting, tearing or otherwise violently altering the original. Geometry usually brings to mind points, circles and squares. This takes us backwards to another time. We expect geometry to change constantly under the influence of new theories and new technologies. Topology is general geometry (general does not mean simplistic). Terms such as 'line', 'circle' and 'triangle', even 'size' and 'shape' have no real meaning in topology. Topological figures are described in terms of 'properties' that exist in relation to other figures. These properties might include having a hole (nonclosed curve), not having a hole (closed curve), having an edge (a surface), and having a homeomorphic relationship to another form determined by deforming, transforming, knotting and linking. Because these are transformations between neighbourhoods with duration they are in effect already the space of experience. The duration of the transformation is the space of experience. 'The invariance of incidence relations provides a basis for the concept of topology as geometry based primarily upon continuity and invariance of neighbourhoods'.[20]

The term 'blob' can be redefined with new emphasis. The surfaces and their boundaries are in fact responsive and effectual and have a distinct relationship to 'nurbs' (nonuniform-rational bsplines). A blob can be considered as a collection of three-dimensional nurbs. A nurb is really just a two-dimensional

Steven Holl, Art Museum

diagram for a potential curved (closed or nonclosed) surface (edge). It is a topological diagram for potential topological space. It is a spline that acquires three dimensions within its own duration. That is to say, potentialising its third dimension is transforming the two dimensions through an exchange of force, really a kind of experience space.

The Möbius House Study was an attempt to construct an experience space curve.[21] In this study, Stephen Perrella and I combined a potential topological space with an arrested topological space. We made a Möbius strip out of a nurb (arrested topological space with the property of one curving surface) and constrained co-ordinates of another nurb (potential topological space) with its own internal set of forces (magnitude – weight, rotation, size – and position), over time. The relationship between the strip and the 'nurb' is a kind of variation on a topological deformation. The Möbius strip was chosen as the figure for the production of a new home. We did this because it can be argued that domestic culture has moved outside the familiar form of the home and onto our screens, where the familiar is already in the form of a strange accelerated repetitious one-sided surface. This is a space of experience already topological, already in a process of continuous deformation both in form and experience, both in terms of the making and the inhabiting. We have some considerations here: an accelerated experience–space of continuous transformation where the actual is already the virtual, and a technologically driven topological transformation between topological forms (experience–spaces that are already actually virtual): an arrested topological space and a potential topological space. In this study, we argue that the form is the space of experience that forces: each line of the actual is in the line of the virtual. This system is in the form of the curving line of time; it is a hyperspace.

The idea of the Möbius strip is introduced in intuitive topology. If we take a surface and we twist it and then reconnect it, it has some interesting properties. Moving along the surface can produce the mirror image of that thing, a new thing. If we fold the surface in on itself and connect it back to itself we get a Klein bottle. The single-sided surface (the surface is really an edge) can in its transformation produce difference. A Möbius strip is an arrested topological space with the property of one edge. We do not want to build the arrested form. We might say the challenge of inhabiting the flatness of this figure is really a topological transformation between experience and space. We can call this kind of ethic a hypersurface. Hypersurface is an ethic of motion.

Notes

1 Brian Massumi, *A User's Guide To Capitalism and Schizophrenia, Deviations from Deleuze and Guattari*, MIT Press (Cambridge, Massachussetts),1995, p67. For a description of the virtual and actual system, see p170.
2 Ibid, p15.
3 'Virtuality' and 'topological transformations' as described by Brian Massumi; 'novelty' as described by Greg Lynn (a 'catalyst of new and unforeseeable organisations'); 'perturbations' as discussed by Reiser + Umemoto, 'Yokohama Port Terminal', in Stephen Perrella (ed), *AD: Hypersurface Architecture*, vol 68, no 5/6, Academy Editions (London), May–June 1998, p22-3; 'new pragmatism' as discussed by John Rajchman, 'A new Pragmatism?', *Anyhow*, vol 7, Anyone Corporation,1998, p211.
4 For a discussion of Built Time see Andrew Benjamin's essay 'Not to Shed Complexity', *Fisuras 3 1/4*, December 1995.
5 Massumi, op cit.
6 I am discussing blobs and event–space as a reinvention of the architectural dialectic form, and experience as a moving diagram – a diagram with time. We can argue that the contextual relevance of this comparison exists within the evolution of organic and dialectic architectures. Gregg Lynn's methodology can be called a formalist continuation of the work of Peter Eisenman. Bernard Tschumi's resistance to an ideology of form and function can be called structuralist. The technique of transposition was typical in 1960s post-war structuralist theories; the historical precedents of this technique belong to the Russian Formalists' approach. The difference in their approach to the problem of incorporating time in architecture can be found within these historical contexts. Lynn incorporates idea and form into a system in which time is imbedded into the form. Tschumi's approach is an attempt to understand the experience through a grid that can be mastered, where experience is linked to language as the primordial symbolic material. See Louis Martin, 'Interdisciplinary Transpositions: Bernard Tschumi's Architectural Theory', in *The Anxiety of Interdisciplinarity*, vol 2, Backless Books,1998, p81.
7 Greg Lynn, 'Geometry in Time', *Anyhow*, vol 5, Anyone Corporation, 1998.
8 Greg Lynn, 'The Renewed Novelty of Symmetry', in *Books by Architects: Greg Lynn, Folds, Bodies and Blobs: Collected Essays*, La Lettre Volée (Bruxelles),1998.
9 Ibid, p64.
10 D'Arcy Wentworth Thompson, *On Growth and Form*, Cambridge University Press,1961, p11.
11 Greg Lynn, op cit.
12 Greg Lynn, 'Blob tectonics or Why Geometry is Square and Topology is Groovy', ibid, p173.
13 For a structuralist analysis of meaning in architecture see Rosalind Krauss, 'Death of a Hermeneutic Phantom, The Materialisation of the sign in the work of Peter Eisenman', *The Anxiety of Interdisciplinarity*, vol 2, Backless Books, 1998.
14 Bernard Tschumi quoted from a panel discussion on infrastructure and distribution, *Anyhow*, Anyone Corporation, 1998, p101.
15 This argument is formally similar to Roland Barthe's paradox of the avant-garde. Louis Martin describes Tschumi's theory of eroticism (pleasure) as a 'perversion of Bataille's position' in 'Interdisciplinary Transpositions: Bernard Tschumi's Architectural Theory', *The Anxiety of Interdisciplinarity*, vol 2, Backless Books, 1998, p71.
16 Tschumi, 'Index of Architecture', in *Questions of Space, Lectures on Architecture*, Architectural Association (London), 1990, p100.
17 Tschumi writes, 'I do not think it is very important to discuss "what buildings look like". It is what they do that is important.' 'Through A Broken Lens', *Anyhow*, vol 7, Anyone Corporation, 1998, p240.
18 Ibid, p242.
19 Tschumi, 'Episodes of Geometry and Lust', *Questions of Space*, op cit.
20 Bruce Meserve, *Fundamental Concepts of Geometry*, Dover Publications Inc, (New York), 1983, p291.
21 Stephen Perrella and Rebecca Carpenter, 'The Möbius House Study', in Stephen Perrella (ed), *Hypersurface Architecture*, op cit.

GIOVANNA BORRADORI
AGAINST THE TECHNOLOGICAL INTERPRETATION OF VIRTUALITY

An image, for Bergson, is 'a certain existence which is more than that which an idealist calls a representation, *but less than what a realist calls a* thing – *an existence placed halfway between the "thing" and the "representation."'*
Matter is not out there, in the world, but a mix of self and world, perception and memory.

For the majority of theorists, virtuality describes the totality of effects and mutations brought about by the information and communication network.[1] Virtuality designates not only whatever happens on, or is generated by, the Internet but includes the impact of the media on the way in which we apprehend, represent and consequently build the world around us. By this definition, virtuality concerns the blurring of the distinction between perception and representation, original and copy.

How does such blurring occur? For many, the explanation lies in the fact that in virtual space objects do not appear as self-contained entities, accessible via sensory perception; rather, mediatised technology fabricates objects as irreducibly represented and reproduced. This irreducibility is the characteristic of virtual space, where objects become 'simulacra'.[2]

I believe this definition of virtuality to rely on a reductionist assumption: if virtuality amounts to a technologically generated set of events, it is in fact reduced to physical states of affairs. I want to call this reductionist standpoint 'representationalist'. By contrast, I see the possibility of developing a nonreductive concept of virtuality, in which it reflects technologically generated events, phenomenologically understood as an aspect of our experience of the world. With reference to Nietzsche's definition of perspectivism as the doctrine for which there are no uninterpreted facts or truth, I shall call this nonreductive alternative 'perspectivist'.

These two definitions, the representationalist and the perspectivist, are based on fundamentally different conceptions of space. In my reading, the representationalist understanding of virtuality heavily depends upon the rationalist notion of space, whose origins are to be found in Descartes' mind–body dualism. The perspectivist alternative is, instead, a critique of the rationalist notion of space in terms of what I name 'virtual spatiality'.[3] Diametrically opposed to the objectification of space as alienated and homogeneous 'outside', this kind of spatiality has as its chief features heterogeneity and movement.[4]

Drawing from the philosophical insights of Nietzsche and Bergson, I shall unfold a heterogeneous and dynamic concept of virtual spatiality in which tensions and qualia override oppositional pairs: in virtual spatiality, direction and movement cut transversally across the distinction between subjective and objective; density and rarity replace the opposition between material and immaterial; latency and expression take predominance over presence and absence.

Virtuality De-Technologised
How does the concept of virtuality intersect with the fields of philosophy and architecture? Is virtuality a contingent or a necessary link between these two disciplines? Most architectural theorists interpret virtuality as a change of technological paradigm and in so doing opt for the thematic type of connection. At a determinate point in time, so their claim goes, architecture begins to be reshaped digitally, in terms of both its technology and its object. Since the paradigm-shift has occurred, architectural design has been increasingly produced through digital means; the spaces architecture has been called to design are themselves virtual; and, even more importantly, architecture has been put face to face with a different spatial sensibility, derived and constantly enriched by the experience of cruising the digital highways. This different spatial sensibility goes together with a new range of spatial needs, the identification of which is still under way, as ever-larger portions of our existence are being conducted on line. The role of philosophy is restricted to helping architecture demarcate this sensibility.

While I am by no means attempting to deny the compelling aspect of technological virtuality, I dissent from reducing it to a contingent historical occurrence, both in the architectural and philosophical sense. To me, virtuality designates a necessary connection between architecture and philosophy, provided that virtuality be de-technologised.

The nontechnological interpretation of virtuality concerns, both etymologically and metaphysically, the Latin notion of *vis* (force), which is a *leitmotif* in Nietzsche's philosophy. Diametrically opposed to the rationalist conception of space, as the container of entities and forms, Nietzsche's idea of space is that of an immanent field of forces. If space is conceived as a field, entities and forms are not simply 'contained' by it but produced by the very differential that constitutes the relation between them.[5] If we understand the nature of these forces to be discursive, virtual spatiality will emerge as the experience of a nomadic discursivity that, because it is yet unexpressed, is virtual.[6] If this de-technologisation of virtuality is indeed pursued in the direction of a new phenomenological definition of the virtual, what will an architecture of virtuality look like?

As the de-technologisation of virtuality should not imply, I believe, an opposition or denial of technological virtuality, but an attempt at interpreting it as a specific mode amongst a larger phenomenological spectrum, the architecture of virtuality should be viewed as intertwined with its metonymical correlative: the virtuality of architecture. By this, I mean the constitutive role that architecture plays in the creation of the human subject, which is what makes virtuality a necessary rather than a contingent link between architecture and philosophy.

The virtuality of architecture suggests that the individual is not just 'always already thrown' into existence, as Heidegger would have put it, but 'always already built'.[7] Architecture, from this

point of view, does not elaborate theoretical, aesthetic, functional propositions 'in' space but becomes the condition of possibility for the primary hermeneutical exchange between the individual self, others and the environment. It is this exchange that makes the human subject a being-in-the-world. The virtuality of architecture relies on the premise that, if we come across ourselves as 'thrown' into the world, we do so in the face of the fact that such a world is built or constructed spatially, as well as socially, historically and culturally. From the standpoint of the virtuality of architecture, architecture builds us as much as we build it.

Why is 'Virtual Space' a Representationalist Concept?

Why is the reductionist interpretation of virtuality also representationalist? What is the coincidence between reduction and representation? If an entity can be reduced to its physical and quantifiable components, it can also be faithfully 'represented' in terms of those components. Since the Renaissance, perspective has been the science of representation, the technique used to rationalise, quantify, order and control spatial relationships.[8]

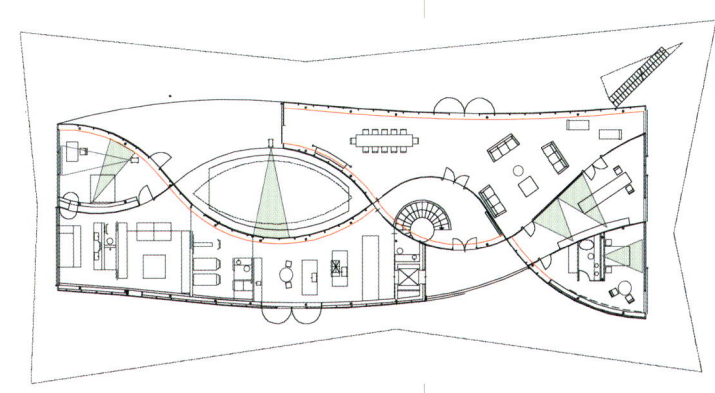

The role of representation in the rationalist lineage is one of the central themes of Heidegger's later philosophy. According to Heidegger, representation can be minimally understood as the relation to a primitive 'presence': the substantial rather than accidental features of an entity.[9] The more representation is granted epistemological transparency, the more the presence of which it is a representation is presumed to be stable, permanent, self-identical. However, stability, permanence and identity cannot exist without that which allows the object to be present: space. Neither reduction nor representation could happen without the homogeneity of the Newtonian and Cartesian space.

Both a reductive and a representationalist apparatus is at work whenever virtuality is understood as the host dimension for simulacra or for effects of simulation. Whenever the blurring of the distinction between perception and representation is justified in technological terms, not only a reductivist but a representationalist position is being offered.

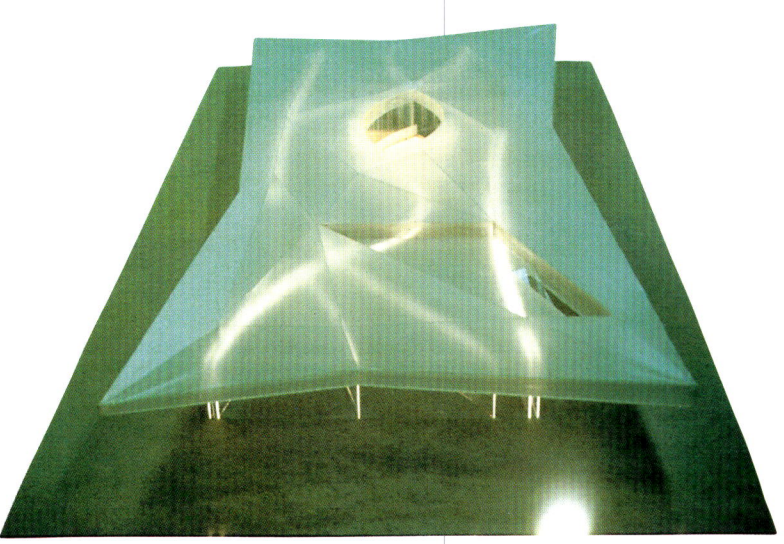

Most of the representationalist positions have a semiological foundation. Simulacra are conceived as infinitely layered compounds of mediated information whose object or reference, assumed as self-contained presence, is ultimately irretrievable. In the vocabulary of poststructuralism, largely influenced by Saussure's linguistics, such an infinite layering of mediated information without a definite object or reference is translated as the endless deferral from signifier to signifier. Whether only simulacra are available, which are neither copies nor originals, or only signifiers are available, which are pointing to each other rather than to a transcendental signified, the categorial framework seems to remain essentially representational.

Herzog & De Meuron, Kramlich Residence and Media Collection, California, 1997-2000. FROM ABOVE: elevation; site plan; model.

The Cartesian Theorem

Cartesian theorem about space could be called the underlying sense of space shared by such different architectural experiences as 19th-century historicism and large sections of the Modern Movement. Descartes' conception of space revolves around the central opposition between the empirical dimension, defined as having spatial features, and the transcendent or spiritual dimension, which characterises mental features. We can doubt everything, he writes in the *Meditations*, except that we are thinking beings, because, even if we think that we are not thinking, we are still thinking. Assumed as self-reflection, thought is freestanding, internally justified, autonomous from all sorts of empirical support. In fact, the inescapability of thinking does not prove at all that we are awake or completely sober. All it proves is that thought is absolutely primary and independent of anything that is extended in space.

To make the transition from philosophy to architecture, let us pair what Descartes calls thinking with the notion of form. The Cartesian theorem entails the mutual exclusion between form and space. Any thinking being – or, in our parallel, any form – exists in its own perfection and balance, completely independently from space. The mind injects space with forms and, in turn, the absolute emptiness of space does nothing but receive them.

The extreme polarisation of activity and passivity, in terms of mind and body, form and space, is essential in the history of representationalist architecture.[10] This polarisation is at the root of the obsession with novelty so crucial to the high-modernist visual avant gardes and made programmatic by architectural modernism. The fact that form is located completely beyond space, as well as the empirical sphere, protects it from any mediation, change, obsolescence and fallibility. Conceived in this way, radical novelty can exist only on the condition that it be transcendent. The new is whatever is possible, and therefore not real (otherwise it would no longer be a possibility). As in the Cartesian theorem, form is not immanent to space but transcends it; it is form that represents the possibility of an installation in space from an ageless and mental 'inside'. Such an inside is purely transcendental and spaceless. In this sense, form is structurally utopian. Descartes is the philosophical ancestor of the modernist conception of the new as necessarily utopian. Utopia, however, only in its literal meaning of nonplace, because the modernist utopia is a political project of social emancipation. The modernist utopia is a nonplace in the sense that it is not-yet real but may become so on the basis of conditions found in the real. The utopian side of modernism coincides with a foreseeable possibility; otherwise it could not encompass an emancipatory project, which is one of its essential components.

Two Conceptions of the New

Both in architecture and philosophy, the representationalist approach entails a conception of the new as foreseeable possibility. By contrast, from a perspectivist angle, novelty corresponds to the actualisation of virtual presences: presences virtually contained in the real but not yet actualised. A representationalist notion of novelty is based on the category of possibility: on what is not-yet real but may become so on the basis of conditions found in the real. Perspectivist novelty is the affirmation of submerged and unexpressed forces, virtually contained in the real but not yet actualised. In other words: while representationalism moves within a system of oppositions based on two classical modalities, reality and possibility, the perspectivist set-up is based on the nonoppositional pair constituted by actuality and virtuality. Moreover, while possibility is larger than reality because it contains whatever could become real on the basis of the conditions found in the real; virtuality is co-extensive with the real, for virtuality is already real, inclusive of the yet unexpressed or non-actualised portion of the real.

Virtual spatiality does not perform the function of space, insofar as it does not provide forms with material and objective stability. While space is the receptor of forms, virtual spatiality is the generator of forms. Virtual spatiality is an active and differentiating dimension rather than a homogenising or alienating one. Forms are not injected into space as if from the outside, but generated within it. While the notion of space implies the installation of the radically new into reality, virtual spatiality implies the affirmation of the yet unexpressed, silent, discursive forces by which reality is constituted. What are these discursive forces? Let us turn to Nietzsche for the answer.

Perspectivism and Force

In Nietzsche's analysis, representation has historically implied the suppression of the notion of force and the dynamics between forces, producing hegemonic outcomes. Instead, representation needs to be looked at as just one of many 'perspectival' alternatives. Perspectivism is the name Nietzsche gives as an alternative to representationalism, that is, to the dogmatic and totalising aspiration of traditional philosophical systems. Why does Nietzsche pick out perspective for this scope? And how does his perspectivism affect architecture?

Perspectivism is laid out as the doctrine according to which there are no uninterpreted facts or truths. Perspective seems thus both a synonym of interpretation and distinguished from knowledge, where knowledge is clearly identified with the detection and rationalisation of some objective dimension. Despite Nietzsche himself using perspective and interpretation interchangeably more than once, there is a subtle difference between them that should not be overlooked by those interested in the contrast between space and virtual spatiality, both from a philosophical and architectural standpoint.[11] While perspective indicates the relativity and uniqueness of our spatial and sensory location within the world, interpretation is an intellectual organisation of perspectives. This is because the juxtaposition of perspectives can be apprehended only at an abstract, intellectual level. Thus, perspective, not interpretation, is the primitive unit of Nietzsche's discourse. Perspectivism reveals the determinacy of our sensory presence within space, assumed by Nietzsche as incompatible with any other. Interpretation is a more constructivist concept, made out of a plurality of perspectives.

Far from naturalising perspective in the representationalist way, as the transparent means of rationalising spatial relationships, Nietzsche attributes to perspective an existential and thoroughly materialistic meaning. In Nietzsche's perspectivist approach, there are as many foci as there are eyes in the world. Perspective is not a technique of representation but the affirmation of one's own actualisation as well as the intuition of the virtual spatiality of others. Perspectivism is both a critical project of displacement of the focus, and an affirmative project consisting in the actualisation of other foci, an actualisation whose scope is to give the undecidable, enigmatic, unpredictable features of existence a new legitimacy. Nietzschean affirmation injects ambiguity into the apparent unity of the actual, opening up fissures of virtuality and becoming.[12] To affirm means to experience the multiplicity of 'perspectives' virtually contained by a present state or form. These perspectives are the virtual lines along which becoming unfolds.

For Nietzsche, becoming affects all facts in the world, whether material, mental or formal. This becoming is the virtual aspect of experience. While form is necessarily actualised, becoming is yet-unformed. The challenge of the architecture of virtuality is diametrically opposed to any formalism. For architecture to be able to connect with perspectivist virtuality, it needs to abandon all formalism, since its challenge would no longer be to simulate or represent existing forms and events but to respond to the yet-unformed. The yet-unformed is pure movement, the movement produced by the pushing of the forces against each other. A movement that, in Nietzsche's philosophy of force, comes before space in the sense that it constitutes spatiality.

The Unformed and the Untimely
The primacy of movement makes perspectivist virtuality available to a thoroughly material, sensory type of experience. But what is movement? How can we 'represent' movement? Can the monumental, archival, memorialising function traditionally attributed to architecture be reconciled with it? The Nietzschean answer would be yes, provided that we shy away from all forms of historicism, including, I suggest, postmodern neo-historicism. Historicism kills movement. History is the first area that architecture has to rethink in its meaning. Next to it, as I shall indicate in relation to Bergson, is memory.

According to Nietzsche, there are two possible connections to history: one is authentic and life-enhancing, and the other is inauthentic and destructive. Inauthentic historiography imposes itself whenever history is taken as a given, as the historicists do by monumentalising and revering it indiscriminately. History has neither determinate meanings nor a unifying scope. Since it is not a self-contained presence, it must be challenged rather than religiously respected. By contrast, authentic historiography depends on the ability to 'make history', which Nietzsche distinguishes from simply 'being in it'. This ability hinges on what Nietzsche names 'plastic power'. Life *is* plastic power, the power to shape new perspectives without becoming self-defensive or losing oneself. Only if this power is affirmed and cultivated, rather than suppressed, will history serve movement and life.

The authentic understanding of history, and of human existence within history, is contingent upon what Nietzsche describes as stepping into the 'Unhistorical'. Such a leap consists in a type of 'creative forgetting', disengaged from the normative power of history, and it is necessary for one's plastic power to strengthen. 'It is possible to live almost without memory, and to live happily moreover, as the animal demonstrates; but it is altogether impossible to live at all without forgetting'.[13] Forgetting means disconnecting from a linear sense of time, described as a series of punctual 'nows', some of which are no-more and some of which are not-yet. This linear description represents selves and cultures as located in time, rather than constituted by it and becoming with it. Switching between the Historical and the Unhistorical, making the present part of becoming, is what secures a healthy, constructive relationship with history, for both philosophy and architecture. What is no-more cannot be objectified as something without an active influence on the present, but needs to be reactivated precisely in terms of these influences. This is the transformative function of time that the Unhistorical is supposed to introduce into the present. Implementing the role

that time, in its transformative function, plays in existence means to implement the contact with a specific ontological modality that is located in reality but is not actualised: virtuality.

The relationship with history opened up by contact with the virtual dimension of experience is neither the radical rejection of the past promulgated by architectural high modernism and the International Style, nor the reverence for the past adopted by the postmodernist appropriation of historical styles. Nietzsche's perspectivist history is not, as it is often all too simplistically interpreted, the generating matrix of an unqualified relativism, that both in architecture and philosophy translates in a neohistoricist kind of sensibility. Perspectivist history presents both the philosopher and the architect with the question of how to interpret the yet-unformed, whether conceptually or spatially. Sensing becoming, responding to movement: these are the new challenges that need to be faced by attempting to capture form as it emerges from the process of its own formation and deformation.

The Tensions of Memory and Perception
Is there a technique of capturing movement, or more precisely, the movement of forms and forces, before their expression? For some, the answer is topology, the digital animation of form, which could lead to 'topological turn'.[14] In contrast to the formalistic orientation promoted by the evolution of modernism into the International Style, topology has pushed architecture to stop viewing form as its ultimate scope but as a by-product of the design process. Topological design no longer consists of a highly polarised activity where the architect injects form and meaning onto an inert, white surface representing space. It has transformed into the interactive experience between a mind and a form, which is interactive because the form emerges from its own generative process. Movement, in other words, exceeds form.

For Bergson, virtuality is the ontological modality of consciousness, or duration. Duration roughly corresponds to what William James, with a famous aquatic metaphor, called the 'stream'. As James's conscious stream is continuous, forward-moving and in constant change, Bergson's duration is the succession of qualitative states of mind, indiscernible as atomic units but only feasible in their interconnectedness and passing. The passing-character is the result of deeper currents that, while remaining submerged, push water towards the surface. Both the deep currents and the superficial motion of the water that they create are real components of our experience. But while the motion on the surface is actual, the submerged currents are virtual.

What does this virtual modality entail? In a word: memory, which Bergson discusses in opposition to perception. Perception and memory are tendencies along which experience 'tends' to organise itself, but do not constitute independent kinds of experience, available separately from one another. Bergson defines perception as the 'abstract' tendency of our experience, referring to what our experience would be like if extrapolated from the effects of time. To stay with the Jamesian metaphor, abstract experience would mean to take the layer of moving water at the surface separately from the deeper currents beneath. This is the kind of experience we tend to produce artificially, when we look at the world objectively, with causal, quantitative, or geometrical models in mind. By contrast, memory embodies the 'concrete' tendency to experience the world as a constant becoming-other than itself. It is experience in terms of the effects of time on it.

Herzog & De Meuron, Kramlich Residence, *California, 1997-2000. Interior perspectives.*

Here, we need to put aside the aquatic metaphor because Bergson indicates these two tendencies as radically heterogeneous to one another. It is as if deep and superficial could not be measured against each other.[15]

> Whenever we are trying to recover a recollection, to call up some period of our history, we become conscious of an act *sui generis* by which we detach ourselves from the present in order to replace ourselves, first, in the past in general, then, in a certain region of the past – a work of adjustment, something like the focusing of a camera. But our recollection still remains virtual; we simply prepare ourselves to receive it by adopting the appropriate attitude. Little by little it comes into view like a condensing cloud; from the virtual state, it passes into the actual; and as its outlines become more distinct and its surface takes on colour, it tends to imitate perception. But it remains attached to the past by its deepest roots, and if, being a present state, it were not also something that stands out distinct from the present, we should never know it for a memory.[16]

Either we are 'in' memory or 'in' perception. We don't reach the past from the present via the extension of the representational model. Quite the opposite. As we intentionally try to recollect something, we step into the past and its virtuality, and we navigate it, not rationally but intuitively, until we meet the virtual current pushing along the memory we are looking for. In order for us to individuate it and recollect it, that specific memory needs to be actualised and transformed in a perception. But, as Bergson warns in the last sentence of the quotation, part of the memory still remains attached to the past, otherwise we would not be able to discern it is a memory. This explains the sense of uncanniness, otherness, vagueness and suspension that memory entails.

The co-existence rather than integration of perception and memory is key to Bergson's relevance to my discussion of space, virtual spatiality and architecture. Bergson articulates such a co-existence within a peculiar conception of matter defined as the fullest aggregate of images, the sum total of all the past, present and future images available. An image for Bergson is 'a certain existence which is more than that which an idealist calls a *representation*, but less than what a realist calls a *thing* – an existence placed halfway between the "thing" and the "representation."'[17] Matter is not out there, in the world, but a mix of self and world, perception and memory. An example can clarify this point.

Even the most simple perception, like feeling cold or hot, takes time. When I analyse perception and quantify it according to objective scales of measurement, I act as if this time, indispensable to experience, did not exist. In the same way, as I try to recapture a memory long past, I won't be able to revive it without transforming it into a perception. The interesting feature of the differential relationship of memory and perception, virtual and actual, is that perception of actuality is arrived at, according to Bergson, from memory or virtuality. The present is accessed from the past, and not the reverse, so that experience is the constant reassessment of the present in terms of the past.

In concrete experience, as Bergson calls it, form is not injected into space as if from some otherworldly, timeless, geometrical outside, but emerges from the generative process of its own formation and deformation. What contemporary theorists identify as the animation of form, via topological techniques, Bergson illustrated as the infiltration of memory in perception. Such an infiltration provides experience with what Bergson names its 'pictorial' character, which indicates the process-like nature of the world. Paradoxically, it is time itself that constitutes experience pictorially, as a cinematic sequence. Thinking in objective terms implies a conception of matter and space as empty, homogeneous and passive, rather than full, heterogeneous and in constant motion: namely, as an aggregate of images in endless tension and becoming.

Let us go back one more time to the metaphor of virtuality as a range of deep currents that, while remaining submerged, push water to the surface. These submerged currents are virtually present to the stream. It is these virtual movements of duration that determine the emergence, or actualisation, of whatever stretch of the stream of consciousness reaches the surface. Bergson's suggestion is that the virtual currents correspond to what the pure past would be like if it were accessible. The emerged stream taken in isolation from the deep currents corresponds, instead, to what the pure present would be like as a self-contained discrete dimension. However, what is true for the dynamics of aquatic currents is true for perception and memory, present and past, actual and virtual. Experience is the theatre of these dynamics, where the invisible, or deeper layer, is always responsible for the emergence of whatever comes into view.

In contrast to the representationalist interpretation of virtuality, according to which virtuality can be 'represented' as the sum total of the effects of communication and information technology on how we know and build the world around us, I have been trying to elucidate an alternative concept of the virtual by phenomenologically understanding it as an expression of intentionality. My perspectivist definition of virtuality describes a constitutive component of experience, irreducible to physical processes as well as to quantification and formalisation. If this phenomenological interpretation is viable, experience contains a virtual dimension that calls into question a whole range of philosophical categorisations and architectural presuppositions. First of these is the Cartesian notion of space as passive receptor of forms, installed by an active and independent mind. If the hypothesis of a stable and controlled space fails, one of the most enduring bridges between philosophy and architecture is swept away. On its remains, a new concept of virtual spatiality emerges.

The relevance of Nieztsche and Bergson for my project lies in their insistence on the irreducibly passing character of our experience: this is what makes them champions of philosophical anti-Cartesianism and architectural anti-formalism. Cartesian space is incompatible with this passing and becoming feature, which is the greatest challenge of the architecture of virtuality.

Notes

1 I shall limit myself to a few references to indicate different tendencies in recent cybertheory. A utopianist, science fiction-type analysis is represented by Howard Rheingold's *Virtual Reality*, Summit Books (New York), 1991. A more scholarly approach, attempting to bind cybertheory to classical philosophical sources, is Michael Heim's *The Metaphysics of Virtual Reality*, Oxford University Press (Oxford), 1997. A comprehensive theoretical account is Pierre Lévy's *Becoming Virtual: Reality in the Digital Age*, Robert Bononno (trans.), Plenum Trade (New York), 1998. John Beckmann's *The Virtual Dimension: Architecture, Representation, and Crash Culture*, Princeton Architectural Press (Princeton), 1998, is an anthology of essays from a variety of disciplines including architecture.

2 The term was first introduced by Jean Baudrillard. See his *In the Shadow of The Silent Majorities*, Semiotext(e) (New York), 1983; *Fatal Strategies*, Semiotext(e) (New York), 1990; *The Gulf War Did Not Take Place*, Indiana University Press (Bloomington), 1995. In the context of this essay, I use it as emblematic of the 'technological' conception of the virtual, which I critique as 'representational'. Greg Lynn has similar views: 'The term "virtual" has been so debased that it often simply refers to the digital space of computer-aided design. It is often used interchangeably with the term simulation. Simulation, unlike virtuality, is not intended as a diagram for a future possible concrete assemblage but is instead a visual substitute'. *Animate Form*, Princeton Architectural Press (Princeton), 1999, p10.

3 I coin this expression in order to mark the difference between the rationalist concept of 'space' and my nonreductive perspective. In my analysis, the notion of 'space' coincides with the idea of a mutual exclusivity between *res cogitans* and *res extensa*, inaugurated by Descartes. The expression 'virtual spatiality' echoes the Heideggerian 'spatiality', which together with 'temporality' and 'historicity', is at the centre of his phenomenonological and existentialist project as laid out in *Being and Time*. These terms imply a critique of the way in which the tradition of Western metaphysics has 'objectified' space, time and history, which amounts to the inability to posit the meaning of these concepts beyond the oppositional framework set up by the subject-object distinction.

4 The critique of the rationalist concept of space as an alienated and inert 'outside' is one of the steadier themes in Heidegger's philosophy, spanning *Being and Time* to 'Building Dwelling Thinking', 1952. Section III of Part I of *Being and Time*, contains the kernel of his treatment of space. The discussion of spatiality is conducted as a critique of what Heidegger calls 'the Cartesian ontology of the world'. If my perspectivist conception of virtual spatiality draws from Heidegger the opposition to spatial inertia, it draws from Bergson and Nietzsche the further characterisation in terms of movement and heterogeneity.

5 It is difficult to locate a single definition of force in Nietzsche's work, since force is one of the most deeply embedded concepts in his philosophy. In this text, I discuss the idea of force as it is developed in the second of the *Untimely Meditations*, 'On the Uses and Disadvantages of History For Life'.

6 The discursive nature of forces cannot be pursued here. I define discursivity in relation to the all-encompassing notion of textuality assumed as a background for both deconstruction and hermeneutics. Since I derive the notion of force directly from Nietzsche, and the question of the nature of those forces remains problematic in Nietzche's own writings, I prefer 'discourse' over 'text' because it describes more pertinently what would be the nature of those forces according to a distinctly Nietzschean line of argument. It is no coincidence that Michel Foucault, who coined the term in the mid-1960s and launched it in the postmodernist and poststructuralist context, did so around the time when Nietzsche appeared on the French scene. Deconstruction was not yet born and Heidegger, along with hermeneutics, was still to make his impact on French philosophy. I wish to anchor the term to that context, in which it meant the implicit knowledge that underlies and makes possible specific social practice, institutions or theories.

7 One of the fundamental notions in *Being and Time* is 'thrownness' (*Geworfenheit*), which refers to the way in which we find ourselves always already 'placed' in our existence – we are not objectively present in it, but have to make it our own place, to appropriate it, give it meaning. It seems to me that within this, architecture plays a major role. The world in which we find ourselves thrown is a 'built' world, which has constituted us as what we are in many substantial ways. Some studies have tried to unravel the constitutive role of architecture along Heideggerian lines. A lucid analysis of this theoretical knot is provided by Karsten Harries in his *The Ethical Function of Architecture*, MIT Press (Cambridge, MA), 1997. See also David Farrell Krell, *Architecture: Ecstasies of Space, Time, and the Human Body*, SUNY Press (Albany), 1997 and Edward C Casey, *Getting Back Into Place: Toward a Renewed Understanding of the Place-World*, Indiana University Press (Bloomington), 1993.

8 See Erwin Panofsky, *Perspective as Symbolic Form*, Zone Books (New York), 1991; Hubert Damisch, *The Origin of Perspective*, MIT Press (Cambridge, Mass.); Alberto Perez-Gomez, *Architectural Representation and the Perspective Hinge*, MIT Press (Cambridge, Mass.), 1997.

9 In the Introduction to *Being and Time*, Heidegger first raises the question of presence (*Anwesenheit*) in conjunction with the Greek interpretation of being in relation to time. Assumed as *parousia* or *ousia*, the Being of beings is both ontologically and temporally understood as presence: a definite mode of time (the present). The identification of a specific temporal modality with the way in which beings are, is for Heidegger a meaningful move on the part of Greek thought, since it indicates a fundamental 'repression' of time's becoming quality. Western thought seeks to confirm being in terms of eternal stability (the notion of presence), which is but the abstraction of a specific modality of time: the present.

10 In the history of architectural theory, the concept of 'space' becomes central only from the late 18th century, as the issue of canonical authority, previously identified solely with Vitruvius, is raised in connection with a universal definition of authority, established on human rationality rather than canonical sources. This question is deeply intertwined with the interdependence of the Enlightenment categories of fraternity, humanity and freedom. The paradigmatic example of the role of space in the Enlightenment debate on the foundation of rationality can be found in Siegfried Giedion, *Space, Time and Architecture*, Harvard University Press (Cambridge, Mass.), 1974.

11 A thorough discussion of this point can be found in the excellent chapter on 'Perspectivism, Philology, Truth', in Alan D Schrift, *Nietzsche and the Question of Interpretation: Between Hermeneutics and Deconstruction*, Routledge (London, New York), 1990, pp144–68.

12 On this issue of ambiguity, I disagree with Brian Massumi in 'Sensing the Virtual, Building the Insensible', in Stephen Perrella (ed) *AD: Hypersurface Architecture*, vol 68, no 5/6, Academy Editions (London), 1998, who sees virtuality and ambiguity as incompatible: 'Ambiguity . . . belongs to signifying structure. It is nothing new for architects to build-in ambiguity in order to make an event of standing form, but ambiguity still addresses the conventional function of the sign-form'. I don't see why ambiguity needs to be interpreted in terms of the 'signifying structure'. Why can't it be felt or sensed? Bergson's definition of memory against perception touches exactly on this point. In order for a memory to emerge at the surface of consciousness, it needs to become a perception. However, there is a fraction of memory that remains attached to the past. This is how we know it is a memory and not a perception. Such attachment to the past gives to memory an aura of uncanniness, otherness, and, I claim, ambiguity.

13 Friedrich Nietzsche, *Untimely Meditations*, Daniel Breaseale (ed), trans RJ Hollingdale, Cambridge University Press (Cambridge, Mass.), 1997, p62.

14 See Perrella, *Hypersurface Architecture*, op cit; Lynn, *Animate Form*, op cit.

15 'Deep' and 'superficial' are typical examples of vague predicates and as such, are unmeasurable. I cannot tell, for example, whether 6 feet of water are deep or not, as I cannot tell whether a 3-millimetre cut in my skin is superficial or not. No amount of conceptual analysis or empirical investigation can settle these matters. See, Timothy Williamson, *Vagueness*, Routledge (London), 1994.

16 Henri Bergson, *Matter and Memory*, trans Nancy Margaret Paul and W Scott Palmer, Zone Books (New York), 1988, pp133–4.

17 Ibid, p9.

HARESH LALVANI
META ARCHITECTURE

Architect-morphologist Haresh Lalvani has developed a technique to modulate sheet metal into a wide range of new configurations that can be easily manufactured using a patent fabrication process he developed with Milgo-Bufkin. Here he discusses the development of his theory of Meta Architecture, his application of the term Hypersurface, and his work with Milgo-Bufkin which is currently launching his new design series.

Meta Architecture is based on manipulating morphologically structured information via algorithms and genetic codes that encipher the formal possibilities of architecture. These possibilities are determined by mapping them in a unified morphological universe,[1] a higher dimensional meta space, which (theoretically) encodes all past, present and future morphologies. It also maps all their transformations. The coding of structures within this universe leads to an artificial genetic code.[2] This is a universal morphological code[3] and acts as a driver for organising, shaping, building and transforming architecture over short-term and long-term time scales. Coupling the code with manufacturing processes, both at the macro level of current computer-aided manufacturing and the micro level of nanotechnologies and genetic engineering, enables the direct translation of the code into the physical process of building. Coupled with biological (DNA-based) or other (chemical, physical) building processes, the artificial genetic code enables growth, adaptation, evolution and replication of buildings, permitting architecture to design itself and eventually liberating it from the architect. Architecture as we now know it will end when self-architecture begins.[4]

Within this overall premise, several examples from my ongoing work in Meta Architecture, and the related visual product, Hyper Space Architecture (or Hyper Architecture), are presented. The work offers an alternative paradigm to 'digital architecture', which has emerged in the last decade. Increasingly sophisticated computer graphics tools have enabled architects to visualise relatively complex spatial environments in virtual space without recourse to physical models or, in some instances (as in Frank Gehry's museum at Bilbao), to digitise complex built models directly. These digital visualisations, all conceived in virtual space, are admittedly visually spectacular and are conceived 'top down', both visually and spatially. However, they are neither informed by construction methods or the properties of physical materials, nor by any morphological principles of space and structure, which impose strong constraints on architecture. Architecture, shaped by these constraints and modelled by morphological principles – including Meta Architecture – is architecture that proceeds from the 'bottom up'.

The works presented here exemplify the bottom-up approach in two different ways: one driven primarily by higher-dimensional geometry, and the other by combining geometry with manufacturing process in making physical form out of real material. Both examples show the unprecedented possibilities for shaping architecture opened up by recourse to basic morphological principles (geometric, topologic, structural, etc). The images demonstrating the first approach are excerpted from my folio 'Hyperspace Architecture', which shows the various applications of higher dimensions for architecture,[5] and the second approach is from an ongoing experiment currently being carried out with Milgo/Bufkin, a leading metal fabricator in New York.

Highly ordered geometry is used in the first approach (figs 1 and 2) as a basis for generating irregular hyperstructures; in this case, hypersurfaces. The term 'hypersurface' here is used according to its original meaning, defined in the strict geometrical (mathematical) sense: ie, having spatial dimensions greater than three. This definition contrasts with the usage in this and the previous special issue of *AD*, edited by Stephen Perrella, entitled 'Hypersurface Architecture', where the term 'hyper' is used as a meta-dimension of the surface and not its spatial dimension. Interestingly, in the first example shown here (figs 1a, b), the term has a double meaning. The two tiling designs are identical in their base geometry, which comprises an assembly of identical crescent-shaped tiles[6] based on two-dimensional projections from five-dimensional Euclidean space. The crescents are thus hyper-tiles. In addition, they have a superimposed pattern of dark lines, echoing the other meaning of 'hypersurface' (as used by Perrella). While the designs appear random, each tile is identically marked in both cases. The image captures the paradigm that irregular and random-looking designs can be constructed from identical modules, an idea of great significance for architecture as it visually blends order with chaos.

Another example (figs 2a–c) further exemplifies this juxtaposition between order and disorder in a three-dimensional structure. The irregular surface, a true hypersurface projected from higher-dimensional space, hovers like a cloud over a space that, when extended, is non-periodic. The structure can be constructed from a single-node design,[7] a single-strut element and flat panels. Additional stabilising features would most likely be needed for its structural stability. This is just one example of the unlimited and varied architectural compositions that can be constructed from this new morphological invention.

Fig. 1a

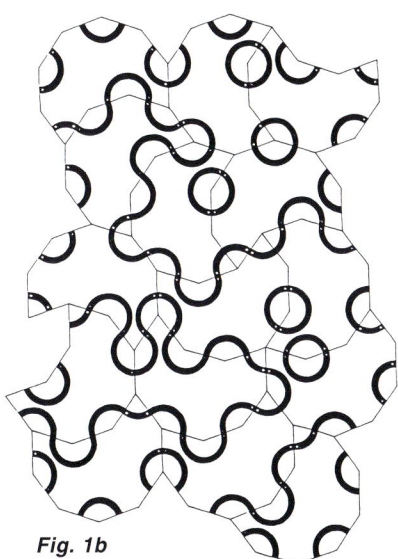

Fig. 1b

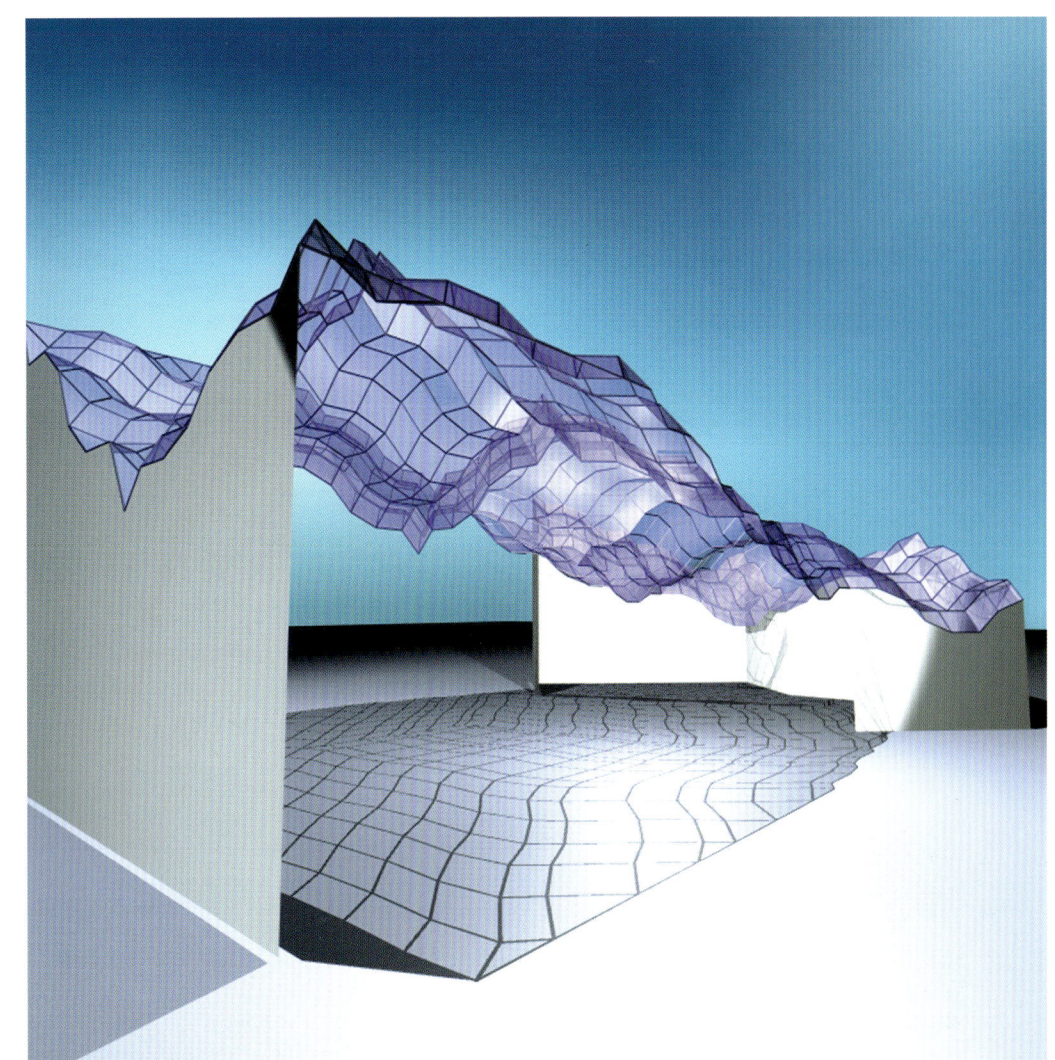

Fig. 2a

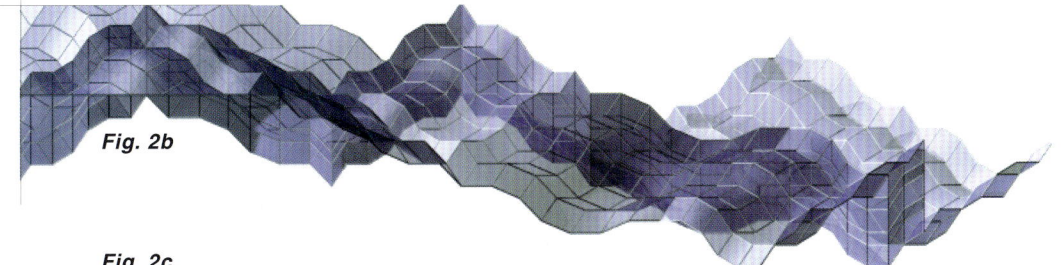

Fig. 2b

Fig. 2c

33

Fig. 3

The next group of images (figs 3a–o) exemplifies the second approach. The project deals with software-driven fabrication of sheet metal for architectural surface structures[8] and is being carried out at Milgo/Bufkin's manufacturing facility. Though columns, capitals, wall and ceiling panels are immediate architectural applications of concern for Milgo's business interests, the project provides a unique opportunity to experiment with broader Meta Architectural concepts, especially the relationship between an artificial 'genetic code' and the manufacturing process. All sheet-metal structures shown here were generated using a morphologically encoded algorithm, which provides the possibility to generate endless 'variations on a theme' by manipulating the code. As a result, no two structures need be alike, so each individual in the world, if desired, could have their own unique structure. A procedure was developed whereby single continuous metal sheets could be marked by computer-driven equipment and then folded (manually, for now). The resulting structures not only have a new look, but appear to be structurally advantageous at the same time. Architectural and industrial design products as well as complete environments based on these structures are currently being developed (figs 4-8). The algorithmic approach permits the structures to be modelled, transformed and fabricated with ease. We expect that the morphologic elegance in the shaping of these structures would also translate into an economy in building.

Fig. 4

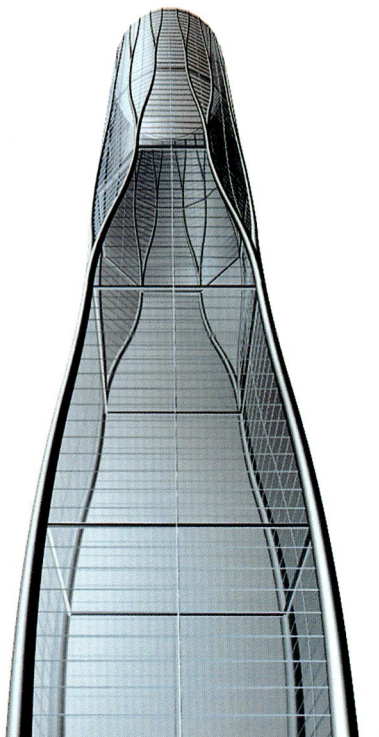

Fig. 5

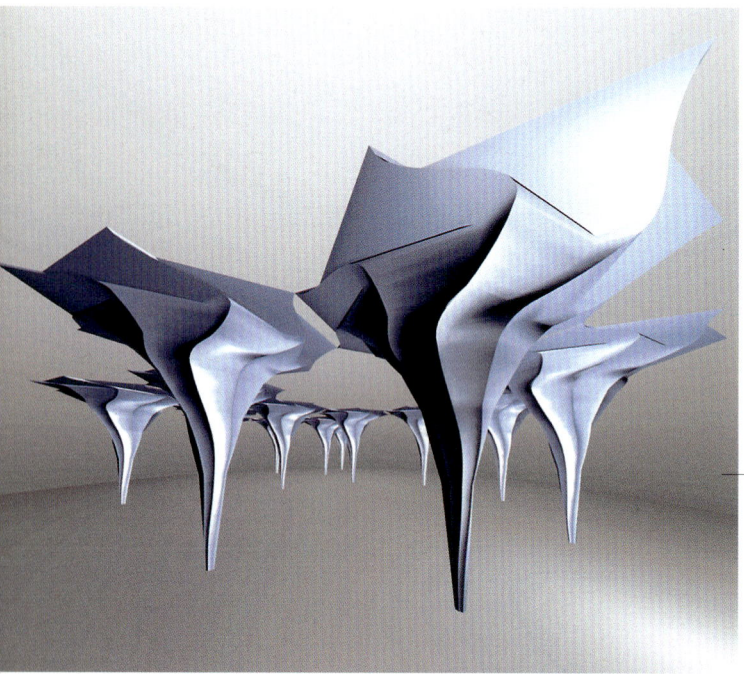

Fig. 6

Fig. 7

Column Museum (fig 4) shows a sampling of the morphologically encoded columnar structures being prototyped and fabricated at Milgo. *Fractal High-Rise* (fig 5) shows a branched fractal column concept applied to a glass skyscraper. *Umbrellas* (fig 6) utilises the twisted fold for a freestanding structure in an open-air environment. *Transitions* (fig 7) shows flat, wavy and irregularly curved walls within the same spatial layout, using the same material and fabrication technology. *WaveKnot* (fig 8) employs a continuous rippled surface for a ceiling or roof, defined by a simple topological knot space.

The undulating look of these structures resulted from an interest in the fundamental behaviour of sheet material under forces. Material 'flows' under its own weight and other forces according to predetermined morphologic laws, which pertain more to fluid motion than to static objects. Constructing architectural elements from rigid rectilinear units (such as bricks and beams), has 'frozen' this inherent flowing nature of architectural envelopes. The wrinkles on our skin, the surfaces of plants and skins of animals, waves and cloud forms, display this fluid-like quality in nature. Curvilinear architectural forms constructed using standard building methods have usually raised concerns of economy.

However, our experiments at Milgo suggest that advanced software-driven manufacturing processes, coupled with powerful morphological underpinnings, can easily and possibly economically generate a wide repertory of new curvilinear vocabulary unavailable to architects in the past. Paradoxically, high technology, representing the opposite pole in the man–nature dichotomy, permits fluid shapes not possible earlier in a simple and elegant manner and, in doing so, brings us closer to forms in nature. This is true not only in visible forms, but also in the concept of the genetic code, which permits each one of us to be unique yet encoded by the same basic genetic alphabets (DNA bases). These sheet metal structures are morphologically coded in a similar way.

Notes

I am indebted to the following for their contribution to the project: computer modelling and rendering, Neil Katz and Mohamad Al-Khayer; photography, Robert Warren; product development, prototyping and fabrication, Milgo-Bufkin with Bruce Gitlin and Alex Kveton. More information on these projects with Milgo-Bufkin, Brooklyn, New York, can be found on their website <www.milgo-bufkin.com> from January 2000.

1. Haresh Lalvani, 'Morphological Universe, Expanding the Possibilities of Design and Nature', unpublished, 1998, based on a lecture presented at ACSA conference, Dalhousie University, Nova Scotia, October 1998, on the theme 'Works of Nature: The Rhetoric of Structural Invention'.
2. My interest in the genetic code of architecture dates back to 1975; my first published work on morphological coding was in the context of Islamic patterns (1982). In 1993, I proposed 'architectural genetics' as an emerging science.
3. I have been developing such a code for over two decades. Early interim results appeared in 'Multi-dimensional Periodic Arrangments of Transforming Space Structures', PhD Thesis, University of Pennsylvania (1981), self-published as *Structures on Hyper-Structures* (1982). Subsequent extensions of this work have been published in various papers, and applications to various structural morphologies have been in progress since the early 1990s.
4. For the origins of 'growing' architecture, see William Katavolos, *Organics*, Steendrukkirj de Jong & Co (Hilversum), 1961; Vittorio Giorgini, 'Early Experiments in Architecture using Nature's Building Technology', in H Lavani (ed), *The International Journal of Space Structures*, vol 11, nos 1, 2, special issue, 1997.

Fig. 8

My work in this concept came via genetic engineering and was proposed in 'Towards Automorphogenesis, Building with Bacteria', unpublished, 1974, the source of which goes back to the question asked by my thesis of 1967: 'Why don't we build with bone and spider silk?' In recent years, John Johansen has been proposing growing architecture using 'molecular engineering'.

5 Lalvani, 'The Architectural Promise of Curved Hyperspaces', 2nd International Seminar: 'Application of Structural Morphology to Architecture', University of Stuttgart, 1994; 'Hyperstructures', in P Dombernowsky and T Wester (eds), *Engineering a New Architecture, Conference Proceedings,* Aarhus School of Architecture (Denmark), 1999.
6 Lalvani, US Patent 4,620,998, 1986.
7 Lalvani, US Patent 5,505,035, 1996.
8 Patent pending.'

38

STEPHEN PERRELLA
COMMERCIAL VALUE AND HYPERSURFACE
Theory, Art and Commerce Considered

Here Stephen Perrella discusses the background to the next three articles on Hypersurface, those by Greg Seigworth, Charlie Watson and Terry Rosenberg. All were inspired by a 30-second commercial for a Mazda car; the advert became known as 'Cool World' and the man behind it was Charlie Watson.

In October 1998, there appeared in our TV diet a car commercial with a curious special effect. This 30-second advert presented a surreal and mutational spatial dynamic: a car zipping through a fragmented cityscape in a way we had not seen before. The image seemed to be alive and in flux, an effective way of representing movement. It was as if the content and camera had melded into one image surface, into a hypersurface, where the affect of meaning occurred because of the way the surface was manipulated. There was a play between image and surface, in one fabric where neither was a plane of reference. And there it was: a consumer hypersurface, a plane of immanence that Gilles Deleuze himself might even acknowledge.

An inquiry was sent out to the ad agency, Doner of Detroit, regarding the specifics of the advert. We spoke to many individuals and creative teams. Then, one day, after many months, a shy young British fellow just happened to call. It was Charlie Watson of the LA special effects company Rhythm & Hues. I explained to him that we were very excited by his work in the Mazda Protégé commercial and that we were architectural theorists working on an idea called Hypersurface. He said he wasn't really sure how he had fallen upon the effect and explained the sequences but not in theoretical terms. Having never heard of Deleuze or planes of immanence, he asked his secretary Sara Foster to purchase a list of books we had suggested. Charlie was very interested in our thoughts and within a few days flew out to New York City to meet us. I didn't think we would get this far into the commercial apparatus.

Simultaneously, Henry Wojdyla and I had begun working with artist Terry Rosenberg on a collaborative sculpture that would tap into the dynamic that Charlie had employed in his up-beat advert. His commercial had been so successful that Mazda vehicle sales increased by 30 per cent. I asked Terry to consider the specific image/surface dynamics in terms of an artistic process that he had been working with, called the Generatrix. Terry's process was to score a sheet of plastic thereby modifying it, enfolding it into a warping object surface. It took several weeks before we had worked out a process for determining the diagrammatic lines we would modulate on the image surfaces of the Protégé commercial that Charlie had allowed us to work with.

Meeting Charlie Watson was surreal. It was an uncanny moment. Suddenly all the theory relevant to hypersurfaces was considered in purely commercial terms: the selling of a car. Doner had emphasised that the commercial had to stand out from other car adverts that all seemed very similar. It was an extraordinary meeting between Watson, Rosenberg and myself. It was an unbased exchange of three individuals with no basis for relation other than this curious and elusive hypersurface affect. What did art, architecture and car commercials have in common?

Also, at the same time, Greg Seigworth, a rigorous cultural theorist from Millersville, Pennsylvania, was asked to consider the Mazda commercial as a theoretical trope, to investigate the consumer spot to open its codes and associations. The result is the following article as a third moment in this emergent ensemble of theory, art and commerce.

Unless otherwise stated, all the images in this series of articles are from Charlie Watson's 'Cool World' commercial for the Mazda Protégé. They were produced using elastic reality computer software to create a hypersurface effect.

RIGHT: *Stephen Perrella,* The Haptic Horizon, *1995*

40

GREG SEIGWORTH
PROTEGULUM
Two or three approximations for hypersurface

It is ... constantly reconstituting itself by changing direction, tracing an inside space but coextensive with the whole line of the outside. The most distant point becomes interior, by being converted into the nearest.   Gilles Deleuze[1]

1. Pro-motional
From here on, constructed space occurs within an electronic topology where the framing of perspective and the gridwork weft of numerical images renovate the division of urban property. The ancient private/public occultation and the distinction between housing and traffic are replaced by an overexposure in which the difference between 'near' and 'far' simply ceases to exist.
Paul Virilio[2]

It begins with an overly bright yellow and black-banded sunburst: infinite horizon. Simultaneously, music is cued: a bouncy, synthetic tune, flatly sung-spoken in a late 1980s slacker hip-hop style. The song tells the tale of four Gen-X travellers and their car. There is Gina (with 'geographic memory'), Karen (dumping her boyfriend), Charley (working in cyberspace where it is 'backslash dot-com all day long') and Pamela (who can't sing but can keep the beat).[3] From the z-axis of the image-viewing space, two words phase in. Initially, they are a blur of motion but, as they recede into the depth of the sunburst-banded colours, they stop mid-screen, becoming legible as 'GET IN'.

Cut to: cityscape (faux-Soho). From tenement rooftops, the camera-perspective (if, indeed, an actual camera provides this view) pulls out and, next, swoops down into the city-space. Buildings and space itself warp and ripple under the effect of the digital swoop-zoom; it is as if, rather than merely passing by the buildings, the city is a single swathe of cellophane and a view is being stretched and extruded through it. From among the buildings, a car enters, travelling along a city street.

Cut to: car interior, a young woman (Gina) is driving. She checks the rearview mirror as the city gently ripples in the car's wake. As it pulls up in front of a tall apartment building (entirely composed of what appear to be – and actually are – unevenly stacked children's wooden blocks pasted over with photographed facades), a female friend (Karen) is exiting its front door. But the dimensions aren't quite right. Oversized, the friend stands a head taller than the building's first floor. When she slams the door, the entire building jostles and, in a quivering jumble, the huge blocks begin to tumble forward. At mid-tumble, our view takes a wide, sweeping stutter-shift to the front of the car, and a third friend (Charley) appears, standing in the right-hand foreground. His coffee cup catches one of the building's massive tumbling blocks (now turned sugar cube) as another hand reaches across from off-screen to take the cup from him. The perspective morph-rotates 180 degrees to reveal that the hand belongs to Karen, now seated to Charley's left in the backseat of the car. This transition is performed as one continuous shot; Karen winks at Charley.

Cut to: profile of stationary car, with its front passenger door swung open. The fourth and final passenger (Paula) is twirling into the car. The stop-frames of her motion have been composited together so that, mid-twirl, she is able to occupy two (or more) discrete frame-spaces at once. Once she is in the car, a cd is passed from backseat to front and into the player, the disc's trajectory is a shimmering series of blended space-time shifts.

Cut to: car exterior. The car's time-motion contrasts with the speed of the other mobile elements in the scene: mostly pedestrians and other cars. Compared to the far more rapid warpings and blurrings of its urban environment, the car is a stable, though occasionally stop-stutter-motion, object. If not for the lilting soundtrack, the city would be vaguely ominous, slightly dark and foreboding. There are quartered clock-faces, each with one of the four blocks left blank. The sidewalks are an uneven and haphazard arrangement of jutting, near-floating surfaces.

Three cuts take the car out of the city. The first shot is back to the car's interior, looking through the front windshield at the travellers bopping along to the soundtrack. The second shows the car in profile, passing along the street, as the tops of buildings flex forward, in feathered, tumble-block formation and then snap back into position – almost as if waving. The third and final shot is low and from behind as the car enters the frame in a continuity edit. The vehicle brakes briefly for a black cat then passes out of the city (which now falls off sharply to its left) through an old archway.[4]

Cut-away: from the cityscape back to the oversaturated sunburst horizon. The words 'GET IN' rise up, as if extruded from the background. 'BE MOVED' zooms in from off-screen, situating itself alongside 'GET IN'. The entire slogan – 'GET IN. BE MOVED' – sits briefly and then splits left and right, each section departing in its own blurred-motion direction in order to make room for the car company logo. Fade to black; fade music; 30 seconds of attention, briefly captured, disperses again in forgetting.

2. Proustian

Well, what nature does from time to time, by distraction, for certain privileged individuals, could not philosophy on such a matter attempt, in another sense and another way, for everyone? Would not the role of philosophy under such circumstances be to lead us to a more complete perception of reality by means of a certain displacement of our attention? It would be a question of turning this attention aside from the part of the universe that interests us from a practical viewpoint and turning it back toward what serves no practical purpose. This conversion of the attention would be philosophy itself.   Henri Bergson[5]

It is, after all, just an advertisement for a car. Not a just ad (is such a thing possible?), but just an ad. The 30-second TV spot is entitled 'Cool World'. The car that it advertises is the Mazda Protégé. Such a perfectly banal and, yet, appropriately sonorous name for a car. Any-car-whatever.

In a prescient moment of Don Delillo's *White Noise*, the novel's protagonist overhears his young daughter murmuring something in her sleep. Transfixed by whatever has burbled up from this dream-state, the father sits by the girl's side waiting to hear it again. When he finally catches hold of it, his daughter's dream-murmur turns out to be two words, a car name: 'Toyota Celica'.

A simple brand name, an ordinary car. How could these near-

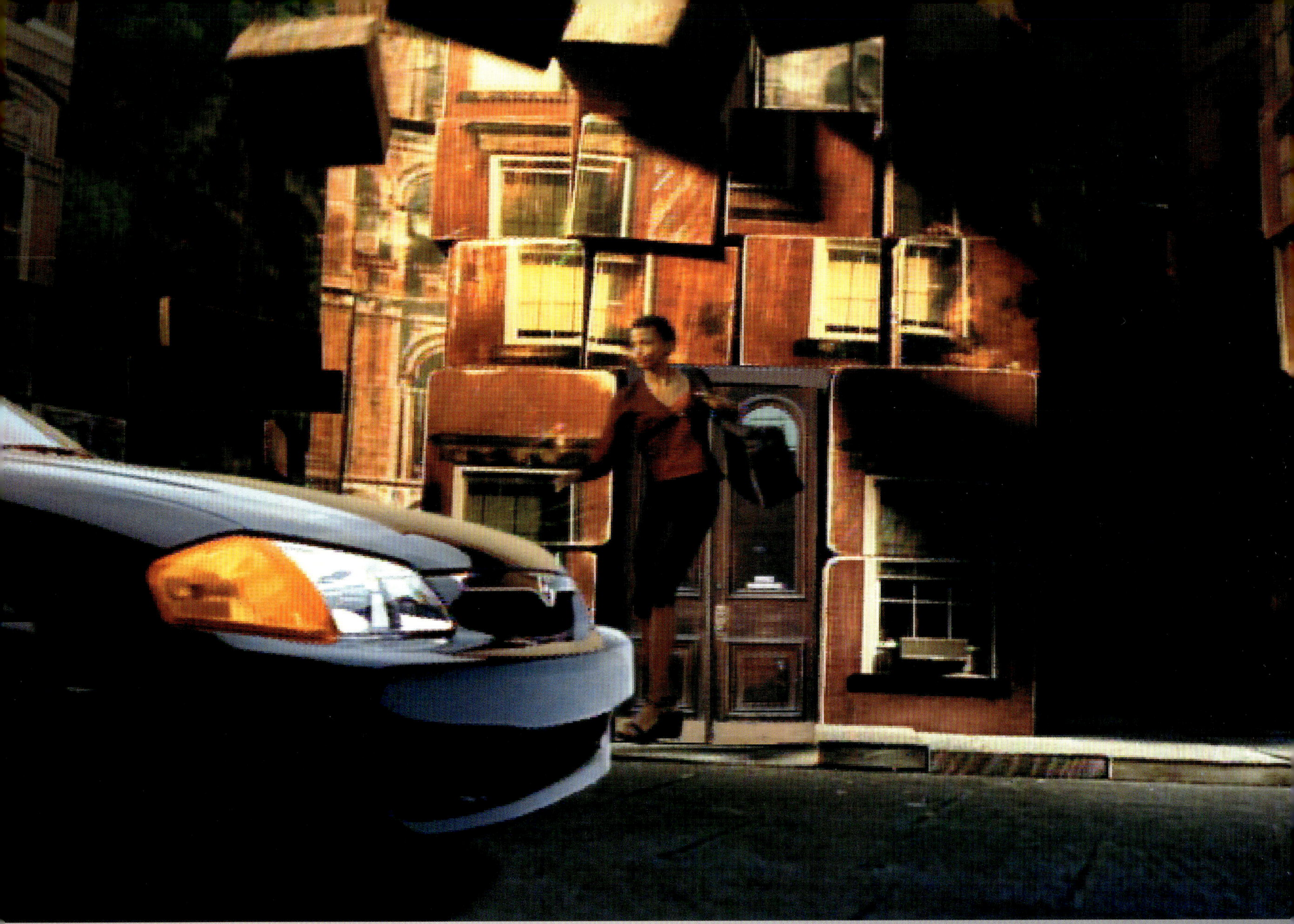

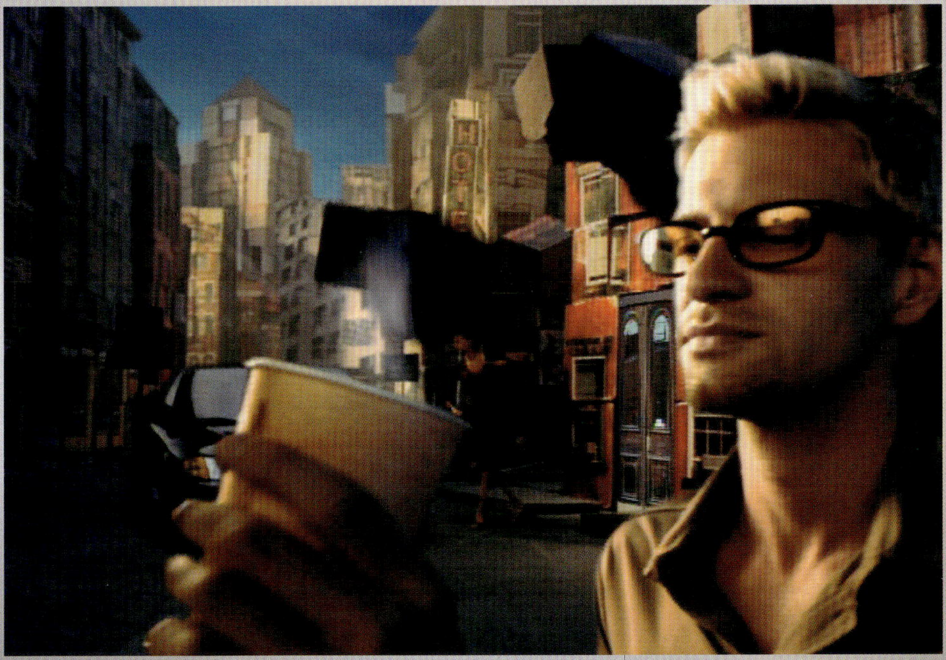

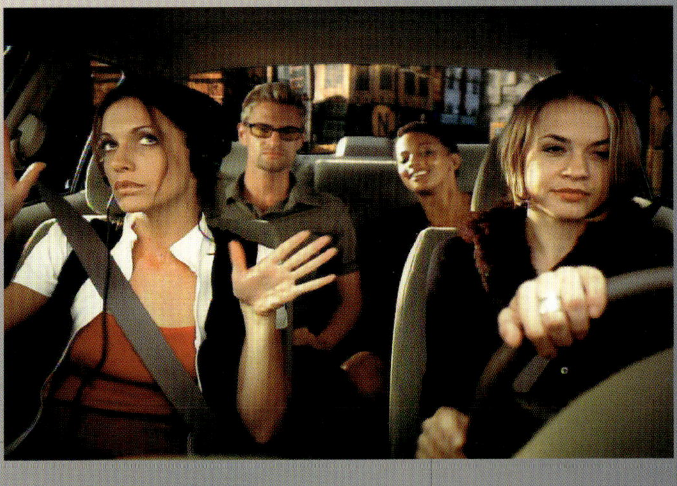

nonsense words, murmured in a child's restless sleep, make me sense a meaning, a presence? She was only repeating some TV voice. Toyota Corolla, Toyota Celica, Toyota Cressida. Supranational names, computer-generated, more or less universally pronounceable. Part of every child's brain noise, the substatic regions too deep to probe. Whatever its source, the utterance struck me with the impact of a moment of splendid transcendence.[6]

The unconscious. The supranational. Between them, a royal road. And, on it, a car. A car with a name like any other car: so matter-of-fact and so much a part of our everyday consumer glossolalia that saying its name is as simultaneously evaporative as it is apparently designative. The 'Cool World' of the Mazda Protégé: in the end, it's just an ad for a car for God's (or Godard's) sake. What might one do with it, besides burble?

In 1928, Walter Benjamin published what might serve as the prototype for any subsequent psycho-physiological analysis of automobile advertisements. Not unlike other patrons of the movie houses in his day, Benjamin found himself periodically ducking for cover as an oversized car careened off the cinema screen and out toward the audience, so strange and yet increasingly familiar was this space of spectatorship. Righting himself in his seat, Benjamin notes: 'It abolishes the space where contemplation moved and all but hits us between the eyes'.[7] How was the critic to compete with such an effect? If criticism was conceived as 'a matter of correct distancing', what happens when all 'things press too closely?' Benjamin's own answer – found in his title for this particular section of One-Way Street – was rather droll: 'THIS SPACE FOR RENT'. While not exactly throwing his hands up, Benjamin concludes this portion of his text by writing: 'What, in the end, makes advertisements so superior to criticism? Not what the moving red neon sign says – but the fiery pool reflecting it in the asphalt.'[8] This was Benjamin's indication that cultural criticism would need to move by other means: not through the distances of signs, but via the fiery immanence of the concrete.

With a 'FOR RENT' sign posted on the old space of contemplation, it was time to reorient the critique's own logic of sense and sensation. It needed to be relocated within a newly emergent sensibility (as reshaped by the sensory modalities that arrived with and alongside, for example, the motor car, the cinema, the flashing neon advertisement), in the different rhythms of embodied and out-of-body sensuousness that had truly begun to cut through and across, not only everyday life but, also, those critical models of contemplation that had dominated intellectual discourse up until the early 20th century. Hence, Benjamin's provocative notion of the 'optical unconscious' serves as an attempt to account for the infinitely diffuse qualities derived via the habitual inattentions and tactilities of modern everyday life. As Michael Taussig maintains, this model of the unconscious may be one of Benjamin's finest contributions to social philosophy: the discovery and description of,

> a very different apperceptive mode, the type of flitting and barely conscious peripheral vision perception unleashed with great vigour by modern life at the crossroads of the city, the capitalist market, and modern technology.[9]

Benjamin's 'optical unconscious' presents both an immanently materialist and incorporeally bewitched model of the unconscious: a fertile and furtive place for the uninterrupted and completely mundane accumulation of the peripherally insignificant. Instead of an unconscious where dreams provide the most royal road of access, it is an unconscious of 'waking dreams', ever open and in contact with its outside.

Any accent on the 'optical' of the optical unconscious is probably misleading since it would seem to over-emphasise visuality.[10] Perhaps better to call it a 'banal unconscious' since it subtends and sustains across the innumerable resonances and unregisterable intensities that pass in the most 'everyday hour'. In his wonderful analysis of Proust, Benjamin asks:

> Can we say that all lives, works, deeds that matter were never anything but the undisturbed unfolding of the most banal, most fleeting, most sentimental, weakest hour in the life of the one to whom they pertain?[11]

From within the seemingly peculiar but absolutely ordinary weave of space-time and motion-sense, Benjamin's optical (banal) unconscious resides. It is a site in which the future insists on the very immediacy of forgetting and on the hair's breadth arrival of the too-soon of the past, and where, no matter the distance, the object-world constantly presses up against us, only in order to turn ever so slightly and continue inconspicuously alongside.

It is this habitual appropriation of mundane and processual space-times absorbed in distraction that, Benjamin believed, revealed the centrality of architecture's contribution to the potentialities of transforming everyday life. Howard Caygill notes that Benjamin regarded 'architecture as the perennial art, the one that is in many respects the most porous and sensitive to change from the outside, whether in technology or in its 'relationship to the masses'.[12] Thus, the ineffable immanence of the concrete affords its own counter-response to the cancelling out of the space of contemplation by the hurtling on-screen car. And so, in what has become an oft-quoted and crucial passage (for architecture certainly) in his essay 'The Work of Art in the Age of Mechanical Reproduction', Benjamin writes:

> As regards architecture, habit determines to a large extent even optical reception. The latter, too, occurs much less through rapt attention than by noticing the object in incidental fashion ... For the tasks which face the human apparatus of perception at the turning points of history cannot be solved by optical means, that is, by contemplation, alone. They are mastered gradually by habit, under the guidance of tactile appropriation.[13]

Here, Benjamin sets out what seems a decidedly gradualist political programme for architecture. Of course, the near-glacial temporality of such a critical-aesthetic approach can appear maddeningly slow given the ever-accelerating rhythms of contemporary life. But no doubt this is the 'time' of architecture – unfurling in the interval where matter and space turn to the substance of encounter with its inter-affectual rhythms, rests, and speeds – at once too near and too far, too fast and too slow, relationships ungraspable even at the very moment in which they're at hand, under foot, enveloping. And, hence, the (literally) unseen powers of architecture: the incorporeal potentials that rise and fall beneath the distances and into the hidden pockets of the most intimate and indifferent attention.

What could be more banal, more fleeting, more prone to sentimentality and more 'insignificant and meaningless' than the virtual (barely acknowledged) ground of everyday life?[14] It is a groundless ground. Our everyday lives are a perpetually shifting, shuffling and stuttering (re-/de-)composition of these virtualities that are, as Gilles Deleuze liked to quote from Marcel Proust as shorthand for 'the virtual': 'Real without being present, ideal without being abstract'.[15] We have always been virtual (long before the arrival of the cinema, the shopping mall, the automobile, or the computer). But, crucially, how the virtual is made available to sensory appropriation and to what degree the virtuality of everyday life oscillates between sensibility and insensibility, between the ordinary and the remarkable, is determined in reciprocal affiliation with the outside. Between, always between, and nothing but a between. And it is this in-between that comes first. As such, its movements are envelope-in and middle-out: continual fold and unfold. Deleuze notes that, while the in-between or middle is often conceived as a 'third line' arising after the arrival of two others,

> this line has always been there, although it is the opposite of destiny: it does not detach itself from the others, rather it is the first, the others are derived from it. In any case, the three lines are immanent, caught up in one another.[16]

For our purposes, it is perhaps better to think of this third line or in-between as 'an infinite fold ... as the exterior or outside of its own interiority: partition, a supple and adherent membrane coextensive with everything inside' or what Deleuze, following Leibniz, calls 'the vinculum'.[17]

At one level, with the vinculum Deleuze is detailing the intagliated and lithesome hinge of virtual–actual and their intervallic exchange-relation. But, even more than that, the vinculum is also a completely sensuous concept. Although it is most easily surmised in the intermixture of the visual and the textural, Brian Massumi has also shown how it intersects with proprioception and a host of other corporeal and incorporeal modes of human existence and non-human inertness.[18] The vinculum is a complicative intermingling, resolutely concrete even in its apparent abstraction. The cross-pollination of Deleuze and Bernard Cache, for instance, is built, in part, around the intuitions and resonances that circulate in the atmosphere of the vinculum. Whether it is Deleuze describing one actualisation of the vinculum as a supple partition turned reflecting wall where optics pass into acoustics and where, thus, an infinity of variables is heard in their echo as a single undulating mass, or whether it is Cache commenting upon how – when a body situates itself before a mirror – vision is permeated by tactility and the body becomes 'a continuity that forms a single surface of variable curvature', the process of emergence outlined by each of them shares this trajectory where life, matter and thought are joined, moving alongside one another, cross-modal/inter-affective.[19] Thought and extension are uttered in the same voice: Spinoza's parallelism and Bergson's spirit and matter with the Leibnizian vinculum running down the middle as a fiery, immanent third line, the very crease of a fold. What must 'hypersurface' be, if not the architectural animation of this supple membrane?

3. Prosopagnosia

To be alive is unreachable by the most delicate of sensibilities. To be alive is inhuman – the deepest meditation is one that is so empty that a smile is exhaled as though it came from some matter.
                                                    Clarice Lispector[20]

Between Mazda's 'Cool World' spot and Stephen Perrella's 'hypersurface', there is, perhaps most immediately and most superficially, a certain shared waviness.[21] Not just a waviness that transpires across an apparent surface, but the kind of waving of folds where non-adjacent areas can come into contact. Where there is a switching of distances, where 'near' and 'far' touch. Where folds touch. Where faux-Soho tumbles into a coffee cup. But all in the intensive magnitude of a single, infinite surface or skin. That is, the imageless matrix moved through or folded is as much a part of the fabric or substance of composition as the more visible figures traversing the surface's undulations. Hence this attention to waviness: where surfaces – with their subjacent volumes and incorporeal shimmerings – rise, crest, fall, ripple, and seemingly do all of the other things that waves do. But what exactly is this affiliation of wave-fold to skin-surface?

In an interview on Michel Foucault, Deleuze links his work on surfaces, especially in *Logic of Sense*, to what he says was Foucault's own opposition of surface, not to depth, but to interpretation. 'Never interpret; experience, experiment ... The theme of folding and enfolding, so important in Foucault, take us back to the skin.'[22] We go 'back to the skin' because the skin provides what in commonsense seems, at first, to be one of the most self-evident barriers between what happens within our bodies (beneath the skin, belonging to an interior space, an interiorised subjectivity, 'I') and what transpires outside our bodies (beyond the skin, belonging to others and the outside world). Of course, though, the skin is also porous. But what if it is porous in ways rarely imagined? What if the skin were part of an even larger membrane: an extruded region of the interaffectual vinculum that composes our non-human line of becoming?

Consider, for example, studies conducted on patients suffering from the neurological disorder known as 'prosopagnosia'. Through galvanic skin-response tests, researchers have demonstrated that one can have 'knowledge without awareness'. When these patients are shown photographs of immediate family and friends, their bodies retain a familiarity with them even when their minds have deteriorated to a state in which they are no longer able to identify them.[23] Obviously, some kind of accumulation (vision to skin) has been called up, evoked, expressed. Afterimages of family and loved ones persist as a virtual presence: of the body but outside consciousness; imperceptible and yet perceived. But one must be careful in saying that it is somehow only the body, as flesh covered by a membrane of skin, that experiences a recognition or remembrance all on its own, since this is not exactly the case. 'It is not the body that realises, but it is in the body that something is realised, through which the body itself becomes real or substantial.'[24] For recognition to occur in people with prosopagnosia, the brain must be involved in the processing of the photographic images presented to them but, quite evidently, it is something more than the brain too. The resonance of the skin revealed in tests is built on the emission of the long-before accumulated intensities that arise again from the contextual interaction of a photograph and receiving body.

Following such results, the old adage 'out of sight, out of mind' should be revised, because even when a thing (or a loved one) is in sight, a portion of it will always be out of mind: outside of awareness but all the while impinging on a body nonetheless. 'Indeed, the virtual must be defined as strictly a part of the real object – as though the object had one part of itself in the virtual into which it plunged as though into an objective dimension.'[25] In the immersion of one's surroundings, the virtual is the 'outside' of consciousness stretched to its farthest expanses and the 'inside' of perception/sensation (as vibratory matter, if nothing else) in its most differentially particulate molecules and their interstices. In cases such as prosopagnosia, the brain has dropped out of mind and re-descended into matter (though it never really left): grey and intagliated with the body.

To take account of the virtual does not mean to elevate matter over mind (no ascendancy or supercession is necessary: parallel will do). After all, the flesh, claim Deleuze and Guattari, is only a developer that dissolves in what it develops.[26] Prosopagnosia studies reveal the virtual as something that, in its own unique way, belongs to its subject as an objective and imperceptible intensity, (re-)registering as an accumulation of passages through a body and across its surfaces. It is a perpetual process of exchange: part-dispersal, part-cocooning. 'Dissolve and envelop', like fold and unfold, is a process that belongs to far more than flesh and brain. Moreover, it is a process that extends through and beyond inorganic life and matter to encompass incorporeal resonances and auratic properties as well. The virtual serves to designate these interweavings upon a single plane as they ceaselessly weave and wave in a contextual forcefield of affects and intensities.

Not coincidentally, Mazda's 'Cool World' and Perrella's 'hypersurface' architecture partake of roughly similar contemporary impulses currently punctuating and permuting the viniculum (offering a sort of resonating galvanic skin-response test for the social-material world) as these impulses variously provoke the most contemporaneous and peripherally fleeting appearances/sensations of the virtual. They are new potential thought-images for the built-environment. Just how these new ways of waving/folding the surface-skin might be made manifest, as historical (and politically progressive) turning points, still remains before us. It is a tremendously gradual transition/transformation, these incidental appropriations, secretions and sheddings of the skin.

And, needless to say, there are some very fundamental distinctions – even at the level of a wav(er)ing surface fascination – that must be drawn between the 'Cool World' and hypersurface projects too. These are distinctions that most crucially pertain to the dominant, emergent and residual conditions of late capitalism: the need to distinguish between what counts (and where it counts) as symptom or as antidote, as proto-acceleration or as homeopathic strategy, as calculated leverage of a capitalising impulse or as an open-ended fabulation of new space-times for a people yet to come. It is for good reason that Deleuze and Guattari were suspicious, if not outright hostile, towards those contemporary marketplace forces that have come increasingly to speak in the name of concept-creation:

> computer science, marketing, design and advertising, all the disciplines of communication, seized hold of the word concept itself and said: 'This is our concern, we are the creative ones, we are the ideas men! We are the friends of the concept, we put it in our computers.'[27]

In spite of this usurping of 'the concept', Deleuze and Guattari advocate a philosophy that responds with 'the giggles, which wipes away its tears' and which then feels itself even more urgently driven to accept 'the task of creating concepts that are aerolites rather than commercial products.'[28] Not the too-timely jaws of a commodity-circuit opening then snapping shut, but an untimely architecture (and not only a thought-architecture) that works as a block of sensation: vibration, clinch or distension.[29] A world of captures instead of closures.[30]

Perhaps this begins to explain why, in the end, Deleuze doesn't sit especially well in the 'Cool World' of the Mazda Protégé. Almost inevitably, the car veers off somewhere else, becoming minimalist sculptor Tony Smith's car 'speeding along a dark motorway lit only by the car's headlamps, with the tarmac hurtling by in the windscreen. It's a modern version of [Leibniz's] monad', says Deleuze, 'with the windscreen playing the part of a small illuminated area.'[31] The four demographically tailorised Gen-Xers in Mazda's 'Get In. Be Moved' campaign seem miles from Deleuze in Smith's car. In part, the difference is the screen.

And it's not just the windscreen of Tony Smith's monad-car versus the Mazda Protégé's surfaces – although there is that aspect too, especially since, during its 30 seconds of on-screen time, the Protégé as surface reveals almost nothing (no resonating skin-conductance) of its environs. It doesn't reflect. It doesn't absorb. If anything, it refracts or repels all adjacent surfaces, skimming through and across the city surfaces like a skipping stone. Buildings and sidewalks might ripple and wave in its wake but the Protégé itself seems to lack the capacity to be affected.

Walter Benjamin may have looked to the fiery pool reflected in the asphalt while Deleuze prefers the tarmac hurtling by in the windshield but the net result of their thought-images is the same: the conjunction of a plane of immanence and affective reciprocity. But, like almost any advertising, this reciprocity will not be found within the virtual space-time of the 30-second Mazda ad itself but in the actual(isable) lived spaces of the viewer-spectator. In other words, the critical discourse of 'interpellation' applies here as it always has. 'Get In. Be Moved' is simply one more way – albeit a technologically sophisticated way – of saying 'Hey You! Complete Me'. So perfectly executed is the interpellative enunciation of the 'Cool World' spot that 1998 sales of the redesigned Protégé climbed 30 per cent from the previous year, with significantly revived interest from Mazda's youthful target demographic. One dealer testified that a couple of kids 'who looked like they were right from the ad' came into his showroom to buy the car.[32] Circuit completed, clamped shut, closed.

Architectural enunciation must follow more closely the meteorological line of flight of the aerolite, not the symmetrical consumerist closure of the commodity circuit. Guattari argues:

> The architectural form is not called to function as a *gestalt* closed in on itself, but as a catalytic operator releasing chain reactions among the modes of semiotisation that we make come out of ourselves and we open up new fields of possibility. The feeling of intimacy and existential singularity adjoining to the aura given off by a familiar framework, an old residence or a landscape inhabited by memories, places itself in the rupture of redundancies emptied of their substances and it can be the generator of a proliferation and line of flight in all the registers of life's desire, of refusal to abandon itself to the dominant inertia.[33]

Although Guattari maintains that he has absolutely no intention of asking architects 'to lie down on the couch of psychoanalysis', architecture and psychoanalysis might share, as he states elsewhere, an agenda:

> a 'futurist' or 'constructivist' opening up of fields of possibility. The unconscious remains bound to archaic fixations only as long as no assemblage exists within which it can be oriented toward the future; and in the future that faces us, temporalities of both human and non-human nature will demand just such an existential reorientation.[34]

The (waking) dream, then, is of an architecture that operationalises the surface-burble of the banal unconscious, that sets its task as

> detecting encysted singularities (what goes around in circles, which insists on nothing, what stubbornly refuses the dominant evidence, what puts itself in opposition to manifest interests ...), and in exploiting their pragmatic virtualities.[35]

Surely, this pragmatic operationalisation – as processual opening onto the outside (not closure of a circuit) – must be one of the necessary components of any hypersurface project. Because otherwise, says Guattari (now taking his turn in the driver's seat): 'The computer voice – "You have not fastened your seatbelt" – does not leave much room for ambiguity'.[36]

Protegulum

In the opening words of his essay 'Architectural Enunciation', Félix Guattari writes:

> Over thousands of years, perhaps in imitation of crustaceans or termites, human beings have acquired the habit of encasing themselves in all kinds of shells: buildings, clothes, cars, images and messages, that they never stop secreting like a skin, adhering to the flesh of their existence just as much as do the bones of their skeletons. There exists nonetheless one notable difference between man, crustaceans, and termites. It is that at present no census has been taken among these last two species of architectural corporations, of the tailors and 'pros' of their media.[37]

Perhaps, then, it would not be entirely facetious to wonder aloud – by way of concluding – what 'hypersurface' could learn, not only from a Mazda Protégé commercial, but also from a phylum among the most ancient of living marine invertebrates known as 'brachiopods' (or lamp shells). Believed to have first evolved about 570,000,000 years ago, the brachiopod is a living fossil that superficially resembles the bi-valve mollusc and, outwardly at least, Stephen Perrella's 'Möbius House Study'. Indeed, while the brachiopod has its own kind of Möbius strip called a 'lophophore' (concerned primarily with the processes of feeding and respiration), even more intriguing is its generative shell structure, which begins in the larval stage as a 'protegulum'. Quite fascinating as natural architecture, the brachiopod's protegulum – as it is progressively formed through a process of steady secretion and accretion – helps to set the on-going relationships for what counts as (and what circulates from) inside and out. It acts simultaneously as surface, hinge, calcified yet active shell-memory and flow-regulator for the brachiopod. Taking a census of the protegulum might serve as a way to bring the remote past of one of the world's first architecture corporations into contact with an overexposed and too upclose future, eclipsing – from an altogether different direction – the once-marked distances of 'near' and 'far' like a hypersurfaced building tumbling into a coffee cup.

Notes

1 Gilles Deleuze, *Foucault*, Sean Hand, (trans) University of Minnesota Press (Minneapolis), 1986/1988, p123.
2 Paul Virilio, 'The Overexposed City', *The Lost Dimension*, Daniel Moshenberg, (trans) Semiotext[e] (New York), 1984/1991, p13.
3 The soundtrack is by a band called the Nails. It was originally a song called '88 Lines About 44 Women'.
4 It is the kind of gateway that, as Virilio writes, cities no longer depend upon for their access (op cit, p13). Barely big enough for a single car to pass through, the archway appears to serve only as an exit.
5 Henri Bergson, *The Creative Mind*, Mabelle L Andison, (trans) Greenwood Press (New York), 1968, p163.
6 Don Delillo, *White Noise*, Penguin Books (New York), 1985, p155.
7 Walter Benjamin, 'One-Way Street', *Reflections*, Edmund Jephcott, (trans) Schocken Books (New York), 1978, p85.
8 Ibid, p.86. On a somewhat related note, see Beatriz Colomina's remark, from a discussion with Greg Lynn and Rem Koolhaas: 'We don't need critics for their sensibility, perhaps for something else, like publicity', in Cynthia Davidson (ed), *Anyhow*, MIT Press (Cambridge, Massachusetts), 1998, p208.
9 Michael Taussig, *The Nervous System*, Routledge (New York), 1992, p143.
10 This is, no doubt, a consequence, in part, of Benjamin's early elaboration of the concept in his essay, 'Little History of Photography', in Michael W Jennings, Howard Eiland and Gary Smith (eds), *Walter Benjamin: Selected Writings Volume 2: 1927-1934*, Rodney Livingstone and others, (trans) Harvard University Press (Cambridge, Massachusetts), 1999, pp507-30.
11 Walter Benjamin, 'The Image of Proust', in *Illuminations*, Harry Zohn, (trans) Schocken Books (New York), 1969, p203.
12 Howard Caygill, *Walter Benjamin: The Colour of Experience*, Routledge (New York), 1998, p115.
13 Walter Benjamin, 'The Work of Art in the Age of Mechanical Reproduction', *Illuminations*, op cit p240.
14 Lefebvre, *Everyday Life in the Modern World*, Sacha Rabinovitch, (trans) Harper & Row Publishers (New York), 1968/1971, p27.
15 Gilles Deleuze, *Proust and Signs*, Richard Howard, (trans) George Braziller Inc (New York), 1964/1972, p57. Additionally, it is Henri Bergson who serves as the pertinent link between the sections of this essay. His conception of an 'ontological unconscious', his call for renewed philosophical attention to distraction, his influence on Proust, his elaboration of the virtual spaces of everyday life serve to undergird many of the viewpoints here. In recent years, Bergson (often via Deleuze) has increasingly come to serve as a prime reference point in certain architectural theorising. See, for instance, several of the essays in *Anyhow*, op cit. Of particular note is a comment from Sanford Kwinter: 'We are interested today in the Bergsonian ontology as an absolute, as a necessity, a dynamic system and phenomenon' (p53).
16 Gilles Deleuze and Claire Parnet, *Dialogues*, Hugh Tomlinson and Barbara Habberjam, (trans) Columbia University Press (New York), 1977/1987, p125.
17 Gilles Deleuze, *The Fold: Leibniz and the Baroque*, Tom Conley, (trans) University of Minnesota Press (Minneapolis), 1988/1993, p111.
18 Brian Massumi, 'The Bleed: Where Body Meets Image', in John Welchman (ed), *Rethinking Borders*, Macmillan (London), 1997.
19 Deleuze, *The Fold*, op cit, p112; Bernard Cache, *Earth Moves: The Furnishing of the Territories*, Michael Speaks (ed), Anne Boyman, (trans) MIT Press (Cambridge, Massachusetts), 1983/1995, p134–6.
20 Clarice Lispector, *The PASSION according to GH*, University of Minnesota Press (Minneapolis), 1964/1988, p165.
21 See Stephen Perrella (with Rebecca Carpenter), 'Times Square, Human Agency', 1995, in John Beckmann (ed), *The Virtual Dimension*, Princeton Architectural Press (New York), 1998, p234.
22 Deleuze, 'Breaking Things Open, Breaking Words Open', *Negotiations 1972–1990*, Martin Joughin, (trans) Columbia University Press (New York), 1990/1995, p87.
23 Israel Rosenfield, *The Strange, Familiar, and Forgotten*, Vintage Books (New York), 1992, p123.
24 Deleuze, *The Fold*, op cit, p105.
25 Deleuze, *Difference and Repetition*, Paul Patton, (trans) Columbia University Press (New York), 1968/1994, pp208–9.
26 Gilles Deleuze and Félix Guattari, *What is Philosophy?*, Hugh Tomlinson and Graham Burchell, (trans) Columbia University Press (New York), 1991/1994, p183.
27 Ibid, p10.
28 Ibid, pp10–11.
29 Ibid, p168.
30 Deleuze, *The Fold*, op cit, p81.
31 Deleuze, *Negotiations*, op cit p157.
32 *Automotive News*, 25 January 1999, p17.
33 Guattari, 'Architectural Enunciation', in *Cartographies schizoanalytiques*, unpublished Tim Adams, (trans) Galilee Press (Paris), 1989, p300.
34 Félix Guattari, 'The Three Ecologies', *New Formations 8*, Chris Turner, (trans) 1989, p132.
35 Félix Guattari, 'Ritornellos and Existential Affects', Juliana Schiesari and Georges Van Den Abbeele, (trans) in Gary Genosko (ed), *The Guattari Reader*, Blackwell Publishers (Cambridge, Massachusetts), 1996, p169.
36 Guattari, 'Machinic Orality and Virtual Ecology', *Chaosmosis*, Paul Bains and Julian Pefanis, (trans) Indiana University Press (Bloomington & Indianapolis), 1995, p89. For Guattari's propensity for forgetting where he's parked his car, see his 'The Refrain of Being and Meaning', Jill Johnson, (trans) in *Soft Subversions*, Semiotext[e] (New York), 1996, pp233–47.
37 Guattari, *Cartographies schizoanalytiques*, op cit, p291.

CHARLIE WATSON
COOL WORLD
'Get in. Be moved.'

The thought process that led to the original 'Cool World' spot was a fairly direct route involving few detours. I was influenced by a variety of sources. When I was sent the original storyboards from WB Doner, they showed the basic narrative of a girl driving a car through a city and picking up three friends before driving out of town. The city was portrayed with an illustrative quality, indicating an invitation to make the ad from an artistic point of view. They were looking for someone to create a city, rather than merely photograph a real one.

In every artistic and creative journey (and in particular creative advertising), there is a significant point at which one asks oneself 'what would I do if this were my own work, entirely free from the influences or requests of other people?' The earlier this question is raised, the better.

I remember thinking, 'Well, what would I do if I were making this for myself, back in some big barn in the English countryside, with all the lights, film, cameras and sets I needed?' I tuned to the things that make me passionate: the photographs, the film-making and lighting, the close-up shots of faces reacting, and the clothes that excite me. And the type of photography I did back at school. I'd film stuff on 16mm cameras and make photographic prints of the frames, then texture the prints – cut some of them up and re-film them. The result was textured film as moving illustration.

I thought of this tactile re-interpretation of the photographic image, of taking that feeling of textured, mismatched photographs and applying it to the commercial in some way. Photographs arranged like a grid. What if the photographic grid were three dimensional? I remembered some old wooden building blocks my mother had as a child. They portrayed scenes of animals, farm buildings, etc. You could arrange a scene by lining up all the blocks correctly. You could then change the picture by turning all the blocks 90 degrees; a new scene was born. What if this formed a city? A four-year-old lad with an over-developed sense of architecture and an abundant supply of building blocks had been left alone for a week in the attic, and had created his own universe.

There is a combination of sophistication and naïvety in this. The naïvety is the lack of rules and boundaries present in a child's mind, the lack of formal structure; only the urge to re-create what he has seen out in the world through the filter of his own imagination. The sophistication comes from how close to reality he manages to get, and the seemingly intimate detail apparent in the three-dimensional collage he creates.

How could life be present in this city? The car and people could be filmed separately and composited into this environment. The appearance of the buildings would already be fragmented, re-interpreted. Some windows would be printed larger than others. Images would overlap. Apply this to movement. The movement of the people could be fragmented. Their images could overlap (the head turns half a second faster than the shoulders do, for example). The car could move the same way, overlapping angles and dissolves. Crucially, this thinking developed into filming a series of still images and bridging them together with morphs, to create the impression of motion. Your mind would fill in the gaps.

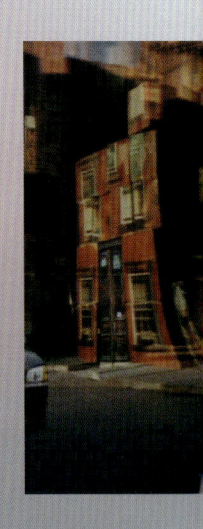

It was a logical step to infect the motion of the camera itself with this feeling. The opening shot shows the camera's descent into the city through a series of locked-down camera positions that are morphed together. The fragmented feeling is enhanced by the way in which one part of a building changes perspective before another part.

Once this flow of motion was clear, more interpretation of collage and fragmentation came to mind. How about applying it to time? Let's freeze time when the girl slams the door to her house. But at the same time, let's keep the story moving. The coffee-cup shot portrayed a guy continuing to drink while the world around him is frozen. We move around him, he drinks; everything else is static. Instead of him revealing the story to us, we reveal the story to him, by moving around him. To me, the combination of two threads of time in the same shot was exciting to create; he only sips for five seconds, but 20 minutes might have elapsed from the time that the girl slams her front door to when she is suddenly sitting next to him and stealing his cappuccino with a cheeky wink. Five seconds for him; 20 minutes for her: stick them together in the same shot. They provide contrast for each other; like everything else that works in the story, the two contrasting elements give the viewer something clear to lock on to. I like the contrasts: of lighting; of sophisticated photography on simple children's building blocks; toppling buildings that appear tall, but in reality are 3 feet high.

I want to contrast this commercial with the next one by not repeating the same formula – for there is now a formula to this 'style'. It's popping up here and there, which is very flattering to all involved, but as soon as there's a formula for something it's no longer fresh or creative. And you can believe that the greatest sceptics at the project's inception are now its greatest experts and 'architects'! I have found that one of the most significant and invigorating parts of my job is to create a new way of looking at things through time and space, limited only by the glass at the front of the screen and the borders that frame it. Everything else is fluid.

ABOVE: Discussing the hypersurface art project, 1999. From left to right: Terry Rosenberg, Charlie Watson, Stephen Perrella.
BELOW: Sequence from Rhythm & Hue's Protégé commercial, 1998

49

HENRY E WOJDYLA
TERRY ROSENBERG – GENERATRIX

In his 'Generatrices' series of sculptures, Terry Rosenberg has developed a paradigm preoccupied with ideas of folding and scoring in relation to the continuous surface. The natural affinity of his work with computer-aided design and assembly and hypersurfaces has led him to collaborate with Stephen Perrella on Cool World.

Gen' er-a' trix (jen'er-a'triks), n.; L. pl. -atrices (-a-tri'-sez). [L.] - Geometry. That which generates; the point, line, or other magnitude whereby its motion generates another magnitude, as a line, surface, or solid. A describant.
Webster's Collegiate Dictionary, 7th Edition

Since 1981, Terry Rosenberg has investigated the implications of emergent approaches that form and inform dimensional surface generation. The media of inquiry are sculptures termed 'Generatrices', which are themselves systems of topological discovery. Generatrices reside in and between the two- and three-dimensional, thus actualising transitory conditions where material and space are concurrent and inseparable. Flat surfaces are scored creating lines of deflection, which transform them into corresponding '2 1/2'-dimensional systems. Produced from sheet materials, Generatrices occur in differing topological phases from tectonic to transparent. The results are more than sculptural, rather informational 'hypersurfaces' that simultaneously define and reinterpret our comprehension of graphics, sculpture, cinematography and architecture.

A group of Generatrices called *Projections* introduce transparent sheet materials such as pigmented plastic, photographic transparencies and woven or perforated metal. These expose the relationships of overlapping surface and space, thus intensifying their informational significance. They are illuminated mobiles that project topological events in actual space–time onto adjacent planes, generating a modulating dialogue of relativities. Various events such as moiré patterns, montages and imaging deflections convey the depth of topological phenomena.

Unique to this work is its redefinition of traditional design methodologies that for the past century have focused on Constructivist philosophies. The Generatrix paradigm elaborates upon ideas of the score and fold in relation to a continuous surface evidencing a natural propensity to computer-aided design and assembly. Rosenberg's collaboration with product development firms has yielded a variety of prototypical manifestations relevant to art and architecture that demonstrate rigorous designs offering economy in labour and ecological implication.

Generatrices are relevant to our future. Their greatest asset is the forcasting of the virtual and temporal as 'hypersurfaces'. This indicates a middle-out approach to form and information interpretation, simultaneously addressing artistic and programmatic issues. As our information-immersed society struggles to develop meaningful cultural attitudes and understandings of the virtual, Generatrices will act as 'describants' of our culture.

Terry Rosenberg, Generatrix *FROM ABOVE: Spray paint aluminium cloth, #11, 1989; Colorine on polycarbonate, projection #1, 1992; Ink on stainless steel screen, #13.1989*

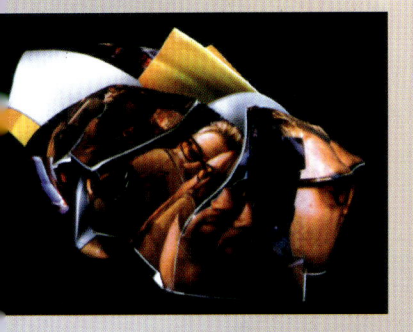

Stephen Perrella and Terry Rosenberg, Hypersurface, Protegé, 1999

HYPERSURFACE ANALYSIS OF COOL WORLD
Terry Rosenberg and Stephen Perrella (with Henry Wojdyla)

The fold activates a middle-out condition along the score line. The inside/outside simultaneously interrelate being two sides of the same skin.

The skin, by nature of the score and fold, additionally acts as bone. The physical properties of the score/fold create structural integrity by their continuous relationship in the sheet material. The layers of surface information describe both the topological motion and re-location of related images.

In the Cool World collaboration with Stephen Perrella, the score-and-fold methods previously used with Generatrices and Projections were pushed to new diversities by articulating the variety of images/structural qualities in the Cool World video. With Cool World, the score/fold transforms the two-dimensional to three-dimensional (with the four-dimensional intact) by the movement, force, directionality, torque and tension of the entire surface. We have made a range of versatile readings of the image/structured surfaces from film to storyboard to moving architecture. The information starts as one sheet (front and back) where plan is/becomes structure and information field in the same sheet.

Navigating hypersurfaces requires an instinctual consciousness because the complexities cannot be reduced to a linear reading as one experiences or creates the condition. With hypersurface, complexities melt into a problematic flux. As one perceives the fractures and folds of the space/surfaces, the body intuitively comprehends (via the motion) the folded complex, thus shedding light on the schizophrenic physical, chemical, cultural, philosophical, aesthetic and commercial everyday reality. In, on and through hypersurfaces, we can navigate the cultural schizophrenia in our accelerating world.

52

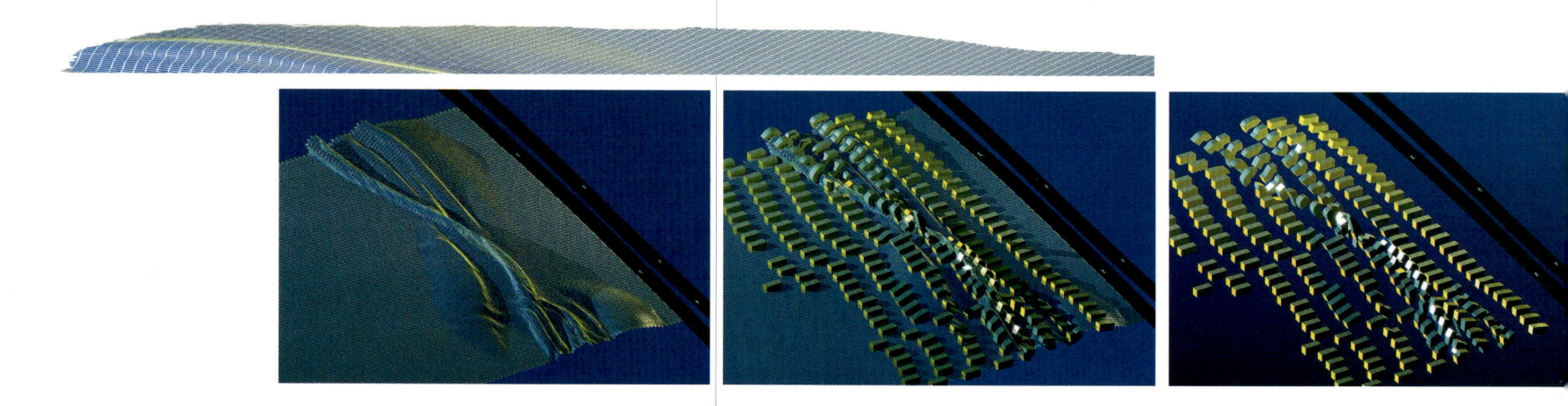

NOX
OFF-THE-ROAD/103.8 MHZ
Housing and Noise Barrier, Eindhoven, 1998

Entering the city of Eindhoven in The Netherlands, a monumental noise barrier symbolically confirms the separation of the technical from the urbanistic and the no-man's land that lies between these two ways of thinking. On one side of this high wall lies the A58; on the other the Blixembosch quarter, founded on the nostalgic typologies of New Urbanism. Our cities (and our thinking) become more and more pervaded with this fatal distinction between bits and bricks, the technical and the visual, media and architecture, waves and ground. In 'Off-the-road/103.8 Mhz', commissioned by the StadBeeld Committee, sound is turned into image.

This is achieved in a completely non-metaphorical way by transforming the profile of the existing noise barrier with animation software into a system of strings: five at the bottom and two thicker ones at the top. In the computer model, these strings are given the same properties as those of a musical instrument, made to vibrate by the sound of passing traffic. The wave patterns triggered in the strings are recorded at certain intervals and 'added up' as a sonoric landscape. The resulting diagram is literally an image of sound that can be simultaneously read along both axes as a musical score in time and an orchestration in space.

With Le Corbusier's Plan Obus (1930) in mind, where the linearity of the highway was celebrated as a de-suburbanistic carrier to enable a maximum architectural differentiation of type, we find here an attempt to make the highway inhabitable, but not simply by reducing the distance between car and house with a single megastructure. The space between highway and residential area is utilised to create a zone of transition, by turning it into a field, a medium, a system characterised by wave patterns, by 'differentiation within the continuous', without the familiar figure/ground relationship.

Instead of distributing typologically differentiated images, the 208 houses follow the exact inflections of the sound patterns, creating a complete differentiation within one volume. The chosen volume of 500 m^3 is flexed in all directions and, accordingly, the programme is also stretched. The number of floors required to make the various forms inhabitable varies between a single one for more-or-less horizontal volumes, and several different ones for roughly vertical volumes. Each residence is therefore different, but not unique because it is always a transformation of its neighbour. This blending of form and programme also takes place at ground level. All houses can be reached by car, sometimes over asphalt, sometimes over sand. Everything is designed so that cars can never develop any significant speed, bringing them to the same level as pedestrians.

All houses are equipped with a sound system. The interior noises (the tingling of spoons in coffee cups, barking dogs, fighting spouses, the folding of a newspaper, the slamming of a door, the sounds from the TV) of all 208 residences are fed into a central computer that arranges these sounds in a real-time composition, which is then relayed to a small transmitter. People driving along highway A58 at this point can tune into 103.8 Mhz, instantly connected to the interior of the houses via car radio.

Just as the shape of the residences interferes with the sound of the cars, the interior of the cars will resonate with the sound of the residences. Here, one could say that object and trajectory coincide and speed becomes inhabitable. In fact, for the first time in architecture, the sound barrier is broken.

V2 LAB (PART OF V2 ENGINE)
Renovation within the V2 Building, Rotterdam, 1998

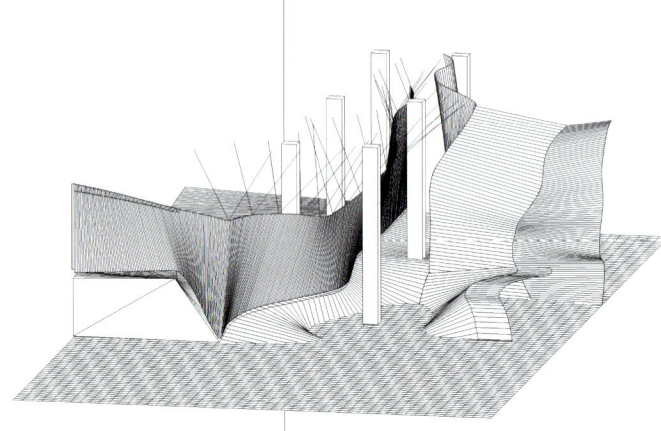

The V2 Lab is part of a larger concept, the V2 Engine. This project is based on the future renovation of the entire V2 building, which will include converting the facade and hall, as well as inserting an extra floor for public activities (bookshop, café and lecture area) in the large exhibition space on the ground floor. This concept has been entirely developed by computer, with animation software that allows for a non-linear, time-dependent architecture.

The V2 Engine consists of a central void, which will be partially finished with synthetic translucent fabric. This will protrude from the facade far enough to be visible from the Witte de Withstraat (a main street nearby). The space will be filled mainly with sounds and images generated by a specially developed software engine that will roam the Internet in search of webcam images of other facades around the world. These images will then be projected from the inside onto the fabric of the facade, together with other images: live portraits of people working at V2, pictures from projects being developed at the time within the V2 Lab.

This concept is not based on the classical distinction between media and architecture where the hole – the void filled with light – is positioned against the material – static and solid architecture. Nor is it based on the even cornier notion of architecture as carrier and media as image.

Instead, the concept is the result of a media criticism of architecture: within a medium, events progress by means of waves, not just within the topological continuity of the medium, but more to induce movement within this continuity by passing on forces within the field. The Euclidean distinction between a point and a line prohibits this, as each point effectuates the separation of lines rather than stimulates their joining. Therefore, with this project, the point constitutes a knot, capable of shrinking and expanding, scientifically known as a 'spring' – a non-static point able to pass on force. Within the computer model that has been developed for the V2 Engine, this spring is the place where the void – the three-dimensional window through which the audience will enter the building in the future – will be located, according to the organisational diagram. All forces within the spring are channelled towards the extremes of the building by way of 'strings', which will be located in the vicinity of the V2 Lab, the extra floor, the new hall and the facade. These forces from the

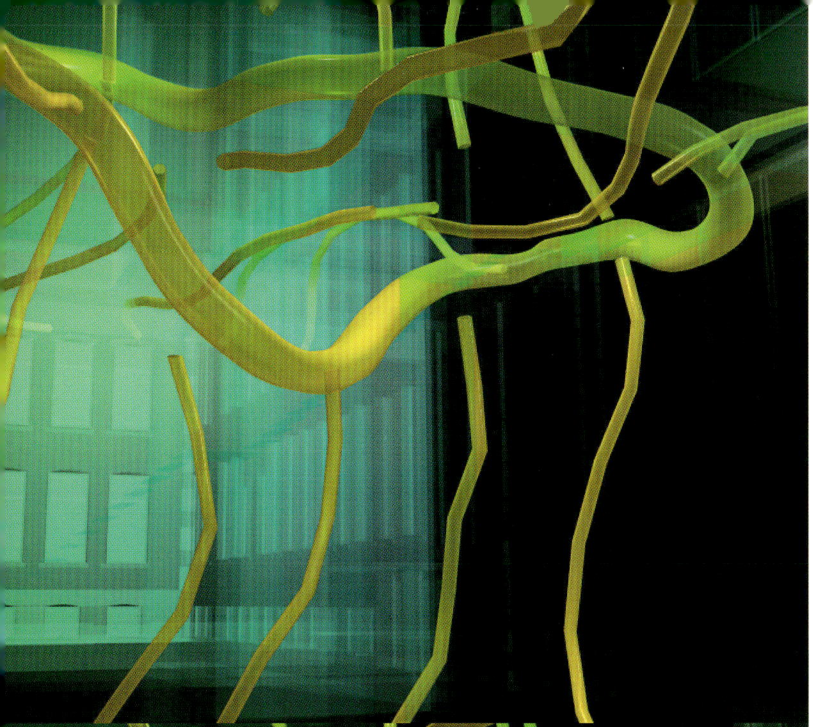
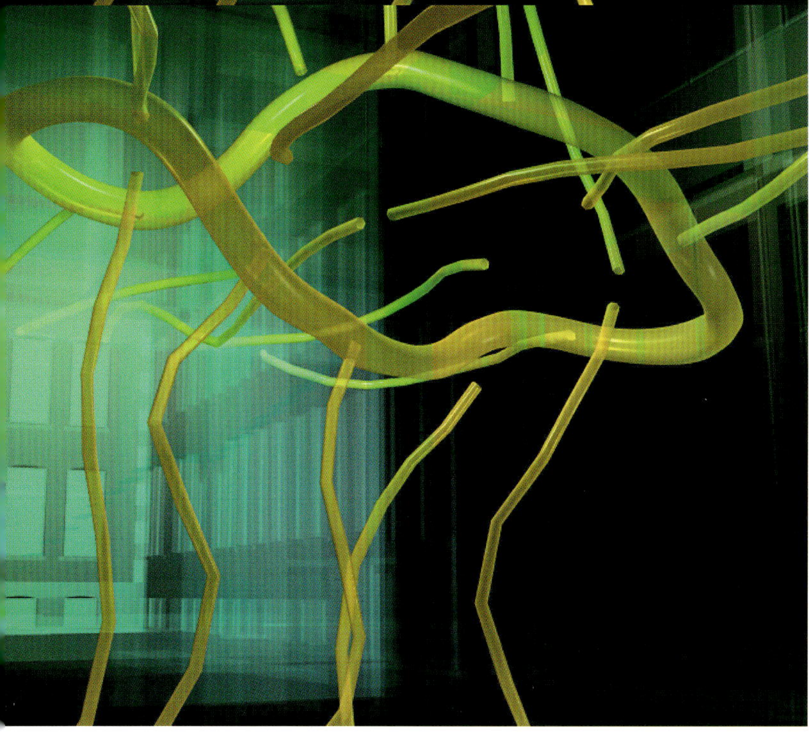
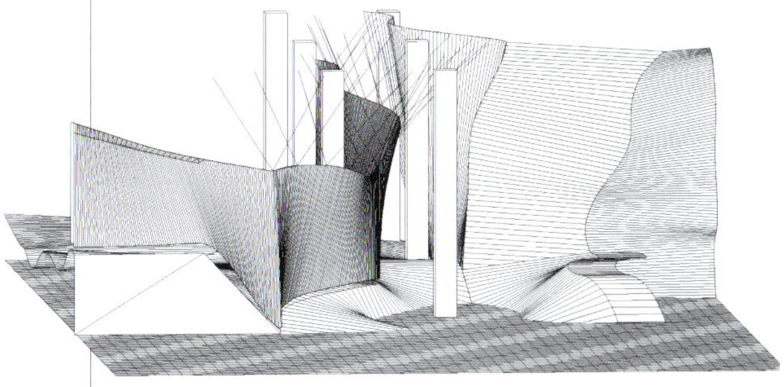
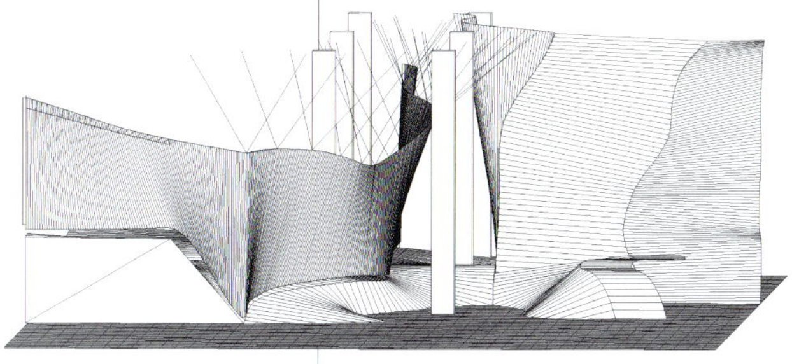
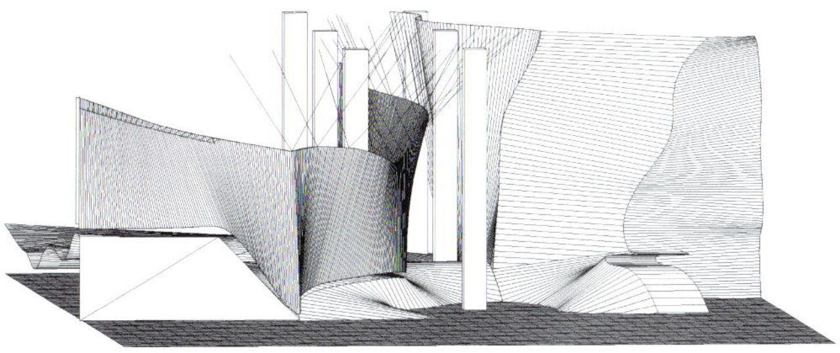
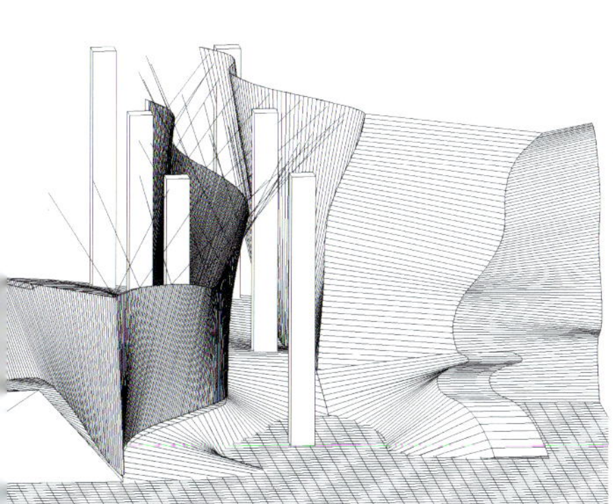
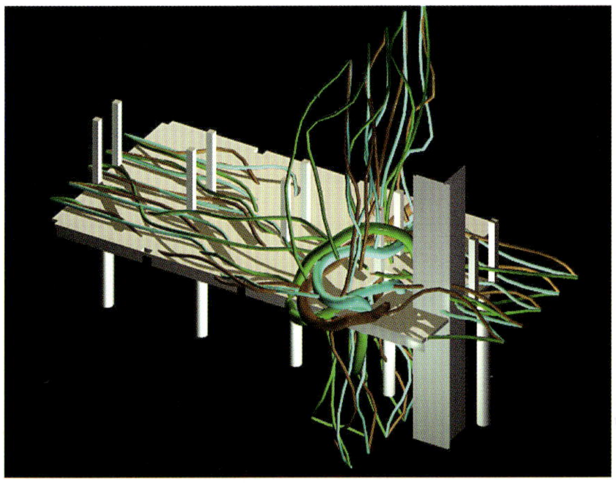
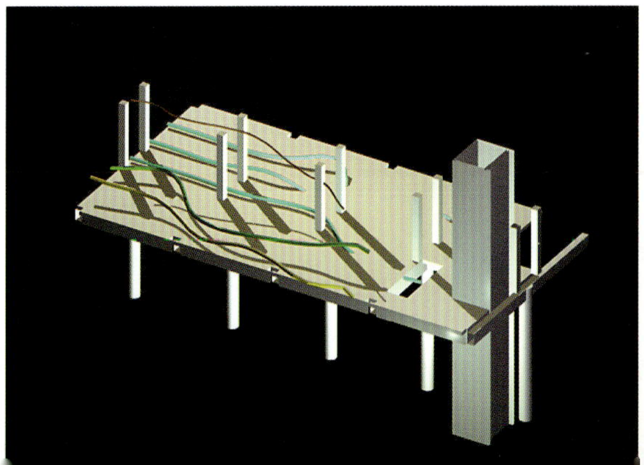

56

central projection space are transported to the extremes by waves, moving in four opposite directions through 20 strings. Continuously returning as waves, and interfering with new forces, eventually, in the topological continuity, active and reactive forces can no longer be distinguished and end up in a process where the inflections of the strings are no longer predictable. The resulting design ceases to be a form that can be overlaid on an organisational diagram, becoming a process in which topological coherence consists of the soft co-ordination of thousands of simultaneously operating diverse forces, making motion and time part of the organisation.

For the V2 Lab and the V2 Medialab – the international Lab for unstable media – this concept is an essential one. For here media are not perceived as belonging to a comfort-creating, servile instrumentalism familiar from engineers, interface designers and system operators, but as accelerators and destabilisers of reality. The virtual is not a so-called parallel world that exists safely on the other side of reality. It is something that continually charges up the present.

Instead of regarding the renovation as that which tranquillises the existing structure and refurnishes it to death, architecture here assumes the attitude of furniture and textile – as that which introduces movement into the existing situation, accelerating it, vectorising, seducing and flexing. In this way, we progress seamlessly from a computer-generated process of forces, vectors and springs, to inflections in plywood sheets and PVC pipes, to (literally) the vibrations in the tables, the undulations of the floor, to chairs with adjustable spring legs, to tensions in the 4-millimetre-thick plastic wall (stretched with steel cables and springs), to the flowing transition between floor and tables and then to the tensions within the human body: the arm and leg muscles that provide a constant neuro-electrical background to all human activity taking place here; a background that may fall outside the diagram, outside the concept of work; a background to all human media showing on the foreground, like piles of paper, coffee cups, old newspapers, the glow of computer screens, clothing, voices. In this sense, the design attempts to produce a shift from the optical domain where architecture is always judged, towards the haptic where everything is proximity.

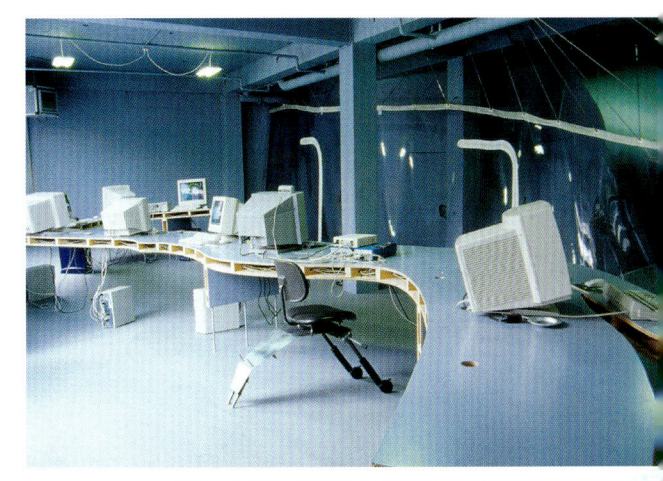

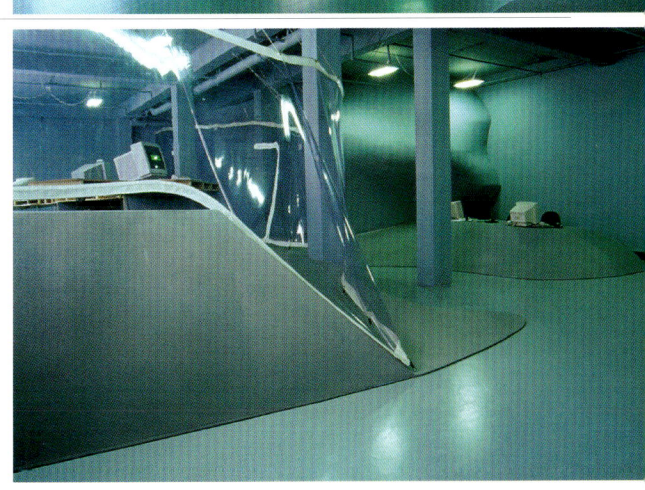

DEEPSURFACE – THE UNVISUAL IMAGE
Exhibition/Installation for the Exedra gallery, Hilversum 1999

Images (The Exhibition)
The projected images in this exhibition are not invisible, but unvisual. If we analyse the NOX projects of the last five years, we can distinguish two areas inaccessible to the eye: the diagrammatic interior of the computer and the neurological interior of the human body. If we try not to pay any attention to the optic, these two dark caves suddenly seem to merge, constituting one continuous haptic space of affects.

The installation shows only these two spaces. All the visual material of the various projects (CAD-perspectives, texture-mapped renderings, working drawings, construction photos, finished photos) will be made available to visitors in a full-colour booklet. The installation shows black and white animated diagrams: on the one hand, the forces within the machine, and on the other, the pulses and tensions in the body, measured in the actual space when built. All projects are analysed within a three-step procedure: from the computed to the built to the experienced, and back again.

In *Phenomenology of Perception,* Maurice Merleau-Ponty introduces the concept of abstract movement, a movement–tension that is always (proprioceptively) present in the body. He calls this a 'background tension', following the Gestaltists from the 1920s. This movement only becomes available to the body through the numerous actions performed in everyday life; it is not given, and one can lose it – movement is made up of movement, and the abstract and the real feed back and forth continuously. The concept of tension is critical of the notion of intentionality, where the body is solely seen as purposeful, as a mechanistic machine that has to start itself up every time a goal comes within view. Every act springs from this background tension, a real, actual movement that 'releases itself from neurological anonymity', within a body where millions of processes go on at the same time. In this view, subject and object must be deeply intertwined, hardly distinguishable, as are action and perception, the motoric and the sensory. In short, it is a deep critique of the architectural programme, the mechanistic layout of all human behaviour within a built system purely viewed as tasks, routines and habits.

Suppose this habituation, this crystallisation of behaviour is instead more a bottom-up emerging of repetition, an order surfacing out of different patterns of collective and individual processes? In that case, an act is never completely certain, it always differs from itself, and is always ready to shift into another act, or even to slide into a 'free' act. When every act, however intentional, is also orientated sideways, much in-between-programme could unfold, both undetermined and unprogrammed. Every path would then have to be part of a field, because every trace is first written within the soft field, the deep surface of the body, as in the classic concept of *chreodes*. The body is a beach too, and architecture can only appeal to this bandwidth of action when it also becomes a beach – at least partly. This topological view of the body, connected to a topological view of programme, connected to a topology of architecture – of structure even – is the explicit agenda of all projects exhibited. Within this system of connections, we should distinguish three movements, related to three different media. Movement in the architecture is created by the conceptual diagram in the computer. This diagram of springs and strings is animated through the scheme of the movement in the building – the organisational or mechanistic diagram (classic architectural tools like bubble-diagrams, organograms, running lines, relational schemes, routing), which quantifies behaviour and square footage. The interference of these two movements results in the actual movements of the body – in the exhibition, shown as plotted diagrams of actual behavioural patterns based on notations of American Sign Language: ruled surfaces of straight lines between the curved motion paths of the different limbs and joints.

In the various projects the 'movement in the architecture' is analysed as the transformation of one architectural element into another: from floor into wall, from line into surface, from point into line, from path into field, from table into corridor, from corridor into room, from floor into carpet, from wall into curtain, etc. All these 'movements', all this morphing, blending, merging, twisting, rotating, delaminating and splitting, are verbs that become part of architectural nouns, actions that become part of forms, creating in-betweens. Objects are nothing but the edges of the in-between. This is expressly generated by the non-fitting, by the interference of the 'movement in the architecture' with the 'movement in the building'; the two are related, obviously, but are not the same. If they formed a perfect fit, ie were orientated in the same direction, this would end up in pure expressionism. If they did not fit at all, being completely unrelated – for example when orientated in perpendicular directions – this would end up in pure sculpturism. To demonstrate that the motions are not 'frozen' into form, but 'passed on' into the movement of the body, not only forward (which is given), but also sideways, into the bandwidth of actions, the animated diagrams show runs and re-runs of different situations in several built projects.

The projects do not just go from concept to percept, from diagram to matter; they make explicit the excitation that spreads out over the matter of diagram and body simultaneously, the non-located affect that draws and redraws, structures and restructures motion.

Surface (The Installation)
The installation was generated in the computer by attaching a number of related forces to a 'textile' surface positioned horizontally at eye-level, where it blocks the view. Not only is this 'textile' made up of different parameters and values indicating its softness and flexibility, it is also a precise construction of springs. It is a tectonics of the responsive, where forces not only go into the soft system of the textile to displace points on the surface into a deformed structure, but where the 'points' are

sensitive zones within the line, which can both contract under pressure and expand again within a certain range. In short, the material has 'character'; it not only absorbs forces, but also responds to them actively in a particular way. This interaction of internal tension and external influences creates a wave-like deformation of the surface over time, and, because of the positioning of the springs and forces along the line-up of the existing structure, makes room exactly where the vertical has been occupied by the columns. The surface therefore stays horizontal at the edges, with a 'facade' of zero-thickness, but in the middle area it tries to elevate, as if the plan itself attempts to become a wall, making the image itself into a space, an image that immerses and envelops, becoming a space of absorption and movement. It is not unlike Jackson Pollock's twist of horizontal action into a vertical image, but then, resisting this climactic freeze, it drops back, remaining in-between and oblique.

These soft tectonics are again analysed in the computer as a buildable structure, where not only the diagrammatic geometry is passed on, but also its conceptual materiality of textile and tension, shifting it into a structure of textile, pulled tight with a number of steel cables. As the forces exerted along the row of existing columns created the complex curves within the surface, these can now only be fixed by inflexible structures of metal, like freed caryatids absorbed by the surface. Obviously, they also create the openings necessary to allow visitors access to the projected images. The tension in the two main cables is measured by two springs connected to sensors, oscillators and loudspeakers. The average tension is tuned to a pitch of 800 Hz. Small differences in tension and slight contact by the visitors create fluctuations between 797 and 803 Hz. Due to these variations, the interference of the two cables is enormously effective, making the sound float in such a way that one cannot really make out the position of the sources, not even whether they are located outside or inside one's own head.

All the gallery's windows, as well as the walls, have been painted white. The textile of the surface is also white, as are the cables and the other accessories. All the images and the animations projected on the surface are black and white.

NOX: Lars Spuybroek with Joan Almekinders, Gemma Koppen, Mike van der Noordt (V2 Lab), Joke Brouwer (booklet) and Bert Bongers (sensors/sound). The installation was made possible by the Stimuleringsfonds voor Architectuur and Galerie Exedra.

DECOI
AEGIS HYPOSURFACE
Autoplastic to Alloplastic

Here we attempt to trace a shift in cultural manner in the transition to an electronic cultural environment in psychological as much as technical terms. The suggestion we develop is that we are moving from a cultural mode of shock (Modernism) to a mode of trauma (suspension of shock) which carries the implicit suggestion of hypo- rather than hyper- tendency: subliminal rather than expressive effects.

Hyper- excessive, overmuch, above, from Greek huper- over, beyond eg hyperbole - a figure of speech which greatly exagerrates the truth hypercritical - too critical, esp of trivial faults
Hypo- below, under, deficient, from Greek, hupo-, hup- under eg hypocritical - of or characterised by hypocrisy a pretense of false virtue, benevolence [1]

The evident formal capacity of new generative *media* in architecture to produce complex or non-standard form(s) is perhaps as nothing compared to the shifts in cognition that such technical change engenders in a subliminal but widespread sense. For what has been claimed as a 'paradigm' shift in architecture is not so much the sudden utilisation of CAD by architects, but the ongoing cultural adaptation of society to an electronic environment.[2] If we consider that 'technology' constitutes the base textile of a culture (its *ge-stell*, or en-framing, in Heideggerian terms - its base language) the impact of any new development is most pertinently measured as the degree to which such terrain is reconfigured in the implication of a new technical weft.

In presenting the *Aegis* project for *Hypersurface* we will therefore consider current technical developments in psychological as much as technical terms, considering shifts in general patterns of cultural (not just architectural) production but also reception. This will suggest a transition from a mode of shock (Heidegger's *stoss*) to a more subtle one of sustained dis/re-orientation – almost a suspension of shock - which we will interrogate consider in terms of *trauma*. Here we will draw in particular from Sandor Ferenczi's reconsideration of Freud's analyses of trauma to suggest a move from an *autoplastic* to an *alloplastic* cultural mode. Implicitly this will shift emphasis to consideration of *hypo-* rather than *hyper*-surface(s) as the prescient (in)forms of electronic genera(c)tion in architecture.

Trauma
In The *Transparent Society*[3], Gianni Vattimo's compelling update of McLuhan's *Understanding Media*[4], he hints that contemporary cultural production relies no longer simply on *shock* but on an effect of sustained disorientation - almost a suspension of shock. For Vattimo the effective event/work endlessly differs/defers cognitive assimilation, marking a shift (for me) from a *reactive* to an *interactive* cultural mode, which I here characterise in psy-

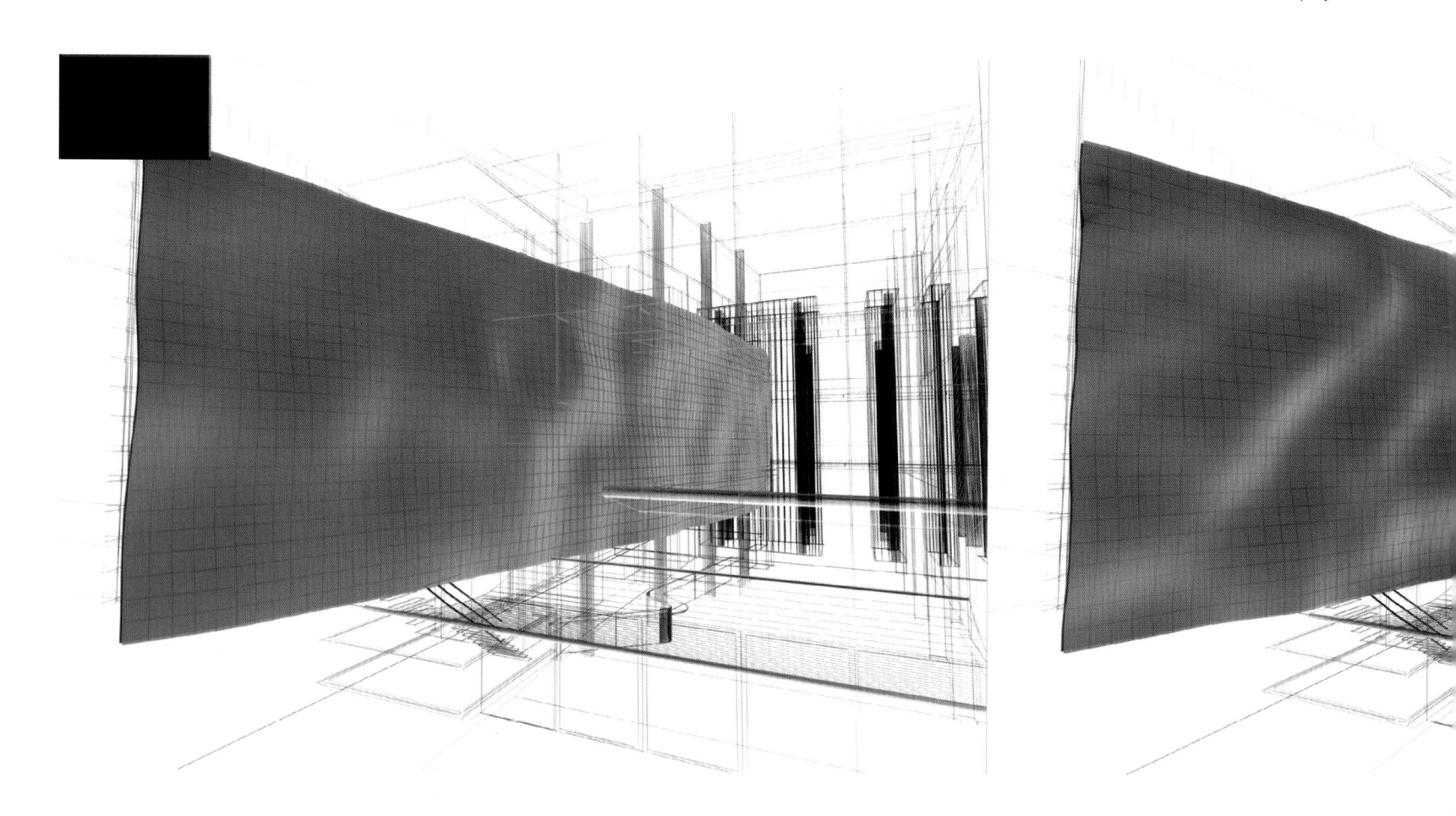

chological terms as trauma (the mind struggling to comprehend a lack). This suggests a substantial shift in cultural pattern - a sharp contrast, for instance - to Gombrich's *Sense of Order*[6] *circa 1960* (subtitled 'A *Psychology(!)* of the Decorative Arts'), in which he continually asserts that disorientation cannot be tolerated and is quickly grounded by representative prediliction (the mind short-circuiting the difficulty).

Vattimo's suggestion that the effectiveness of strategies of shock seems to be giving way to 'softer, more fluid' modes of operation, corresponds to current cultural strategies throughout the arts, which I'd characterise as being those of *precise indeterminacy*. Such thesis draws from Heidi Gilpin's suggestive essay, '*Abberations of Gravity*'[6] where she attempts to account for the bewildering effect of William Forsythe's indeterminate creative strategies (where he asks his dancers to 'represent loss', 'sustain the reinscription of forms', 'capture an absent presence', etc) with the *effect* they engender, accounting for cultural effect in terms of trauma. Both production and reception, now as extensions of one another, are traumatic in that there is no *a priori*, no representational *dictat* - they 'stage that which does not take place' in Forsythe's terms.[7]

Shock has long been considered the *modus operandi* of the Modernist arts, writers from diverse fields (Heidegger, Benjamin, Barthes,etc) all accounting for the effectivity of art-works in terms of 'the shock of the new' and the dis-orientation that it engenders. In considering the effects of a profligate and radical new productive electronic media that rapidly infiltrates all aspects of the cultural field, an 'art in the age of electronic (de)production' as it were, one senses that there is a dissipation of shock-effectivity. Rather than this being due simply to the over-proliferation of such strategy, it seems that different patterns of cultural registration are emerging, engendered by an electronic media which reconfigures the field subliminally. For shock implies comprehension for it to be effective, the resulting disorientation figured consciously as a strategy of *reactivity*, and frequently as a strategy of re-orientation. But much contemporary work, in its genera(c)tive profligacy, disenfranchises comprehension in an absence or over-abundance of evident reference, the trace of its coming-into-being 'digitally' indeterminate. The ensuing disorientation differs from that of shock in that it aims at no particular assimilation, instead offering itself as an endless transformation of the same, engendering a range of *effects* propitiated in the struggle for comprehension: this a strategy of *interactivity*.

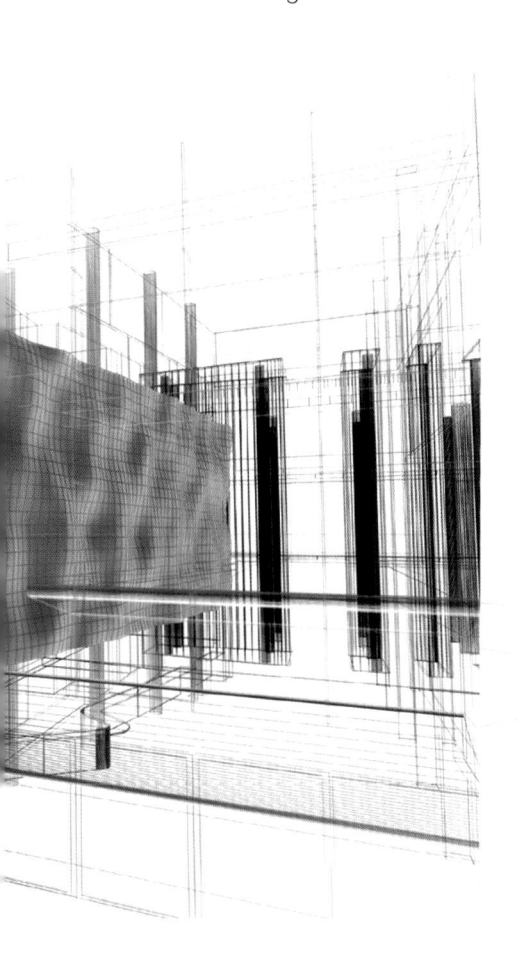

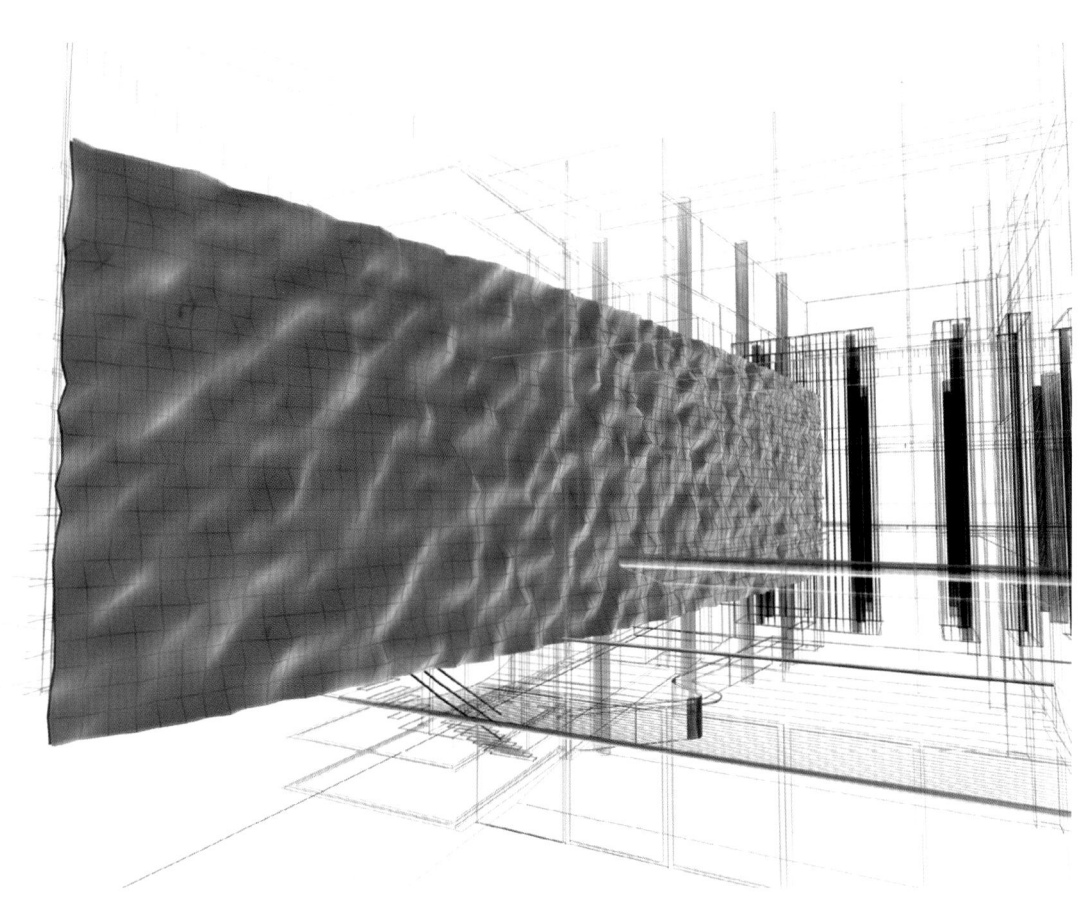

Psychological accounts of trauma are varied, but generally it is characterised as stemming from a moment of incomprehension or cognitive incapacity.[8] At a moment of severe stress, for example, there is a frequent shut-down of the conceptual apparatus (as if for protection), which creates an *anxiety of reference*. Cathy Caruth, who has written extensively on the relations of trauma and memory, suggests that 'in its repeated imposition as both image and amnesia, the trauma thus seems to evoke the difficult truth of a history that is constituted by the very incomprehensibility of its occurrence.'[9] Trauma, that is, develops not as a direct response to shock, but through the very inability to register it conceptually – through the absence of its assimilation and the struggle of the mind to account for this cognitive incapacity. 'While the traumatised are called upon to see and relive the insistent reality of the past, they recover a past that enters consciousness only through the very denial of active recollection. The ability to recover the past is thus closely and paradoxically tied up, in trauma, with the inability to have access to it... an event that is constituted, in part, by its lack of integration into consciousness.'[10]

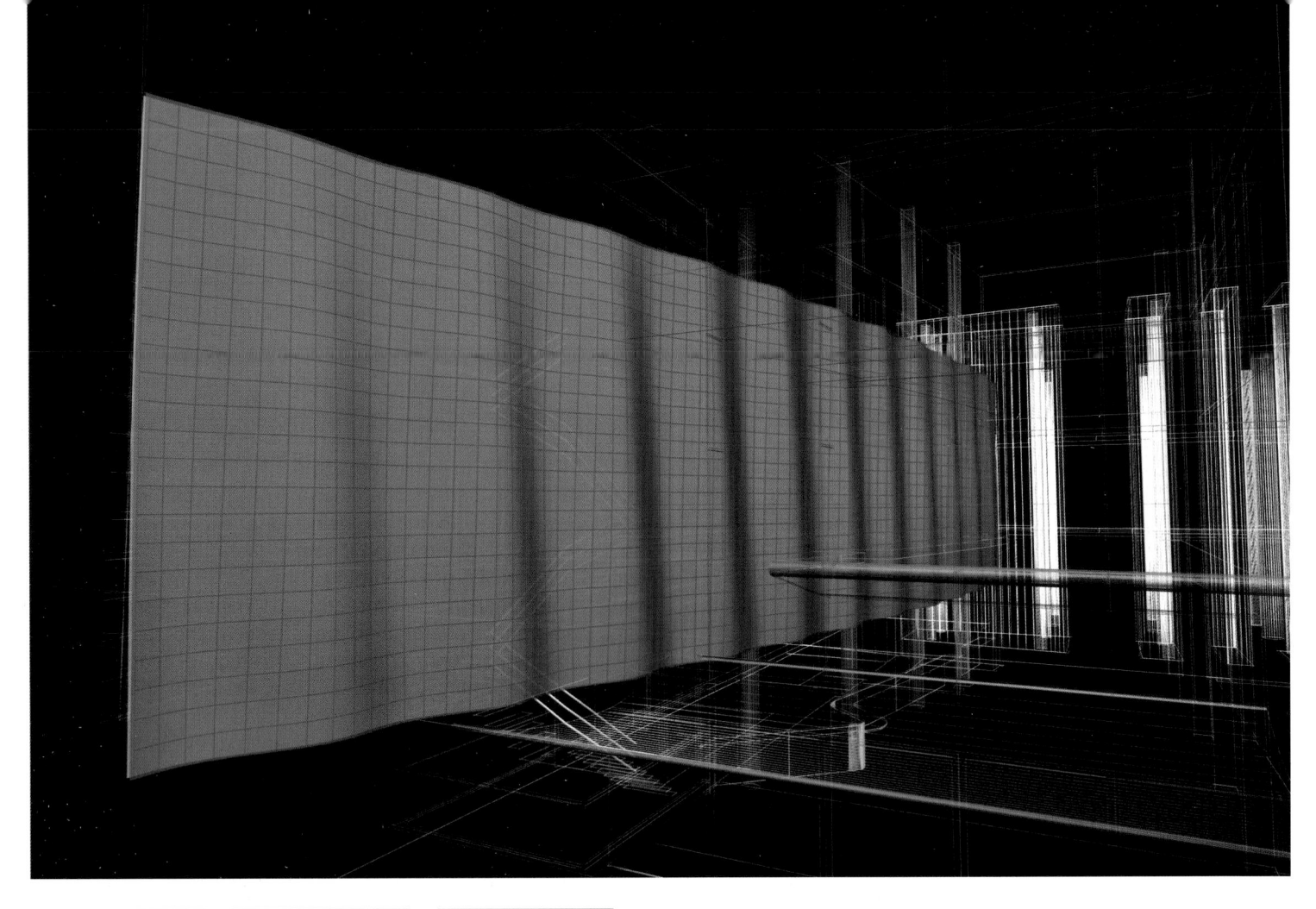

As we enter a mode of electronic production that implicates time in multiple ways, to the extent that the generative patterns of creativity are left as indeterminate traces of transformative process – transformation displacing origin and dispersing its vertical legitimacy across a now limitless electronic territory – so such accounts of trauma seem redolent.

But if it is the very lack of cognitive assimilation from which derives trauma, then it produces a variety of effects, not all of which are debilitating. For instance, there is a compulsion to account for the apparent lack (a stimulus) and a frequent heightening of bodily awareness, as if the very lack of cognitive assimilation dispersed thought throughout the sensorium, stimulating neglected modes of cognition as an intense 'sampling' of experience. This raising of the body to a cognitive level, a chemic as well as optic mode of thought, metonymic as much as metaphoric, Forsythe characterises as a proprioreceptive mode of production/reception, a 'thinking with/in the body'.

This posits a linkage of trauma with technological change, not simply in our incapacity to assimilate the rapidity of its development, but in its realignment of conceptual capacity. A recurring theme throughout 20th century discourse has been that technical change shifts the privileging of the senses in relation to cognitive thought. William Blake perhaps originated this idea in light of cultural changes propagated by rapid industrial development, and it was expressed cogently by Marshall McLuhan in regards to the development of electric media. Latterly, Derrida has sought to refine and requalify McLuhan's speculations, his experimental writing a highly suggestive matrix of sensorial realignment - a re-qualification of cognitive privilege in light of a now fully electronic media. This suggests whole new genres of cultural strategy and effectivity - a 'shift in the balance of the sensorium' that I have pursued elsewhere[11], trying to account not only for an apparent shift in cultural receptivity, but also of changing modes of creativity emerging in the interstices of technical change...

Evidently, then, such technical transformation may be considered through a variety of conceptual frameworks (psychological, philosophical, art historical, etc), but perhaps most evidently through the apparent break-up of representative strategy. The current generative environment, in which 'the image becomes primary'[12], dislocates familiar patterns of comprehension and the referential strategies they seem to imply. The turmoil this engenders for *determinate* creative strategy - both productive and receptive - then poses profound questions for cultural (and not simply technical) activity.

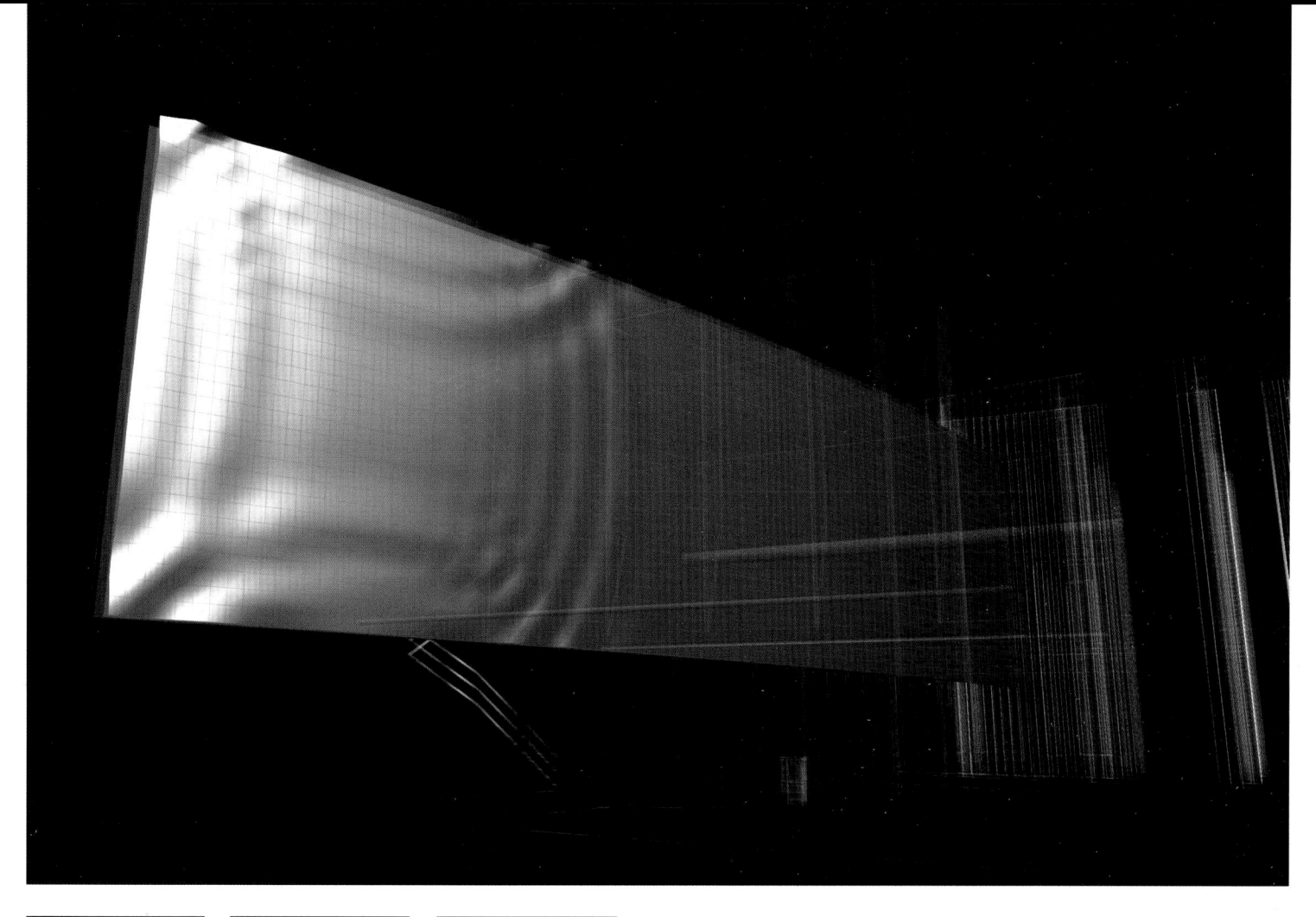

Autoplastic / Alloplastic
Drawing from Ferenczi's analyses of trauma, one might characterise this as a shift from an *autoplastic* to an *alloplastic* mode of operation. Autoplastic being defined as a self-determinate operative strategy, and alloplastic as a reciprocal environmental modification. Classically in trauma alloplastic response is predetermined by the inertia and indifference of the environment: 'for trauma to have effect, no effective "alloplastic" action, that is, modification of the environmental threat, is possible, so that "autoplastic" adaptation of oneself is necessary.' [13]

As we enter a period where the operative cultural tendency (whether through technological change or otherwise) seems to be a mode of trauma - as trauma becomes operative, in a sense - there is a shift from autoplastic to alloplastic mode, both in a productive and receptive sense. Creatively we operate within an alloplastic 'space' as one begins to work in a responsive, conditional environment, sampling and editing the proliferating capacity of generative software. But increasingly this also extends to our physical context, which is itself interactively malleable, and where our very determinacy is placed in flux: there is a reciprocal negotiation between self and environment - an interactive uncertainty.

Asked what his 'ideal' theatre might be, Forsythe suggested that it would be an indeterminate architecture in which the surfaces themselves would ceaselessly reconfigure, even the floor offering differential resistance and support which would compel the dancers to continual recalibration and requalification of movement strategy. Some measure of this was given in an experiment with accelerators attached to the dancers limbs: movement created an electric current which produced a synthesized sound which transfigured an interactive ribbon on a screen, programmed to distort with changing sound frequency. [14] This in turn was 'read' by the dancers who improvised sequences from predetermined alphabets of movement according to the 'letter' they recognised. This in turn led to new accelerations, new sounds, new distortions ... a circuitous and non-linear creative path which, in its utter disqualification of temporal priority (of either movement or music), led to a conceptual vertiginy which sustained itself to the point of a sort of physicalised feedback loop, traumatic for dancers and audience alike. [15]

Aegis
The *Aegis* project has developed as a speculation on such alloplastic condition, and as a vehicle for foregrounding current operative design strategies. It was devised in response to a competition for an art piece for the Birmingham Hippodrome

63

theatre - specifically for the cantilevered 'prow' which emerges from the depth of the foyer to cantilever over the street. The brief simply asked for a piece which would in some way portray on the exterior that which was happening on the interior - that it be a dynamic and interactive art work - an idea which we have extrapolated for Aegis.

Already in 1995 in our *Prosthesite* project (Nara/Toto *World Architecture Triennale*) we had suggested the possibility of responsive and reconfiguring surfaces, both at an urban and architectural scale, and these ideas have been taken forward in the conception of *Aegis*, which is a dynamic surface capable of physical deformation (ie it literally moves in reponse to environmental stimuli).

The project is simple in its conception: one might even say that it is nothing or that it highlights the nothing - the everyday events which occur in the theatre around it. It is a simple surface - metallic and facetted - just one of the walls of the prow which penetrates from exterior to interior as a gently curving surface. Frequently the surface is inert - just a shimmering backdrop to events. But it is a surface of potential, carrying a latent charge which may suddenly be released. In response to stimuli captured from the theatre environment it can dissolve into movement - supple fluidity or complex patterning. It is therefore a translation surface, a sort of synaesthetic transfer device, a surface-effect as cross-wiring of the senses. It engenders its effect as a precise yet indeterminate strategy, a swell and fall of significance, playing on the margins of perception.

As a translation surface it is in principle readable, a sort of glyphism, but now as a real-time event. Like the hieroglyphs it drifts between pattern and writing, proffering and deferring a promise of meaning as a sensual and rhythmic form of electronic writing. It's 'resolution' and speed will emerge from the actual parameters of movement, but it will be capable of registering any pattern or sequence which can be generated mathematically. It can also hold an image or video sequence which then vanishes-as-trace, playing the field of art as it alternates between foreground and background states.

The surface deforms according to stimuli captured from the environment, which may be selectively deployed as active or passive sensors. It is linked in to the base electrical services of the building which are to be operated using a coordinated bus system, such that all electrical activity can feed into its operational matrix, allowing it to register any aspect of electronic capture. But additional input from receptors of noise, temperature and movement are will be sampled by a programme control monitor which responds by selecting a number of base mathematical descriptions, each parametrically variable in terms of speed, amplitude, direction, etc. This produces a near infinite series of changing permutations which overlap continually, drifting in and out of sequence. The surface is therefore not designed, not determined as such: it is genera(c)ted by a random sampling, a deployment of electronic sensory-input, the designer's role becoming that of editor or sampler of a proliferating range of *effects*.

The design process, which implicated many people from a variety of fields, threw up a further possibility: that of qualitative filtering. The mathematician generating the formulas began assigning them names which coloured or stained the abstract formulation - gave them a human dimension. We enjoyed the congenital breach of abstract codification, the mischief of a mathematics let loose: 'large aspirin in a foil packet', 'cat under the mat', 'go right (go right dammit!)'. From this we began to devise alphabets of patterning, and categories of deformation as emotive lists. These then offer a further selective filter which may be introduced into the generative matrix, such that visiting companies can select, say, three categories which capture in some manner the mood or artistic direction of the company adding modes of damping or inflection to the patterning.

As a device of translation upon translation, the project highlights the extent of writing systems in their utter saturation of the cultural field, writing now become *primary*. The basic premise of the project - to capture a technical shift in cultural experience by foregrounding the extent to which writing and translation mechanisms figure in contemporary processes (that we're wrapped by endless writings) - suggested a creative process that itself involved translation and multiple writing. Interactivity is predicated on mechanisms of translation - the evident or instant transfer from one medium to another (movement to sound, sound to light, etc). Aegis, conceived through the translation between multiple writings will then operate in response to many other forms of writing - musical scores, flow charts, temperature scales... But the project seeks to emphasise the irreducibly human aspects of such iterative processes, playing on the slippages between domains and the pleasures of forms of notation (the 'elegance' of programmatic description, for instance).

Hyposurface

The surface is poised between physical states, undecideable not only as a writing-effect, but in its physical statelessness - its oscillation between solid and fluid. As such it may be held to be in a *smectic state*, that point of liquid-crystal indeterminacy at immanent crystallisation or meltdown - the fluctuating limit-case of objectivity. This smectic surface is neither object nor image, but haunts both territories: it follows, in an architectural register, the logic of LCD imaging, be it the latest flat-screen technology or vitreous plate-glass opacity-switching, all of which rely on the ferroelectric reversibility of the interstitial molecular structure of certain smectics. Here, though, it is not an imagery which derives from a physical indeterminacy, but the collapse of physical determinacy into processing: we generate neither object nor image, but *effect*, transformation displacing the notion of origin (of representative *a priori*). The piece tries to capture the sense of contemporary technologies which propitiate entirely new cultural forms, *processes*...

Our previous *Pallas* house was developed as an investigation of the demise of representative priority in numeric design process, marking a release of chance-calculus imagining. [16] The name of the project refers back to the emblematic *Palladium*, fashioned by Athena in memory of the double she had murdered (Pallas), a figurine which lies at the heart of all problems of representative doublature. [17] The anxiety of the Palladium relates to the uncertainty of originality, both in terms of the originary sin it represents, but thereafter in its endless repetition (originally in order to protect the 'original' from plunder). Athena, haunted by the ghost of duplicity, can be seen as the very figure of *eidetic* ambiguity - poised between *eidos* (form) and *eidolon* (phantom) - abstraction and rationality latent within her glittering form (the very image of optic priority).

The genera(c)tive development of the Pallas house, calculated as a series of non-standard (and therefore non-repetitive) glyphic motifs, marks a transition to the 'primacy of the image': a process, as it were, that needs no Palladian sanction - becomes indeterminate. In this sense the skin of Pallas carries an enigmatic, absent quality - an endless deferral of serial (in)significance – it, too, an *eidetic* image...

Trauma, as we've noted, is not marked by an overfullness or excess of significance, but by an absence of conceptual registration. This suggests that the prefix *hypo-*, which is characterized by deficiency and lack, by a subliminal incapacity, might be more appropriate in considering the effect of such numerically-generated surfaces than *hyper-*, which denotes excess or extremity. Doubtless, since the terms are those of relative fullness or depletion, these should not be considered as exclusive oppositional terms ('expressivity' and 'inexpressivity' will frequently cohabit according to context), but held in flux. But the Pallas house, which seems to numb its own expressivity – to engender a sort of inexpressive plasticity (which I've called on occasion an 'Asiatic' sense), would seem to shift to the sublimity of hypo-surface. *Aegis*, then, as a surface of variable significance - a literal distortion of reference - would seem to carry this further, fluctuating between hypnosis and hallucination, the limit cases of optic sense. It will be interesting to guage the resultant displacement of conceptual registration and to inquire as to the possibility of an emergent genre of *hyposurface*.

An *aegis* is implicated in both instances that Pallas figured in the life of Athena, and both encounters involved duplicity. It was the moment that the childhood Athena stood stock still, spear in hand, confronted by her own likeness in the form of her friend Pallas that Zeus, sensing a danger, threw down his *aegis* (originally the skin of the monster with fiery breath, *Aegis*). The momentary distraction released Athena's spear which mortally wounded Pallas, whose body the remorseful twin fashioned in timber and wrapped ambiguously in her own *aegis*, placing it in her own place next to her father, Zeus.

The adult Athena then encountered the giant Pallas who lured her to an attempted rape by pretending to be her father. Athena, slaying the giant, added his scaly skin to her aegis, as she was always adding to it trophies of her adventures. The enigmatic surface, alternately hard and soft, both warning device and defensive shield, fused with the figure of Athena, the rational female-warrior. The aegis, then, as the very figure of inflection, a beguiling surface of reciprocity, harbours a latent memory, is significantly alternate - mute or vociferous - a device of trapping (in the double sense of both capture and decoration). We then select this image/object as ambiguous appelation for the subliminal hyposurface which unfurls around us in the interstices of technical expressivity, *eidetic* image of a reciprocal environmental calculus...

Credits: dECOi, Mark Goulthorpe, Mark Burry (parametric modelling), Arnaud Descombes, Oliver Dering with Alex Scott (mathematics), Peter Woods (programming), Chris Glasow (systems engineering), Univer (pneumatic systems). Consultant Engineers: Ove Arup & Partners, David Glover (Structural Engineering), Andy Sedgewick (Electrical Engineering), Sean Billings (Facade Engineering) for PACA/Birmingham Hippodrome.

Notes

1 Taken from Longman's English Larousse
2 I developed this argument in a twin essay, *The Active !nert: Notes on Technic Praxis* in AA Files 37, Autumn 1998, p40 where I offer a loose comparison of the work of Greg Lynn, FORM and dECOi in their response to the effects of technological change on the cultural scene.
3 *The Transparent Society*, Polity Press, 1992. See for example, *Art and Oscillation*: ...the aim of this is not to reach a final recomposed state. Instead, aesthetic experience is directed towards keeping the disorientation alive, p51.
4 Marshall McLuhan, *Understanding Media: The Extensions of Man*, MIT Press, 1994. Even here, in a text which is highly optimistic about the influence of electric media, McLuhan hints at quite disturbing psychological undercurrents: 'having glanced at the major trauma of the telegraph on conscious life, noting that it ushers in the Age of Anxiety and of Pervasive Dread, we can turn to some specific instances of this uneasiness and growing jitters' p252.
5 Ernst Gombrich *The Sense of Order: a Study in the Psychology of Decorative Art*, Phaidon Press, 1979: for example, 'no jolt should take us unawares... the most basic fact of aesthetic experience is the fact that delight lies somewhere between boredom and confusion... a surfeit of novelty will overload the system and cause it to give up...' p9
6 Heidi Gilpin, *Abberations of Gravity* in Parallax
7 My knowledge of William Forsythe and the Frankfurt Ballet derives from study of their work over a number of years, and many discussions with them.
8 The 'classic' texts on trauma are those of Sigmund Freud which deal largely with the neuroses associated with vividly disturbing events. Sandor Ferenczi offers a more subtle interpretation, extending Freud's thought to a wide range of everyday events, in effect using the discourse on trauma as a means of developing a generalised psychological theory. In my view such 'extension' does not imply opposition to Freud's basic thought – rather, a requalification - and in seeking to extend Ferenczi's thought to consideration of cultural reception I would note the basic similarities of both thinkers in their descriptions of trauma. A good account of their respective differences is given by Jay B Frankel, *Ferenczi's Trauma Theory*, The American Journal of Psychoanalysis, vol 58, No &, 1998.
9 Cathy Caruth, *Psychoanalysis, Culture, and Trauma* (part 2), The American Imago, vol 48, #4 (Winter 1991), p 418-9.
10 Cathy Caruth, *Unclaimed Experience: Trauma and the Possibility of History*, Yale French Studies 79, Literature and the Ethical Question, 1991, p 187.
11 Derrida's multiple interests in technological change (and 'technology' itself) are well articulated in Gregory Ulmer's stimulating, *Applied Grammatology*, The Johns Hopkins University Press, 1994. In particular Ulmer emphasises Derrida's interest in the possible 'shift in the balance of the sensorium', and the extent to which Derrida appears to extend and correct McLuhan's interpretation of technical change. To my knowledge this aspect of Derrida's work has been largely unacknowledged.
12 This is an expression of Bernard Cache in *Earth Moves: The Furnishing of Territories*, MIT Press, 1995, describing the extent to which the computer image is no longer a representation of something prior, but begins to develop a life of its own – to become primary, or generative, in the creative process.
13 Sandor Ferenczi *Notes and Fragments* in Final Contributions, 1930-32 Hogarth, 1955, p221. This is the third volume of his collected notes and papers, published posthumously.
14 These experiments were carried out during rehearsals of Eidos/Telos, 1995, which I studied whilst running Intermediate Unit 2 at the Architectural Association.
15 See my essay *An Architecture of Disappearance* (*Une architecture de la disparition*) in Contredanse, 1998.
16 See, ANY: Public Fear, #18, Pallas House p57
17 Here I borrow from Roberto Calasso's insightful re-interpretation of Classical mythology in *The Marriage of Cadmus and Harmony*, Vintage, 1994.

66

BERNARD CACHE
OBJECTILE
The Pursuit of Philosophy by Other Means?

In this text, written to commemorate Gilles Deleuze, Bernard Cache explores how philosophy can be pursued as a means of production. His project Objectile, founded with Patrick Beaucé and Jean-Louis Jammot in Paris, is dedicated to the production of nonstandard objects calculated by computers and industrially produced with numerically controlled machines.

The title of my essay should be taken as an open question. 'Objectile' is the name given by Gilles Deleuze to the investigations I am carrying out, with other researchers – especially Patrick Beaucé and Jean-Louis Jammot – on the development of industrial means for producing nonstandard objects. By that, I mean objects that can be repeated as a function of their difference from one another, like a family of curves declining the same mathematical model; objects in flux, inflected like the signal modulating a carrier wave; lines and surfaces of variable curvature, like the foldings of Baroque sculpture or like the *rinceau*,[1] whose transformational capacities Alois Riegl so convincingly demonstrated in his history of ornamentation.[2]

'Objectile: the pursuit of philosophy by other means?' This could only suggest philosophy pursued as a means of production and not as a contemplative activity, nor as a kind of reflection, and even less as an instrument of communication. A pursuit by other means? The phrase clearly alludes to Karl von Clausewitz, recalling not only that philosophy acts as a war machine against all apparatuses, but also invoking the restlessness of the Prussian general, an avid reader of Kant, who realised to what extent one's means can divert one's ends, and how fitting it is that one's ends should be subject to denaturing. Something to rejoice in, perhaps: neofinalism as a philosophy of denaturing!

How exactly is philosophy subject to denaturing? In many ways, probably, since neither causes nor opportunities are lacking. Yet like everyone else, I perceive an over-riding factor: the computer. This denaturing force is certainly not new. For the computer was not conceived in the calculating rooms where Gaspard Marie Riche de Prony worked on the trigonometry tables that Charles Babbage was later to succeed in mechanising. Nor was it conceived during World War II, in the new rooms where the trajectories of shells were calculated, a process that was also to be mechanised. Nor was it conceived lately in Silicon Valley garages. It took a philosopher like Leibniz to anticipate all that contemporary computer science is only just beginning to realise. Take his clear and brilliant statement that any form, no matter how complex, can be calculated. That statement is what authorises our current attempts to design digitally, as well as our conception of objectiles as declinations of parametric surfaces.

This suggests philosophy as a calculus of reason and of forms. Granted this goal, what are the means? Means logical and material (software and hardware) are required. On the logical side, mention must be made of Joseph Fourier (1768–1830), a largely forgotten giant in the history of science. His theorem provides the means by which to decompose all periodic phenomena into a series of trigonometric functions. It was Fourier who discovered the mathematics for accomplishing Leibniz's programme. All that was left was to cast the algorithms in silicon in order to automate the calculation of series whose manual execution is by no means a trivial matter. FFT: Fast Fourier Transform. A French engineer sets up shop in the US: C-Cube Inc, which develops the first digital compression circuits. The MPEG or H261 source code behind such new inventions as digital television and the videophone is nothing but the ultra-high-speed execution of Fourier transformations by integrated circuits. The question is how these integrated circuits succeed in denaturing philosophical affirmation by executing a theorem every split second behind our screens? This is just the kind of problem, of the speeds and slownesses of thought, Gilles Deleuze so loved to pose.

Let us rejoice in the face of this algorithmic Fourierism. For it signals, perhaps, that we have come to a turning point. A turning point that challenges us to make the most of the fact that mathematics has effectively become an object of manufacture, and that when components become photonic rather than electronic, thought may indeed be confronted with an absolute speed of calculation. But, the question is no longer simply one of the speed of calculation. Once we have grasped that its execution will be limitless, the question turns to the very power or potency of calculation. Must we then believe the prophets of Artificial Intelligence who predict the day when machines will think in our stead, and who claim that our consciousness is nothing but an epiphenomenon, little more than a parasite of algorithmic calculation? Is machinic thinking reducible to information processing? Are we on the brink of a third generation of knowledge, verging on that absolute or lightning speed of thought of which Deleuze spoke with reference to the Fifth Book of Spinoza's *Ethics*? Or, are we heading instead towards a kind of thought boom where, having broken the calculus barrier, we will soon discover a world in which algorithms no longer hold sway? In broaching these questions, one must begin by saying that a computer does essentially two things: it calculates and it memorises. Calculus and memory. We shall see that this is not far from Matter and Memory. Let us examine each of these aspects in turn.

Start with calculus. Turing himself found a set of problems for which no algorithmic solution exists. As an example, we can cite a problem that seems very simple. Given a set of polygons, which ones are suitable for tiling a plane? That is a problem for a tiler or a mason, almost a child's game: 'How do you cover a surface with a small number of basic shapes without leaving blanks and without overlaps?' But it is also close to being a philosophical problem: 'How do you construct space out of shapes rather than points?' The atomists had based the problem of constructing space on the point, understood as the passage to the limit of a shape so small that it is devoid of both form and parts. What daring! It is clear to us today how complicated the problem is when you begin with divisible components, ie, components with actual extension and form. Even in restricting oneself to very simple elements – the juxtaposition of identical squares – the problem of tiling a plane and, worse yet, that of space, has no algorithmic solution, due to the appearance of nonperiodic elements. Such combinations of squares, known as polynominos,[3] will not form infinitely repeatable basic patterns, the examination of which would suffice to allow one to tile a plane correctly. It was Roger Penrose, a British mathematician, who explained that the critical step in demonstrating the algorithmic insolubility of tiling problems came down to showing that there is no general procedure for deciding when to switch off a Turing machine. Completely deterministic models of the universe with well-defined rules of evolution do exist, but their digital simulation is impossible to achieve. Penrose states, further, that the understanding of mathematics is irreducible to computation, and that understanding itself is a nonalgorithmic activity of the brain or mind. The most important consequence of Gödel's theorem is not the existence of undecidable propositions, but the existence of the uncomputable in thought. Moreover, this consequence can only be shown in the most formalised realm, namely, mathematical invention. Penrose proceeds on the basis of an argument advanced by John Searle. Suppose one were to capture each one of the basic commands of a computer programme, as carried out by someone who understands nothing of computer programming. Partisans of Artificial Intelligence would like to think that the computer 'understands' the algorithms it is executing, whereas it is clear that its user, who is – in this case – also executing the programme, persists in understanding nothing at all. This leads Penrose to propose the following: intelligence requires understanding; understanding requires an immediate knowledge differing in nature from the execution of an algorithm.

In light of this, we wonder whether the real result of the invention of computers might not be to free thought from algorithms and memorisation. Leroi Gouran explained how the act of standing upright had freed human hands from tasks associated with locomotion and jaws from prehensile and utilitarian functions, thus blazing the trail for the vocalisations of sounds to become the articulations of speech. In similar fashion, I think that *homo cyberneticus* is well on the way to developing the strange new faculties of an amnesiac and analgorithmic consciousness. If Gilles Deleuze deserves the title of Philosopher of the 20th Century, it is because he knew how to ford the stream of mnemonic and algorithmic unconsciousnesses, by stepping on tiptoe from stone to stone – from Bergson-stone to Ruyer-stone – between the few who affirmed the value of a consciousness of self-survey. Since we are, definitely, unreasonable, why then must we *also* be conscious?

What the 21st century may discover is that *consciousness* is what is strangest about thought. We may be about to perform a tremendous philosophical twist, only to have consciousness make a comeback as a locus of interest, no longer for the sake of reason, but for the sake of an irreducible unreasonableness. Enlightenment thinkers took consciousness to be the seat of Reason, and took unreason to be a deficit of consciousness, limited in actual fact, but unlimited in principle. Then came the Romantics, who intuited only too well the intrinsic limits of consciousness, in the face of an irrational whose throne would soon be relegated to the unconscious. Freud would attempt to save the situation by explaining that the unconscious is itself a second Reason, well before the structuralists came along to tell us that this unconscious is not only the reason for a troubled consciousness, but Reason itself: Engram with a capital E, and Algorithm with a capital A. Nevertheless, it was clearly not the unconscious that annoyed Deleuze with respect to psychoanalysis, but rather the absolute reign of the engram and of the algorithm in the analysis of childhood memory traces and, later, in linguistic, anthropological and mathematical structuralisms.

What can it mean to transfer an irreducible unreasonableness to the heart of consciousness itself? How to make sense of this? It means that the time has come to oppose the ideology of Information with a philosophy of Incarnation. For, in order to execute an algorithm, it first has to become incarnate (become flesh). Telecommunications engineers are well aware that source coding is only half the job. Any image, no matter how complex, can certainly be sampled and reduced to a highly compressed digital series thanks to Fourier transformations, but this digital series still has to be carried by a physical support. The source coding is doubled by a channel coding. In fact, any text, any sound, any image may in future be reduced to a digital series, but a bit stream – a series of ones and zeros – is nothing until it is recomposed in or on a given support, at a pre-determined clock time. This is how a digital series can effectively become a sound on a stereophonic membrane, or an image on a video screen; this is how the digital verb becomes analogue flesh. And that is what gives rise to our new digital montages, where it is no longer a matter of coupling a given sound to a given image like in the good old days of cinematography, but where sounds are visualised and images are heard as one descends into the fine-grain of perception.

For the most minute perception is itself already composed of a multitude of vibrations. Bergson reminded us that the simple fact of seeing a colour or of hearing a sound was already an act of memory that contracted a quantitative multitude into a qualitative multiplicity. But this contraction-memory is an entirely different thing from the engram-memory of our computers. The Engram is nothing but a sequence of bits, whereas a contraction-memory is the act by which we constitute our present/presence by contracting a series of moments into the thickness of a duration. It is the act whereby a bit of information is incarnated through a perceptual support: retinal persistence, or on-screen after-images of our consciousness. How does number become sound or image? This process is impossible to understand if matter itself does not in turn become the object of the kind of distinction applied to memory. For matter is also two-sided:

> [It was] Bergson who praise[d] Berkeley for having identified body with idea: because matter 'has no inside, no underside ... it hides nothing, holds nothing ... possesses neither power, nor virtuality of any kind ... it spreads itself out as surface and holds together at every moment in what it offers'.[4]

Matter is thus at once that by which everything is given, reducible to pure quantity, like Lucretius' black atoms, as well as that which constitutes the most relaxed membrane, the qualitative residue without which quantity does not exist. It is the minimal colour without which there is no black nor any white, the fundamental noise without which there is no signal.

The computer forces us to rethink the boundary line between the two major Bergsonian concepts, Matter and Memory, and also between Leibniz's two levels, a boundary, which Deleuze used to explain the fundamental difference between the two couples virtual/actual and possible/real.[5] These two levels no longer separate monads from bodies, nor matter from memory; instead, they establish a *chiasmus* that allows us to place the algorithm and engram together on the side of Information, while membranes and temporal frequencies are coupled on the side of Incarnation. Thus, on one side you find all that is computable and writeable, while on the other, you have that which appears negatively as the noncomputable and the nonsamplable, but which takes on a positive aspect as Duration and Membrane. This works so well that we are tempted to propose a new version of the diagram sketched by Gilles Deleuze in *The Fold*, where he juxtaposes two very different processes: the actualisation of the virtual and the realisation of the possible. Anything is possible when it comes to the engram and the algorithm: information technologists tell us so – all the time. And the possible asks only to become real, its realisation subject only to the logic of economic optimisation as guided by the invisible hand of the market, which promises us, as a bonus, to select only the best, out of all the possible contenders. This is to forget, however, that there is an undecidability factor in algorithms, and that there are propositions of which it cannot be said whether they are contradictory or not, or, more exactly, whether they are compossible or not with another set of propositions. This is the irreducibly uncomputable. On the other hand, the possible cannot become real without becoming corporeal, without incarnating itself in a membrane and changing its nature, according to the clock-time stimulus driving it to realisation. 'That which cannot be divided without changing nature.'[6] That is how Deleuze described the second process, by which the possible cannot become real without something of the virtual becoming actual. This is why duration has its own thickness, and reality cannot be anticipated through the possible.

Membranes and frequencies: these are the singular figures through which the virtual is actualised at the same time as the possible becomes real, without any guarantee that the best will be selected. Kandinsky used the term 'resonance' to designate what is spiritual in art. Elsewhere, he also clearly perceived the advent of information technology. 'As these means of expression [abstract forms] are developed further in the future ... Mathematical expression will here become essential', he announced in *Point and Line to Plane*.[7] He also warned,

> There is, however, the danger that mathematical expression will lag behind emotional experience and limit it. Formulas are like glue, or like a 'fly paper' to which the careless fall prey. A formula is also a leather arm-chair, which holds the occupant firmly in its warm embrace.[8]

Written in 1923,[9] these remarks sound like warnings for those of us who spend our days in front of a computer screen.

Calculus does provide the means for designing forms like modulations of abstract surfaces, forms whose frequency and membrane remain indeterminate for a time. Following Kandinsky, we take Leibniz's affirmation that all forms are computable at its word. And, the only means needed to achieve our ends are those prescribed by Fourier, that is, series of trigonometric functions. To design volumes, we use whole periodicities that cause surfaces to curl up on themselves. The first stage thus consists in devising mathematical models, which allow for declining infinite kinds of possibles. In order to approach these 'worlds' whose functions are comprised of as many dimensions as parameters, we have developed exploratory tools, generating series of video images that correspond to trajectories running through these multi-dimensional universes. Objects generated by this process initially resemble still-frames from video footage.

But in order to move from these virtual possibilities to actual realities, we have to switch scanning techniques and substitute the numerical command router that manufactures any material for an electronic gun, which activates the pixels on our video screen. If we hear the term 'virtual reality' so often, it is because video scanning comes across as the minimal machinic operation of the extremely ductile and supple membrane that is the video screen. But we have to insist on the dual nature of this operation: first, it is already an incarnation and, secondly, the screen is just a membrane amongst membranes, which is why we can effectively speak of virtuality. For video sequences are only a primary or first actualisation. The mathematical models we are exploring still belong to the order of the possible, and hold no surprises except in the measure that our power of calculation remains limited. What we will never be able to predict is the relationship between a frequency and a membrane. To select a still image amounts to assigning a value to the parameters of our periodic functions, in view of manufacturing a specified material to produce singularities in a series of objects.[10] By what power to determine whether the amplitude of a modulation on the surface of wooden panels in a given architectural context will be smaller or larger? By what power to determine whether a different modulation will curl into a three-lobed volume in the middle of a room? By what power to determine whether the phase difference of an electronic undulation will enter into a relationship with the texture of a pre-determined membrane? Solutions to these problems cannot be anticipated, for in each case the actualisation differs in nature from all others, and in no case is the selection optimisable.

In a certain sense, none of this is really new. In his *Harmonie Universelle* of 1636, Marin Mersenne had already asked how it would be possible to compose the best song on the basis of an investigation of combinatory possibilities. He concluded that it could not be done, citing the overabundance of possibilities. Thus, the number of melodies foreseeable with 23 non-repeating notes already stands at factorial 23. How amazing is the confidence with which composers choose their sounds! To cite another example of combinatories, let us take chess. The number of legal moves in this case stands at 10 to the power of 56, a figure so large that it exceeds the number of electrons in the universe. The calculation of all of these moves would thus remain unfeasible as long as computers are driven by current technology. If today's computers perform relatively well against flesh and blood opponents, it is because they use software that is purveyed with heuristic devices simulating a player's intuition on the basis of probabilities. But, this matters little, for if we can see the day when a quantum computer becomes unbeatable by virtue of the exhaustion of all possibilities, this is because the problem of chess remains simple and eminently computable. It is a purely algorithmic problem based on a comparison of possibilities in view of the selection of the best outcomes, thus, purely a problem of realisation. Mersenne's musical problem is of an entirely different nature. We have long known that harmony is not defined once and for all, and that a given relationship between two notes that is consonant in the soprano range, will be dissonant in the bass range, and that a chord that one composer classifies as dissonant will be considered consonant by another.

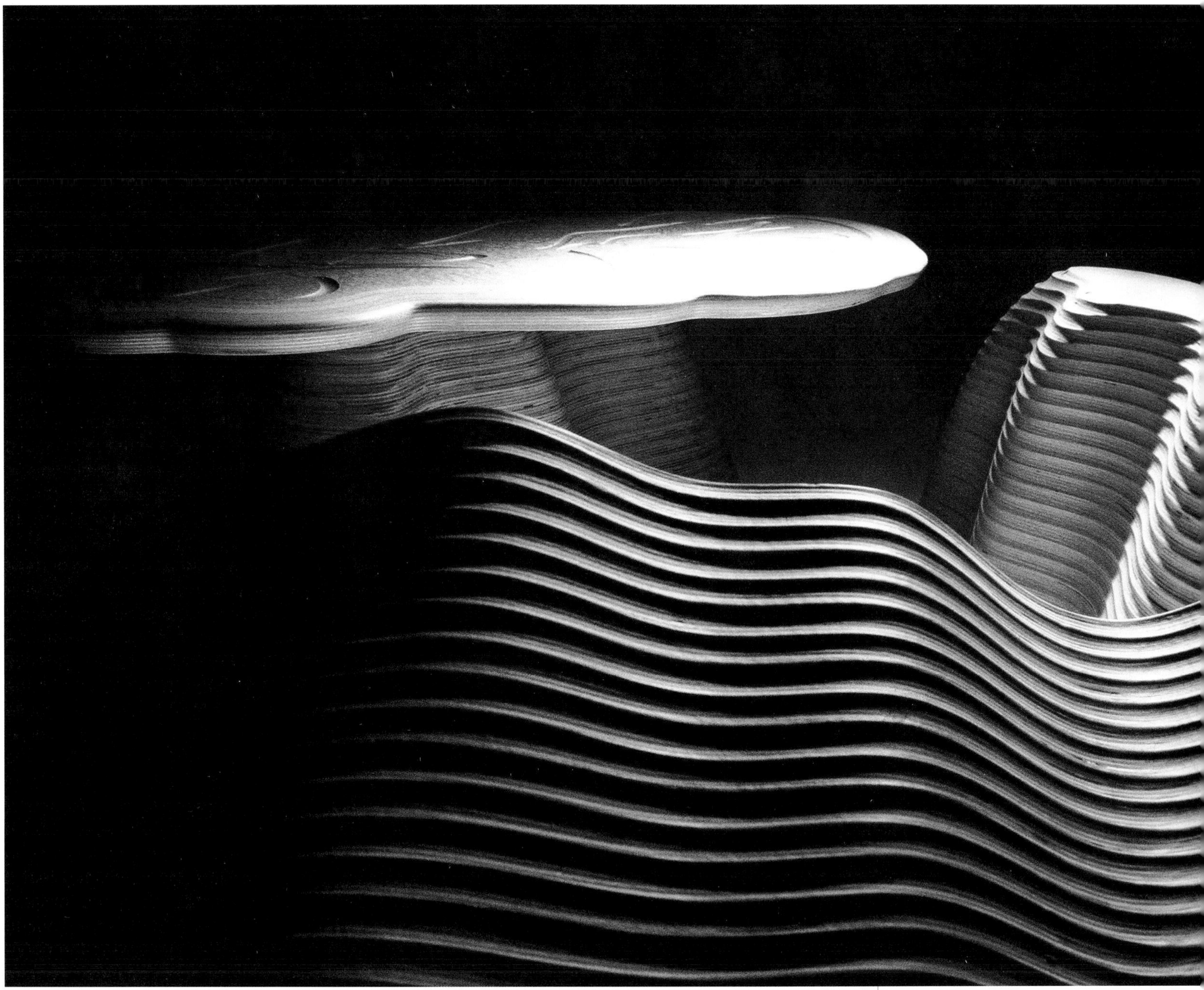

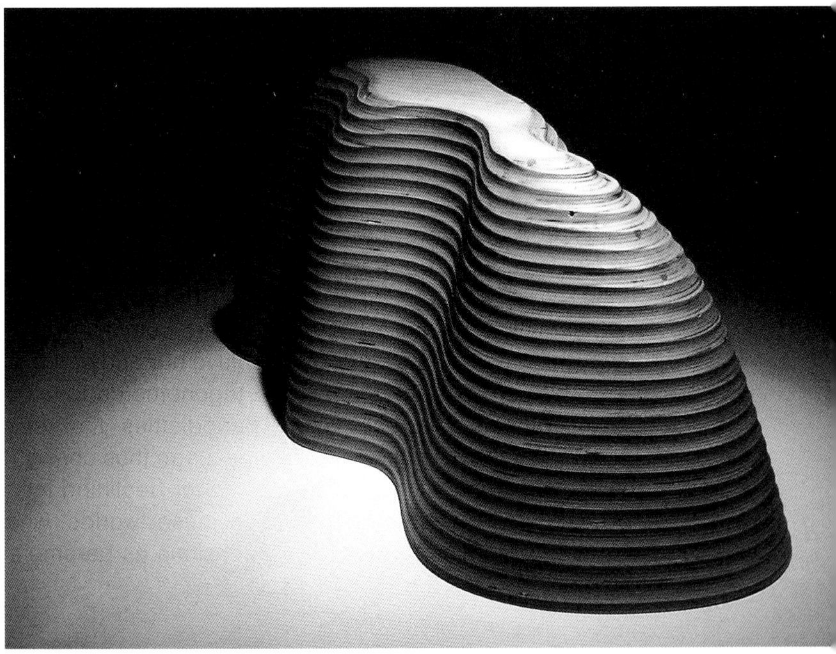

There is no common reference by which to compare musical modulations in the way we can select chess moves. For the existence of a perfect major chord in one monad implies the existence of a minor or dissonant chord in another. What has changed is that the screening procedure whereby possibles are selected for realisation as a function of 'the optimal' works less and less well. Dissonance in one monad thus no longer implies consonance in another to the benefit of universal harmony. For, on one hand, there is something uncomputable in algorithmic possibilities that impedes selection by criteria of optimisation, and, on the other hand, virtualities cannot be actualised without changing in nature the membranes incarnating them and the frequencies animating them. Worlds jostle one another while the real endures ever more divergent actualisations. What is coming to light is a vision of harmony as singularity and not as a universal. From this follows our attempt to put into practice a means for producing the nonstandard.

Translated by Karen Okana.

This paper was first given at the 'Immanence et vie' conference on 27 January 1997, in Paris, to commemorate Gilles Deleuze on the anniversary of his death.

Notes

1. Defined as 'ornamental bands of undulant and recurving plant motifs' in the *Illustrated Dictionary of Historic Architecture*, Cyril M Harris (ed), Dover Publications Inc (New York), 1977.
2. Alois Riegl
3. 'polyomino, n. The plane fiture formed by joining unit squares along their edges. Polyominos all of which are congruent to a given polyomino that uses four or fewer squares can be used as tiles to cover a plane (ie monominos, dominos, trominos, tetrominos)', in *Mathematics Dictionary*, fifth edition, James and James (ed), Chapman and Hall (New York, London), 1992.
4. My translation. Gilles Deleuze, *Bergsonism*
5. See especially ibid, pp42–3 and Deleuze, *The Fold*
6. See *Bergsonism*, p40.
7. Wassily Kandinsky, 'Point and Line to Plane', in *Kandinsky, Complete Writings on Art, Volume II (1922 – 1943)*, Kenneth C Lindsay and Peter Vergo (eds), GK Hall & Co (Boston), 1982, p544.
8. Ibid.
9. According to Kandinsky's Foreword to the first edition of 'Point and Line to Plane' (*Punkt und Linie zur Fläche*), the final version of this book was begun in Weimar in 1923 and finished in Dessau in 1926, while the original notes were taken in Goldach on Lake Constance at the outbreak of World War I.
10. See demo on www.objectile.com

MARCOS NOVAK
EVERSION
Brushing against Avatars, Aliens and Angels

Iannis Xenatis has written that, ' to make music is to express human intelligence by sonic means'.[1] *Here, architecture and music are considered in parallel; conjoined into 'archimusic', they express human intelligence by spatio-temporal means.*

Aliens I: Transmorphosis
Entries for a future glossary: liquid architectures, transarchitectures, transmusic, extreme intermedia, disembodied dance, habitable cinema, navigable music, nanomusic, nanotonality, eversion, transmodernities, the production of the alien.

In my work and writings, I trace a sequence of developments in the poetics of new technologies that begins with architecture and spreads to culture at large. This sequence articulates what I perceive to be a growing cultural tendency towards algorithmic indirection, liquid variability, non-retinality and, eventually, full virtuality. The ascendancy of the liquid over the fixed is a phenomenon that is emblematic of an intellectual condition in which previously irreconcilable, even inconceivable, opposites coalesce into strange but ultimately tenable alloys. More alien fusion than mere Hegelian synthesis, this phenomenon is also thriving in popular culture. Elvis Presley moves backwards, meets Abbot and Costello and becomes Elvis Costello, then moves forward, meets Adolph Hitler and becomes Elvis Hitler. Marilyn Monroe encounters Charles Manson and becomes amalgamated into Marilyn Manson, who in turn presents an identity-construct that is at once familiar and alien, androgynous and unsexual, shock performer and polite, articulate talk-show guest. Meanwhile, global citizens are nomadic resident-aliens, teenagers, affiliated by alienation, morph into tribes of self-destruction, bringing terrorism to high-school cafeterias, and transgenic doctors threaten to clone themselves with the help of their spouses. Telomerase research seeks to make us immortal; nanotechnology promises not only to replicate but also to miniaturise us; and terraforming Mars is a concrete project whose outcome will surely be the production of terrestrial Martians.

Easy opposition involves redundant bipolarity. Like two faces of a coin, polar opposites imply one another. A more interesting form of opposition consciously seeks what Charles Peirce would call 'thirdness', or what Magritte would search for using Goethe's notion of 'elective affinities', forming a third position somewhere off the axis of an existing continuum. It is possible to go farther still: whereas bipolar opposition relates two elements already on some common axis, or even the axis of a constructed 'thirdness', the form of opposition I have in mind does not find offsets along extant continua, but posits continua where none previously existed, creating alloys that are *between-above* their constituting, previously unrelated elements. Although these alloys soon reveal themselves to be alien to their origins, they rapidly establish themselves as materials from which to launch additional 'transmorphings',[2] which we are encountering with increasing frequency. In this climate, it is the familiar that is suspect.

If the operations associated with the idea of the liquid suggest that parameterisation leads to radical variability within a continuum implied by a thing and its opposite, or even its near opposite, the operations associated with the metamorphic 'trans' suggest something more powerful: that a continuum can be established between *any* two things, even if those things would otherwise cancel each other out. It is useful to distinguish between *bipolar* opposition, which admits to a continuous variation between two given poles – a *field* condition – and *binary* opposition, which only allows discrete, disjunctive selection between one pole or the other – a *state* condition. To give an example: in glass, solid and liquid are opposed in one sense, but belong to the same continuum. Presence and absence, on the other hand, are opposed in quite a different way, though they still share a common axis. There can be continuous variation between solid, liquid, vapour and gas, but presence and absence seem inherently binary. What then, of *liquid-absence*? What would be between these poles? What above? And what of the more distant positions that are so easily imagined? The notion of 'transmorphosis' anticipates that technology will soon allow combinations of precisely this kind. However, whereas the liquid simply suggests a *becoming-continuous*, transmorphosis suggests a *becoming-alien*.

Thus, while the notion of the liquid leads us to oppose the stability and permanence of architecture with a radical variability, and to propose 'liquid architectures', the notion of 'trans' leads us to oppose previously unrelated aspects of solidity/liquidity and presence/absence, and to propose 'transarchitectures' that are not present in any ordinary sense. These are architectures of partial, variable and contingent presence, not only in cyberspace, but right here, in ordinary space. Already this statement seems perplexing. What could this mean? And yet, as we shall see, it is exactly this that is the new potential for the arts of space.

Aliens II: From Immersion to Eversion
Eversion is the obverse of immersion. Literally, it means 'to turn inside-out' and differs from the more common 'inversion', which signifies 'turning outside-in' or simply 'turning over'. Eversion also has mathematical and biological uses, which provide other fruitful associations and resonances, but these are beyond the scope of the present text.

As captivating as the concept of immersion into virtuality has proved, it focuses on our entry into information spaces and has an unfortunate but strong connection with a narrow understanding of virtual reality. More importantly, 'immersion' is not a complete conceptual apparatus: it lacks a complementary concept describing the outpouring of virtuality onto ordinary space. Since there is neither reason, desire, nor likelihood that we will abandon ordinary space soon, if ever, and every reason why we should augment it now, such a companion concept is necessary. Eversion is this complementary concept and signifies a turning inside-out of virtuality, a casting outward of the virtual into the space of everyday experience.

First, let me offer some context for this term. Eversion is one of a growing set of concepts I have proposed in describing the cultural and poetic circumstances brought about by the exponential growth of information technologies. There can be little question that we are tending towards a culture of ubiquitous virtuality. As modernity encounters the high slopes of exponential change, it undergoes a phase of transition into a new stage I call 'transmodernity', or, better yet, 'transmodernities', placing emphasis on the inherent multiplicity and diversity that the proliferation of possibilities offers and requires. The transition from modernity to transmodernities is not a sequential development, as postmodernity presumed itself to be, but a change of state when modernity encounters sufficiently great and accelerating change. Also, as I envision them, modernity and transmodernity exist in parallel. What is implied here is that modernity is capable of multiplicity and internal variability. If ordinary modernity is characterised by the production of the 'new', which is, in any case, an ongoing cultural project, transmodernity is characterised by the production of the 'alien', a much more focused concern, in its many forms, both literal and metaphoric, both popular and unsuspected. So far, we have experienced this exponential change primarily through immersion into information technologies. As change accelerates, the technological becomes cultural and the immersive becomes everted. Hence, the transmodernity that has so far been brewing within information technologies is already being cast onto the world at large by the very same forces that drive the economics and politics of technology. In other words, eversion makes the encounter with transmodernity as inevitable as television.

Second, the notion of eversion complexifies the already altered nature of our relationship to space. The word 'space' is now just shorthand for 'spacetime', and 'space' is no longer innocent. Cyberspace implies a space laden with intelligence. For the time being, the metaphor and technology of immersion keeps cyberspace apart from our conventionally embodied experience. Eversion, as I have described it, predicts that the phenomena with which we are familiar in cyberspace will find, indeed are finding, their equivalent, everted forms in ordinary space. Thus, phenomenologically, the nature of space itself, *this* space, *our* space, is already undergoing significant changes into what I call 'newspace', the sum of local, remote, virtual and interactivated space. Hence, we will encounter the *transmodern-alien* in a space already contaminated by the eversion of virtuality.

Faraday's Garden, Maxwell's Demon, Theremin's Antennae
The history of our changing relationship to space goes back at least to Michael Faraday. In 1820, at almost exactly the same time as Nikolai Lobachevsky was writing about non-Euclidean geometry and Victor Hugo was declaring that the book would kill the building, or that bits would triumph over atoms, as Nicholas Negroponte would articulate it in our time, Michael Faraday understood that space was not empty.

Faraday developed the idea of the magnetic field run through by lines of force, demonstrating that space was not always vacant, unstructured or innocent. He went further to recognise the connections between space, field, force, electricity, magnetism and even light. Building on Faraday's work, James Clerk Maxwell reconciled electricity and magnetism through his field equations, making it clear that light itself was simply a form of electromagnetic radiation. His findings were, in turn, central in Einstein's conjoining of space with time and mass with energy.

Maxwell also studied the behaviour of gases and, through the thought-experiment known as 'Maxwell's Demon', became one of the originators of what would later come to be known as cybernetics. Maxwell's Demon was conceived as what we would now call an 'intelligent agent', located at the aperture between two chambers filled with gas, initially at the same temperature and pressure. The Demon would sense fast-moving molecules and selectively allow them to pass from one chamber to the other, eventually overcoming entropy and creating a disequilibrium that could be used to provide power. Although it was later shown that this process would consume more energy than it produced, for a while it seemed that Maxwell's Demon could overcome entropy with information. The relationship between energy and information has remained problematic ever since.

In 1920, Lev Sergeyevich Termen, better known as Leon Theremin, created the first truly electronic musical instrument. The 'Theremin' produced electromagnetic fields around two antennae. The fields acted as sensors, detecting the presence of a performer's body and modulating the frequency and amplitude of oscillators that produced sounds. Careful motion within the fields produced music. No direct contact was necessary. The Theremin was the first expressive instrument to be played solely through presence, that is, through engaging a new conception of interaction with invisible *form-in-space*.

If we connect Iannis Xenakis' conceptions of music as being 'inside-time', 'outside-time' and 'temporal', and allow ourselves to see music as extended form, we can look at a physical performance on a Theremin and realise that not only can the interaction of human presence and sense-activated space create music, but also that the actions that perform music on a Theremin have distinct three-dimensional shapes as 'music-outside-time', linking spatialised music to temporalised, animated liquid architectures.

In fact, writing about 'metamusic' – and, I would argue, 'transmusic' and 'transarchitectures' – Xenakis anticipated a visual music of quanta of light, localised in space, fired by photon-guns. We will return to this later.

Of course, the electromagnetic Theremin still operates in analogue fashion. Present-day sensor technologies employ analogue phenomena to detect a variety of conditions and, via sampling and quantising, make the collected sense-data available to digital computation, conjoining analogue space to digital space, interaction to computation.

'Faraday's Garden' is an interactive artwork by Perry Hoberman. It consists of a room full of numerous electrical appliances, in which a viewer can walk as if through a garden. Strewn among the sundry appliances are sensors that inform computers of human presence and activity. As one walks through the room, machines turn on and off in glorious cacophony. Old gramophones and fans, lamps and power tools, announce that space is not only not empty, but actually attentive and intelligent. Meanwhile, thousands of satellites and pieces of space debris orbit the Earth like a halo of alien flies. We see ourselves through their eyes.

Aliens III: Exponential Growth and The Production of the Alien
The word 'alien' is derived from the Latin *alius,* which in turn comes from the Greek *allos*, from which the word 'else' also

derives. When, in computer language, we write a conditional statement, *if x then y else z*, we are, in effect writing if *x then y alien z*, which expands into something of this form: *if condition x is true, then make outcome y true; if condition x is not true, then produce the alien outcome z*.

It has frequently been said that modernity is characterised by a fascination with change. It is also often noted that we live in a time of exponential change. Moore's Law predicts that computational power will double every 18 months. It is further argued that, because improvements in technology provide the means for further improvements in technology, there is reason to believe that this rate will continue unabated and spread far beyond its initial enabling technologies into all aspects of culture, following what Kurzweil calls 'the Law of Accelerating Returns'.[3]

One implication of exponential change is that the ratio of technological advancement to perceived cultural effect also changes exponentially. If we consider the familiar graph of an exponentially rising curve as a diagram of the growth of the cultural impact of technological change, placing the amount of technological advancement on the horizontal axis and reading the amount of cultural impact on the vertical axis, we can see that for most of history, it would have taken a large amount of technological advancement to produce a small amount of cultural impact, spawning predictable changes with little or no surprise. As the slope of the curve changes, this balance shifts until we reach a stage in which these terms are reversed and the opposite becomes true: a small amount of technological advancement produces an increasingly large amount of cultural impact. At the extreme, if exponential growth continues unabated, each infinitesimally small amount of technological change will produce an infinitely large amount of cultural surprise.

While modernity as a cultural outlook has always been understood in terms of its relationship to change, what has now become apparent is that this relationship is not fixed, but changes character as we move along the curve of exponential growth. Up to a certain point, the impact of change remains predictable, but beyond a certain point, even the smallest increment of change is amplified into a condition sufficiently removed from its origins to warrant being called 'alien'. The popular fascination with aliens is but a symptom of this transition, a vernacular awareness of the proliferation of flavours and species of 'alienness' and alienation.

Hence, we must ask what the 'alien' might be with respect to any particular cultural endeavour. In the case of architecture as an art of space, we must ask this for each term: architecture, art, and space.

Sensor Surface
By definition, a sensor is a device intended to activate an inaccessible region of reality in such a way as to make it available to our senses. This activation has specific spatio-temporal extension, or, in other words, specific shape in spacetime. Like Faraday's fields and their 'lines of force', analogue sensor space has overall contour and internal structure. Every sensor has an implicit focus, contour, surface, volume, or hyper-volume. Our ordinary impulse is to use sensors as transducers and components of control systems, and to concentrate our attention not on the spatial extension of the sensor-field but on the task at hand. Another view is possible: sensors interactivate space.

Analogue sensors have a relatively fixed form, and their internal structure is determined by the particular physical principle that they employ. Infrared sensors, for example, can detect degrees of intensity of projected or reflected infrared light whose spatial extension is a series of concentric isosurfaces. If one works directly with the analogue signals generated by such sensors, one is limited to the specific shapes implicit in their modes and principles of operation.

Digital sensors are analogue sensors whose output is not made available to us directly, but is mediated by a layer of abstraction that helps generalise their spatial extension. For example, triangulation and other techniques of exploiting redundancy and overlap are used to infer specific location. An overlay of sampling and quantising converts analogue sense signals to digital data. Once this is accomplished, the shape of the sensed field becomes an abstract region of space with a co-ordinate system that is relatively independent of the original shape implicit in the underlying analogue phenomena that are sensed.

Not only is the overall form of the sensed field altered by this, but the internal structure also changes. Whereas previously the internal 'lines of force' had to conform to the physical principles underlying the sensor's operation, and to the grain these principles imposed, now the internal shapes become totally programmable, like pixels on a screen.

In fact, let me coin the term 'sensels' to describe the elements of a sensed field, by analogy to familiar 'pixels' (picture elements), 'voxels' (volume elements) and 'texels' (texture elements). Just as we can use an array of pixels to create any image we please within the confines of a screen, or a three-dimensional array of voxels to create any form within the confines of an overall volume, so we can create a precise *sense-shape* with an array or volume of appropriate sensels. Such a shape would be exact but invisible, a region of activated, hypersensitive space.

All the techniques of computer graphics can be brought to bear upon the creation of *sensed-form*. Moreover, all the techniques of computer animation also apply, as do those of real-time simulation. Because sensels are not bound to exist on a screen, however, and because, as sensors, they are inherently intended to mediate between the invisible world and our own senses, they open up entirely new aspects of expression. To make architecture is to express human intelligence by spatial means.

From Sensels to Sense-Selves
Consider this: you reach into a sensor space. As your fingers cross into a selected region, sounds are triggered. Curious, you try to trace the extent of the region that causes the sounds. Soon you discover that it is a tall, elongated, shape, tapering at both ends. Exploring, you begin to realise that it is a sculpted form, an invisible rendition of Constantin Brancusi's *Bird in Space*.

What has Happened Here?
What I am proposing is that a new form of sculpture has been born, which reverses most of the ordinary expectations we might have about sculpture: since there is nothing to see, voyeuristic visuality has been replaced with Duchampian non-retinality. The still prevalent prohibition against touching the work has also been destabilised, since the object can only be known by touch: untouchability has been replaced with hypertactility. However, this sense of touch is problematised: there is nothing there to touch. Tactility becomes virtualised and synaesthetic.

Now let's follow this a step further. Instead of making the region of space a simple shape, let's use a three-dimensional scan of a classical bust. Rather than render it in pixels, or voxels, let's render it in sensels. Now, when we interact with the sensor region, we can accurately trace our fingers across the face of the sculptural portrait. Although we cannot see the face of the person, we can, ever so lightly, caress their features. Voyeurism is replaced by intimate touch.

Let's take a further step. We know that not only can we represent a model via computer graphics, we can also animate it. The invisible portrait can be animated either passively, as a precomputed animation, or actively as an interactive real-time simulation. By animating sensels rather than pixels, we can create dynamic and coherent regions of space that can sense the world and our presence in it and that can take any definite form we wish to give them. Again, the now animated sculpture is not visible. It is something we can only sense through a form of synaesthetised touch.

One more step: why stop at the head? Why not scan and animate an entire body? Several bodies? Now we reach a significant landmark: we have established *avatars-in-our-midst*, invisible presences that perambulate near us, acting as stand-ins or agents. One of the strangest predictions of the idea of eversion becomes true in the most direct of ways. We have moved from sensels to sense-selves.

What are these invisible apparitions? What are the origins of our imagination of such entities? Spirits and ghosts, avatars and aliens, phantasms and spectres: these are the naïve conjurings of what we are now technologically able to release amongst us.

Brushing Against Angels I
In Wim Wender's film *Wings of Desire* (1987), angels walking amongst humans eavesdrop on them, hearing their inner dialogues, their thoughts and fears and worries. Occasionally, the angels place an ethereal hand on a heavy shoulder and soothe a person. More often than not, they merely observe.

Now consider this: a gallery space with an installation that is entirely invisible, consisting of animated, autonomous sensor-presences. Walking into the gallery, you see nothing but empty space. But should you persist and remain in the gallery, perhaps you will brush against one of these presences, triggering synaesthetic clues of your encounter. Perhaps, alerted to this presence, you will reach out to touch the unseen visitor. The sensor-field of the invisible presence can be as detailed as we wish it to be: you can reach out and touch the face of an angel. Feeling gently, and paying attention to carefully correlated synaesthetic clues such as sound, voice, light, or projections, you will be able to read every feature and expression on the angel's face.

Nanospace
Physicist Richard Feynman's 1959 lecture entitled 'There's Plenty Of Room at the Bottom' predicted that design would proceed all the way down to the scale of atoms. In the intervening time, nanotechnology, the discipline that has emerged to study how such design capability is to be realised, has made numerous concrete accomplishments in the creation of nanomachines. These successes have in turn fuelled additional speculations as to what is possible once the frontier of scale is crossed. Below nanoscale (billionth of a metre), there are pico- (trillionth), femto- (quadrillionth), even atto- (quintillionth) scales, at each of which design and computation can be envisioned.

One of the most provocative proposals to emerge from nanotechnology is J Storrs Hall's 'Utility Fog'. Hall invites us to consider a 'foglet', a nanomachine that is a cross between a supercomputer and a nano-robot or nanobot. As a computer, it is a full supercomputer designed specifically for massively parallel processing and communications. As a robot, it consists of a dodecahedral structure with six telescoping and gripping arms, arranged so that it can grasp and hold other foglets under algorithmic control: intelligent nanorobotic Velcro.

Now consider the scale at which Hall imagines this can be built: a foglet is about the same size as a human cell. We are ordinarily unaware of the enormous number of molecules, atoms and particles that make up ordinary matter, and it will therefore be useful to suspend disbelief until some of these numbers are considered. A cubic inch of space would contain 16 billion foglets. As fantastic as this may seem, it is conceivable because, with a reach of only 10 microns, the foglet would still consist of 5 trillion atoms, plenty of material for both its mechanical and computational requirements.

'Utility Fog' is a collection of such foglets sufficient to fill a space, say a room. If the foglets are relaxed and distant from one another, they are invisible. If they are contracted, they take on aspects of solid matter. Under algorithmic control, they can vary smoothly between one state and the other, morphing from apparent nothingness to objecthood, or from one form and behaviour to another. Hall builds on this informed speculation and performs some of the calculations necessary to make a persuasive argument that this is indeed possible in some not too distant future. Kurzweil estimates that it will take 50 to 100 years to achieve this.

We do not have the technology to build 'Utility Fog' at present, but we need not reach the limits of physical possibility to see what this implies. Even if we could only build 16, rather than 16 billion such machines into a cubic inch, even if each foglet occupied an entire cubic inch by itself, the implications for our relationship to space and architecture would be profound. At the scale that Hall envisions it, 'Utility Fog' is an intelligent 'meta-material'. It seems reasonable to assume that before we get to that level, we will build intelligent 'meta-components', elements of a generalised space-frame construction system that can sense its environment, adjust, and even reconfigure itself dynamically. Intelligent meta-components suggest that we can build liquid architectures in real space; combined intelligent meta-materials and meta-components hint at the transarchitectures of alien transmodernities.

A Romance of Many Dimensions
The subtitle of Edwin A Abbott's *Flatland* is 'A Romance of Many Dimensions', the word 'many' directing our attention to the more general problem of understanding a space of n-dimensions by thinking analogically of spaces of $n+1$ or $n-1$ dimensions.

Information space, whether immersive or everted, is inherently multidimensional. Physical reality, as presented to us via superstring theory and its superset, membrane theory, is also inherently multidimensional. At one point, it was believed that there could be as many as 26 spatial dimensions, but at present, the number is believed to be merely 10. In nature as in artifice, there is much more to reality than meets the eye, so perhaps the eye needs to learn to see more than it normally does.

Brushing Against Angels II
In my earlier discussion of the gallery in which regions of space were activated in the forms of intelligent presences, I likened the presences to 'angels'. This was not motivated by any religious

consideration, but because of their symmetry with the angels in Wenders' film and with the larger history of interaction with invisible presences. Although I understand these presences to be everted avatars, it may be useful to give them a distinct name. So, angels, yes, but alien angels of a technologised spirituality.

I have long argued that it makes little sense to replicate the outside world in cyberspace. It makes even less sense to take a poor replica of the familiar from cyberspace and evert it onto the real. Just as it is more challenging to explore the ways in which the virtual exceeds the real in cyberspace, it is also more interesting to evert our cyberspace discoveries from virtuality onto ordinary space. I have explored spatial ideas that are inherently non-visual: n-dimensional geometries, curved trans-Euclidean spaces, abstract artificial life, fitness, landscapes. Musically, I am trying to understand what n-dimensional sound may be like, how it would propagate, what musical form and formation would be appropriate to it, and how its shadows would play in our spacetime. This parallel consideration of architecture and music is necessary: when space and time combine into spacetime, architecture and music conjoin into 'archimusic'. To make archimusic is to express human intelligence by spatiotemporal means. When spacetime is understood as n-dimensional, archimusic must be considered n-dimensionally as well.

Higher dimensional phenomena behave in ways that we find difficult to comprehend, and this strangeness carries through to the projections or sections by which we know higher space. In three-dimensional space we can understand rotation about a point or about a line. In four-dimensional space, objects can rotate about surfaces; in five, they can rotate about hypersurfaces. Since we have no direct equivalent, our understanding of these higher rotations is necessarily partial. Sound is also affected: an n-dimensional sound of uniform loudness and frequency, emanating from a single source in higher space can register to us as a multiplicity of sounds of varying pitches, timbres and intensities emanating from numerous moving sources in our space, simply on the basis of how it happens to drop into, intersect with, or project onto our space. Should the n-dimensional sound be part of n-dimensional music, the pattern becomes richer with every drop in dimension, until, in our three-dimensional world, even the simplest four-dimensional music sounds complex and intricate. Many such phenomena are waiting to be studied.

Transmodernity will surely take the new dimensions offered in cyberspace or discovered by physical space as raw materials for constructing new, multidimensional species of the alien, first in virtuality, and soon thereafter, via eversion, in real space augmented into newspace. Sensels will give interactivated form to this everted virtuality; parametric sound systems will localise the corresponding sound, photon-guns such as those Xenakis envisioned will provide a visual-musical correlate, if that is desirable or necessary, and developments of intelligent meta-components and meta-materials will allow the creation of n-dimensional liquid architectures in newspace.

To register the ramifications of all this, let us revisit the hypothetical gallery in which we first brushed against our alien angels. My initial observation was that eversion implied that sensels would interactivate regions of space, and that we would learn to detect the shape of those regions synaesthetically. Pressing forward now, we can see that the implication of components derived from nanotechnology is that the gallery itself becomes liquid and can change form dynamically. Pressing even further, the implication of materials derived from nanotechnology, such as Hall's 'Utility Fog', is that the distinction between space and boundary finally fades into a programmable continuum. In effect, every location in space becomes a voxel of variable presence or absence, permeability or hardness, attribute x or attribute y. At this level, the gallery itself takes on the capacity of a three-dimensional screen, upon which anything can be projected.

If space itself becomes a screen upon which anything can be projected, not as a hologram but as a variation in density and material presence, then it becomes possible to project onto space the computation of the behaviour of liquid, n-dimensional architectures, inherently virtual designs now made palpable in familiar space. An archimusic of varying densities and qualities of space animates the space of the gallery, which is itself fluctuating, and we can touch the archimusic. Our alien angels need no longer be anthropomorphic, but can take on forms appropriate to their origins, and, strange though these forms may be, we can still touch them too.

And, finally, our gallery can move outdoors. Since eversion is about puncturing the barrier of computer screens as we know them and letting virtuality pour out and saturate newspace, there is no longer a need to remain confined to dark interiors. Eversion brings virtuality to sunlight.

Notes
1 Iannis Xenakis, *Formalised Music: Thought and Mathematics in Music* (Revised Edition), Pendragon Press, 1992.
2 I introduce the notion of 'transmorphosis' to describe an operation between-and above 'transformation' and 'metamorphosis'. 'Allomorphosis', 'xenomorphosis' and 'exomorphosis' belong to the same cluster and are useful in describing species of the production of the alien. 'Diamorphosis' and 'paramorphosis' are related concepts describing other aspects of morphosis/genesis that range from the pedagogical to the monstrous. 'Transmorphosis' is intended to collect these various notions of formation and to call attention to their transversal connnection to the alien. That the word is hybrid, combining the Latin prefix 'trans' with the Greek 'morphosis' is only appropriate. A parallel set built upon the word 'genesis' is also possible, leading to 'transgenesis', 'allogenesis', 'xenogenesis' and so on. The terms require consideration of the differences between the evolutionary 'morphosis' and the creationist 'genesis', but this is beyound the scope of the present text.
3 Ray Kurzweil, *The Age of Spiritual Machines: When Computers Exceed Human Intelligence*, Viking Press, 1999.

References
Peter Anders, *Envisioning Cyberspace: Designing 3D Electronic Spaces*, McGraw-Hill, 1999.
Bruce Clarke, *Allegories of Writing: The Subject of Metamorphosis*, SUNY Press, 1995.
BC Crandall (ed), *Nanotechnology: Molecular Speculations on Global Abundance*, MIT Press (Cambridge, Mass.), 1996.
Brian R Greene, *The Elegant Universe: Superstrings, Hidden Dimensions, and the Quest for the Ultimate Theory*, WW Norton & Company (New York), 1999.
N. Katherine Hayles, *How We Became Posthuman: Virtual Bodies in Cybernetics, Literature, and Informatics*, University of Chicago Press (Chicago), 1999.
Naomi Matsunaga (ed), *Transarchitectures in Cyberspace: Ten Architects who Stimulate the World*, Nikkei Architecture (Tokyo), April 1998.
Marcos Novak, 'Next Babylon, Soft Babylon: (trans)Architecture is an Algorithm to Play in', in Neil Spiller (ed), *AD: Architects in Cyberspace II*, vol 68, no 136, pp11–12, Academy Editions (London), November–December 1998.
Marcos Novak, 'Transarchitectures and Hypersurfaces: Operations of Transmodernity', in Stephen Perrella (ed), *AD: Hypersurface Architecture*, vol 68, no 133, pp5–6, Academy Editions (London), May–June 1998.

DILLER + SCOFIDIO WITH PAUL LEWIS
JUMP CUTS
United Artists Cineplex Theater, San Jose, California, 1995

Jump Cuts is a permanent public art installation. It grew out of an interest in the increasingly blurred boundaries between art and commerce. Following the resurgence of extravagant lobbies in theatres, this newly built cinema on the Paseo in San Jose has a huge, open circulation space speared by freestanding escalators and flying pedestrian bridges. The installation straddles the glass wall along the major facade. A steel armature appended to this facade supports a series of 12 liquid-crystal panels over the street. Correspondingly, at the interior, one projector stationed before each of the panels is fed by a string of live cameras positioned along the multiple levels of escalators in the grand lobby, either looking down in plan or across in elevation. The mechanical movement of the escalators past the stationary cameras supplies a succession of bodies on parade. As patrons zig-zag through the lobby on the moving stairs, they are electronically reconfigured to appear as if travelling across the facade. The continuous stream of bodies is interrupted only by movie trailers.

Re-interpreting the function of the traditional theatre marquee, the apparatus of *Jump Cuts* informs passersby in the street of events within by flipping the building inside-out electronically. Candid views of movie-goers milling through the lobby are given equal status with more established forms of entertainment. Drawing inspiration from the tradition of grand social antespaces like the Paris Opera, in which circulation area exceeds theatre area by 5:1, the installation re-frames the question: on which side of the stage is the spectacle?

Glass architecture in combination with surveillance technology allegedly produced a transparent world. But did this transparency lead to new tactics of secrecy? Or, more interestingly, did visual availability lead to new tactics of display? Glass and surveillance screens have become calculated surfaces onto which performance can be projected. Perhaps the paranoia has shifted from the fear that someone is watching to the fear that no-one is watching. Postmodern narcissism may have turned yesterday's pathologies into today's signs of good health.

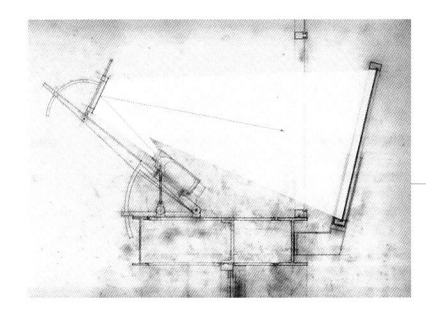

MARK BURRY
PARAMORPH
Anti-accident methodologies

Since 1979 Mark Burry has been Consultant Architect to the commission completing Antoni Gaudí's Sagrada Família in Barcelona. The richness of Gaudí's reiterative design development procedures have inspired Burry to develop computer-based design research propositions sympathetic to Gaudí's own. Citing his work on the Sagrada Família here, he argues more broadly for a greater understanding of the computer's potential at a profound level in architecture. He rallies, in particular, against the apportioning to the computer credibility in 'design through accident', as against 'design through design'.

> *A world that is open to continuous change and to becoming different, requires an* ars accidentalis. *The creativity and the productivity of the accident, the break and the fall, have to be understood as the potential to achieve new forms of heterogeneity and of the disjunctive synthesis. Imprecision, haste, and forgetfulness are only some of the characteristics of this romantic discipline. The* Art of the Accident *is not looking for conclusive answers. It investigates the project in the face of failure.*[1]

Given our continuing ill-defined relationship with computer-derived design, it is hardly surprising that the accidental effects achieved thereby are given substantial visual status and appreciation. Many computer-based surface representations – hypersurfaces – are nevertheless deliberately and not accidentally provoked and they too are sponsoring revised theory and new architectures coinciding with but possibly more in opposition to the outcome of the *ars accidentalis* school. Many observers recognise the difficulties from a traditional point of view in establishing appropriate aesthetic theory for what are often rather esoteric and spatially unfathomable surfaces. When we review contemporary literature it does not seem to be a priority to delve too deeply into the ways and means whereby the computer is used to generate highly contemporary images of multidimensional spatial boundaries with some measure of explicit user control. Emerging critical theory therefore has no embarrassment in accepting, or benignly accommodating or even celebrating the accident or the error.[2] The intellectual value of a perverse giving-up of authorship ('design') is neither judged with quizzicality, nor seen as a potential artistic impropriety:

> *Yet, malfunction and failure are not signs of improper production. On the contrary, they indicate the active production of the 'accidental potential' in any product.*[3]

With the exception of those familiar with using digital media themselves, many critics of contemporary design are in the unusual position of being removed from the design process. In contrast an art critic may not be a painter, but they at least know what paint is, and how it gets onto the canvas. This essay therefore involves itself in production issues rather than the productions, and production through design, not through accident as casual champion. Architectural design where the constituent geometry is mutually linked (so-called 'parametric design' or 'associative geometry') is hardly mainstream, yet the principles involved have been understood for many years and exploited by vehicle and product designers able to profit from the necessarily substantial investment in software and appropriate hardware. As prices start to fall markedly to the advantage of architectural practice, parametric design procedures can be advanced as both friend as well as potential pariah to the digital designer, should it come out of its rather curious obscurity into our arena.

Art through Accident
Can we apply a test of 'repeatability' as a means to distinguish art from architectural design? For instance, the panache of a Jackson Pollock paint-splash contributes to the final valued product. Its inexact definition (the combined dribbles and splashes) and nonrepeatability is its uniqueness, and its value. The equivalent in surface representation within the virtual realm comes from deliberate tinkering with on-board algorithms, or through programming which incorporates random numbers or some aspect of chaos theory or from serendipity. In most circumstances the results are unpredictable and unrepeatable. With some unrecorded and poorly remembered series of operations, surprising results nevertheless emerge. There may be conspicuous merit here where such images become elevated and appreciated as art or virtual architecture produced through accident, or designed accident – the ultimate oxymoron. To be taken further, to the building of the structure represented, a better understanding of what has been represented will be required: not only what the image *is* but how it came to be. In many cases, architectural design favours a linear process where design can build upon itself. Any reiterative process will require some ability to go back in the design process in order to proceed forward in a different direction. This of course is rather difficult if the process is accidental and less well understood than the outcome.

Art through Design
Looking at design as a process that leads to production requires a shift in our current focus to issues broader than 'flair' the definition that has privileged the word 'design' and therefore 'designed' (as opposed to accidentally produced?) objects in common parlance since the 1980s: 'design' as in 'designer jeans', for instance. A design for something, however, is not the outcome but the means to its end. An object that has been designed reflects deliberate decision-making, not a serendipitous

Fig. 1

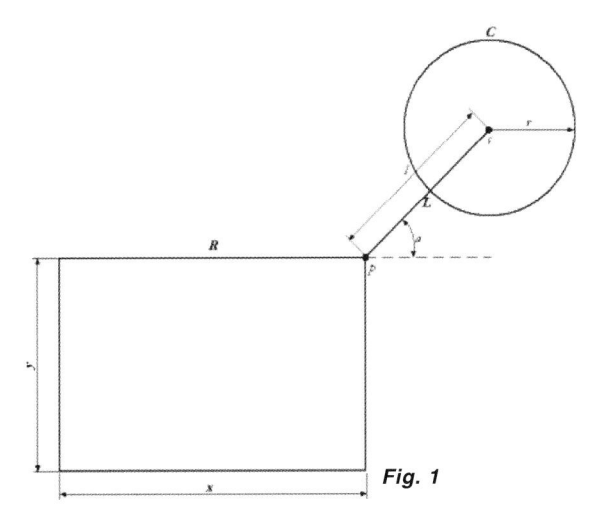

occurrence. Design to manufacture or design to build is surely a deliberate act, not an accidental happenstance.

In our pluralist times it would be odd to suggest a formulaic approach to building design, but the need for a collaborative understanding implies a system, an order to the proceedings, anything other than chaos. Little wonder then that architectural production remains steadfastly orthogonal in the main despite regular challenges to the straight and vertical during the postindustrial age. Cyberspace-hypersurfaces confined to cathode ray tubes or print risks remaining aloof from the built world: hypersurface as hyperbole. Can it be otherwise?

The *paramorph*[4] presented here is an experimental incursion into a context of unstable spatial and topological description of form – unstable form but stable characteristics (parameters). In this context, and loosely contained within a definition offered by Stephen Perrella,[5] a paramorph might be the unstable stability that hypersurfaces imply when attributed to representations of buildable form. It is contended here that hypersurfaces are buildable. Describing unstable representations of form is of course a challenging and counterproductive enterprise without syntax. Parametric design through associative geometry provides such syntax.

Parametric Design through Associative Geometry

Parametric design is an anathema to the accidental formalist. It is predicated on the design being so well understood that the derivation of its constituent parameters can be recorded historically along with relationships between geometrical entities. Figure 1, a circle C of radius r can be linked by a line L of length l between the circle's c centre down to a point p of a rectangle R measuring x by y. C is an 'object', and c is a parameter. In a carefully considered design, a so-called explicit design, parameters have declared values. In almost all CAD packages the design is explicit, regardless of how the software user might have produced it, with the parameter represented as a direct... 'Grip points' give the impression of parametric variability – which to an extent they are. The user 'grips' the centre of C at c and moves it with the mouse to a new position. But the line L remains in place in its original. If the geometry is associated the situation changes quite distinctly. If entity C, for example, moves through the redefinition of the position of c, the end of line L whose end is linked to c moves with it while remaining attached to the rectangle.

'*Parametric design*' is such that it is the parameters of a design that are declared, not the shape. A circle described as an ellipse with coincident foci is automatically made into an ellipse when the foci – parameters – are moved apart.

The parameter values are tweaked via the screen. Values of and relationships between parameters are stored in the graphics software database and are referred to the user through a visual representation on the screen. The size of an element is represented as a dimension that can be changed. By clicking the mouse on a particular value, for instance, it is changed interactively and the model can be regenerated in its new configuration.

Equations are used to represent the relationships between objects. The ability to define, determine and reconfigure geometrical relationships is of particular value. In the example given above, the relationship between x and y can be determined by an equation such as: $x = 1.5 * y$, where x is one and a half times the value of y.

Relationships such as the angle a between the rectangle and the circle can be linked as, for example: *if $x < (2 * y)$ then $a = 45$ degrees else 30 degrees*, such that if x is greater than twice y then a is forty-five degrees otherwise it is thirty degrees.

This is known as constraining the model. It is easy, however, to over-constrain such that by unilaterally attempting to change the length of one side of a rectangle otherwise constrained by all angles being 'set' to ninety degrees, an impossible form is attempted.

The parametric designer can nevertheless reiteratively experiment with an assembly (a design) to taste, and repeatedly should an earlier design be favoured over a later. Otherwise, designers have to resort to erasure, not reformation of a construct. Unless the conventional designer has saved an earlier version, they will have to remember how they produced it, if they need to go back to it should later explorations have proved counterproductive.

The parametric designer can move backwards and forwards at will – a peculiar attribute of this way of working with the computer. There is no haptic equivalent, and parametric design is a rare example of a design process that is uncharacteristically linked to the computer. But there is a cost, which is that design becomes formulaic.

Returning to our example of the circle linked to a rectangle while the circle can be parametrically altered to an ellipse, and the rectangle to a square by simply altering the values of their parameters, the parameters themselves cannot be altered. Having related the circle C to line L, itself related to the rectangle R, a cylinder might be associated with each of the corners of the rectangle. If the rectangle is moved and changed to a square by making x equal to y, the cylinders will follow the fortunes of the rectangle.

A different reconfiguration can be based around the geometry of the objects, not just their parametric values. For instance, the original decision to place a rectangle can be revisited, and the rectangle is replaced with a pentagon. In all likelihood the 'command tree' will be extinguished from that point forward – there will no longer be a line, circle and cylinders associated with the original figure. Artificial Intelligence is not at the level of

79

predicting subsequent decisions following a compositional change of this order. With the introduction of the extra node, ought the modelling software to be able to predict that five cylinders are now required? A moot point and a deficiency that immediately compromises the effectiveness of parametric design should the approach to the software use be the same as to any other design process.

Clearly, to avoid such pitfalls the designer needs to have a strategy. The strategy could include factors of indeterminacy. Even if the design is likely to be based on a quadrilateral, possibly square, possibly rectangular, it could be based initially on a pentagon on the basis that a side could be subsequently removed. The modeller can accommodate the change from five to four sides inasmuch as the computer can handle absence better than super-presence. The removal of the fifth node means that from a logical point of view, the fifth cylinder can not find a home and is therefore not included. The reverse situation does not present the same logical condition: an extra node may or may not require a cylinder. It is in fact a dilemma that can only be resolved by the designer.

Early references to parametric design recognise this apparent inflexibility in presuming that parametric designers adopt the same methodology as they might using other media.[6] More generous sceptics have conceded a usefulness, at least for design resolution at a detailed level. Figures 2 and 3 show this to be the case. Both figures show the assembly of hyperbolic paraboloids that form the 3.1metre high triforium columns for Gaudí's *Sagrada Família* Church in Barcelona. These columns have been modelled parametrically such that all the proportions and characteristics of the columns can be changed at will until the digital version matches exactly Gaudí's original as represented in surviving 1:10 gypsum plaster fragments. The laboriousness of this task can be appreciated; a considerable amount of reiterative erasure and remodelling can be semiautomated using parametric design software. This approach gives a more intuitive feel to the digital manipulations. In this example, reconfiguring all twelve columns for the model and rendering them takes less than 30 seconds.

A further example of detailed design resolution being aided using parametric design is outlined in figures 4 and 5. Figure 5 shows the interrelationship between the rafters of a reciprocal

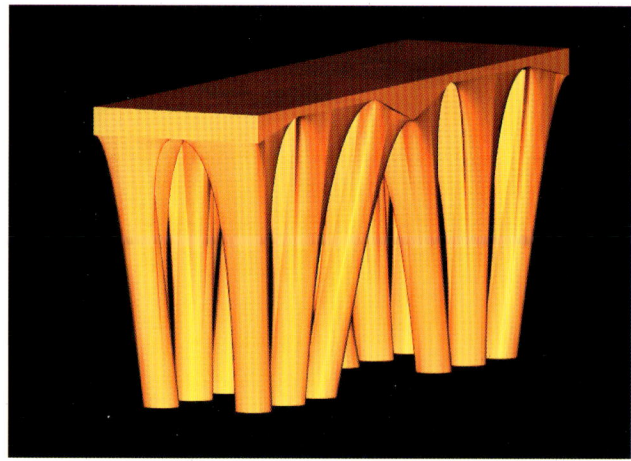

Fig. 2: *Intermediate version of triforium columns for Gaudí's Sagrada Família Church*

Fig. 3: *Final version of triforium columns for Gaudí's Sagrada Família Church*

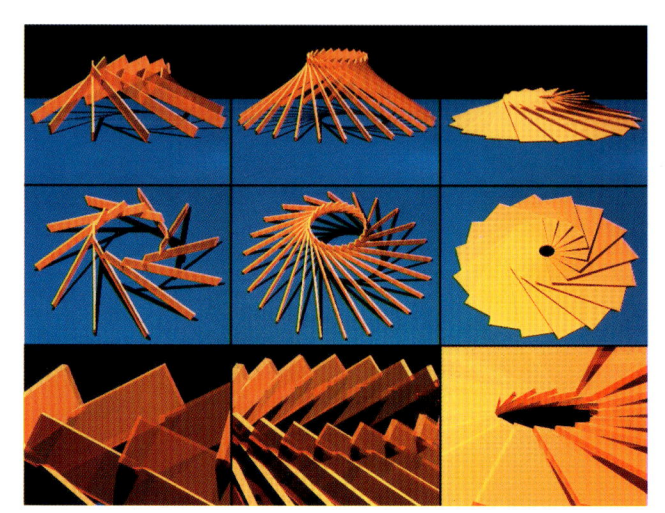

Fig. 4 *Reciprocal frame truss. Various configurations for reciprocal frame trusses all derived from the same parametric model. Each variant takes a matter of seconds to generate and represent. Parametric variables include the number of rafters, slope, and height.*

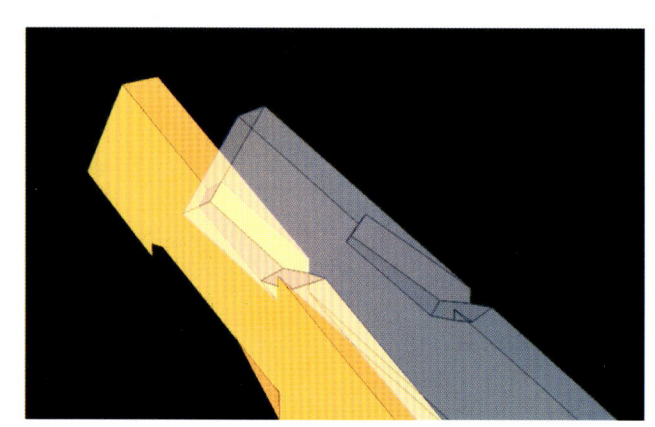

Fig. 5: *Reciprocal frame truss. Notching calculated automatically during the reconfiguration such that the seat is a given depth and is always horizontal regardless of changes in the configuration. A highly complex cut is nevertheless generated automatically and can be made using CAD/CAM. The joint can be viewed as a 3D VRML at http://www.ab.deakin.edu.au/paramorph*

frame truss, the sort that Jujol used in Casa Bofarull in the Tarragonès. Each joist supports the previous while being supported itself by the following.

The number of rafters, their depth, the degree of notching, how close the supporting function is to the supported object expressed proportionally in relation to the whole assembly all combine to determine the slope of the roof. Doubters of the sophistication required in order to obtain a prescribed slope and occulus by deriving the optimum values for each of these parameters above (for the designer will have 'values' for both in mind) can experiment using chopsticks over a bowl. Still more difficult is modelling the assembly using CAD, especially the joint of given depth (Figure 5) such that the seat is always horizontal regardless of the angle of the rafters.

The examples provided in figures 2-5 are details of one aspect only of an architectural form: structure. The user-controlled variability makes these non-committal structures hyperstructures (they could support anything – they support only themselves), and it is only when they become inseparably implicated with a skin that they become hypersurfaces in a formal architectural sense. Being neither surface nor substance, supporter nor supported, their ambiguous declared architectural status means that each variant is unstable as a formal description. They become stable once the design is committed as a building, probably best stabilised as a kinetic building to reflect optimally the possibilities that the parametric model implies.

Figures 6-9 show members of a parametric family that makes up a typical paramorph. Each variant is an example from an iterative experimental sequence with their 'birth times'. All the spatial characteristics and positions in this example are governed by Cartesian co-ordinates. Their values can be governed individually or grouped by equation. In this case a spreadsheet is used to generate streams of values for identified parameters transferred seamlessly to the modeller as an exported *ascii* script which the parametric modeller imports as an executable file. The process takes seconds, as does the regeneration; the rest of the time is accounted for as design reflection time. At once the paramorphs are explicitly tectonic if the hypersurface implies a structure, but they can be tectonically neutral by a sleight of parametric modification where a simple reductivist state (the paramorph precursor) suggests neither surface nor structure, simply volume.

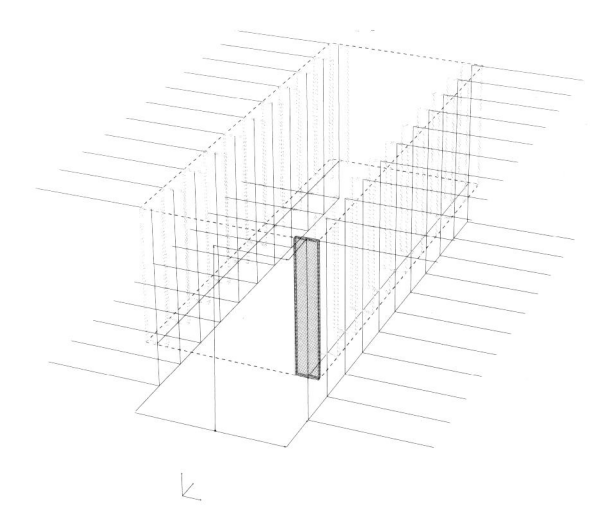

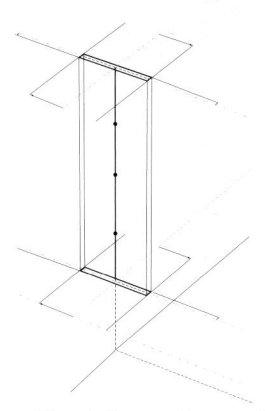

Fig. 6: *General layout from the basic structure of one of the paramorph elements (Structure 1).*

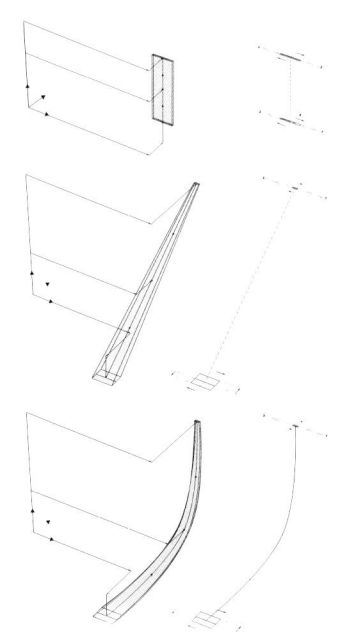

Fig. 7: *Typical parametric structure (Structure 1) showing the variation in geometry through altering the parameters of each structure.*

Fig. 8: *Paramorph general layout diagram. Notional structure 1-11 and 12-22 (with layout of typical parameters and guides for Structure 1).*

There are therefore two neutral-active states to the paramorph: apparent tectonic neutrality in the precursor (fig 10a) and states of heightened tectonic expression once the form is transformed from the precursor (figs 10b–10e).

In summary, the figures show the tectonically neutral state of the precursor with a selection from a range of hypersurfaces all generated from the one apparently neutral but in fact parametrically unstable state. In this case, all the hypersurfaces are ruled-surfaces pointing to ready description and facility for construction. The designer has absolute authority over their design, and limitless possibilities for iterative design development experimentation in this medium and context.

Concluding Remarks

The crisis of art and architecture is a symptom of the deep ambivalence of human mentality: committed to reason as a tool for dismantling nature and learning secrets of her power; unable to offer to reason an unreason that does not smell of nightmare and death. The artist is sensitive to this dichotomy, and can deal with it independently in ways the architect cannot.[7]

The procedure outlined here is different from others, but so too is the paramorph. The paramorph is not an accident but a hypersurface made through design. The difference between a paramorph and the accidental nonintended outcome of other approaches to design is intention. Are we to judge one system requiring considerable controlled technique unfavourably when compared with the captivating dalliance with the accident? I suspect that we will continue to form our own opinions but not to the exclusion of dabbling with parametric design given the opportunity.

Separating technique from art is a risky business, especially when the art leads to a building. Visiting galleries I am reminded of the relationship of technique to outcome. Who is not stopped in their tracks by Bernini's rendering of *Apollo and Daphne* at the moment when Daphne has already partly metamorphosed into a tree, a virtuoso representation of hyper-materiality in cold marble yet rendered living by technique alone? The computer is offering new facilities in artistic production, in relatively uncharted waters. Pausing in our cycle of benign accommodation or active encouragement of the monkey typing *Hamlet* we can reflect on previous dilemmas not so different from our post-computer technology psychosis. Saarinen, for instance, observed the following on the use of free forms for architecture in 1957, predating any computer virtuoso output:

> Technology has made plastic form more easily possible for us. But it is the aesthetic reasons which are driving forces behind its use. What interests me is when and where to use these structural plastic shapes ... Plastic form for its own sake, even when very virile, does not seem to come off.[8]

There is benefit from a constant reminder of the implications of the attainment and application of higher levels of technical skill to art production. Such reminder can temper the triumph of the mishap in the face of conspicuous endeavours evidenced from the past, where art is married to technique through light but active control.

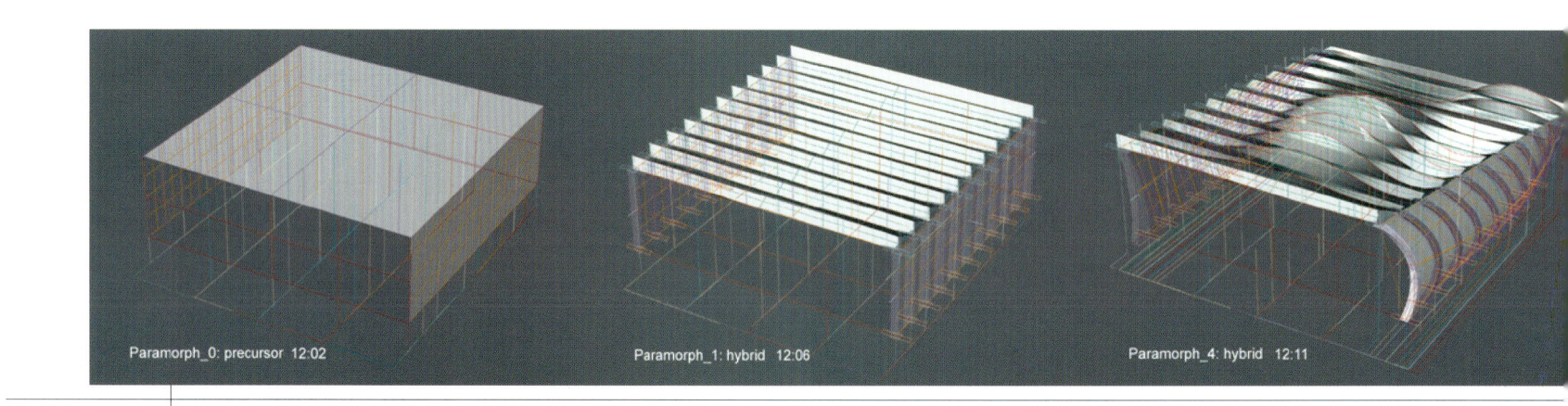

Fig. 11

Notes

'Triforium columns' and 'Reciprocal frame truss' were modelled by Mark Burry and rendered by Gregory More. 'Paramorph' was modelled and rendered by Mark Burry and Grant Dunlop.

1. Taken from, 'Ars accidentalis', introduction to the catalogue *DEAF98, 'The Art of the Accident'*, NAI Publishers/V2_Organisatie Netherlands 1998
2. Pérez-Gómez and Pelletier: 'The tyranny of the computer-aided design and its graphic system can be awesome: because its rigorous mathematical base is unshakeable, it rigidly establishes a homogeneous space and is inherently unable to combine different structures of reference.' The authors proceed to identify a tendency for error to be enfranchised as a legitimate design outcome. Pérez-Gómez, A and Pelletier, L: *Architectural Representation and the Perspective Hinge*, 1997, The MIT Press, Cambridge, Massachusetts
3. Ditto endnote 1
4. A paramorph is described as a pseudomorph (something the shape of somethingelse with a different chemical composition – eg a pertrified tree) formed by a change to the physical charactersitics without a change in chemical composition.
5. 'A hypersurface is the informed topology of an interstitial terrain between the real and the unreal (or any other binary opposition) which then flows transversally into a stream of associations.' Perrella, S: 'Hypersurface Theory: Archi-tecture><Culture', *Architectural Designs* London 1998
6. Parametric design is dismissed here for the reasons of apparent inflexibility given by Miller, F.C> (1990) in 'Form Processing Workshop: Architectural Design and Solid Modelling at MIT' In (eds) McCullough, M. Mitchell, W.J. and Purcell, P., *The Electronic Design Studio*, pp441–55, The MIT Press, Cambridge Massachusetts
7. Maxwell, R., *Sweet Disorder and the Carefully Careless Theory and Criticism in Architecture*, Princeton University Press, New York, 1993.
8. Saarinen on plastic form in architecture (June 1957): *Ero Saarinen on his Work*, ed Aline B. Saarinen, Yale University Press, 1968

Fig. 9

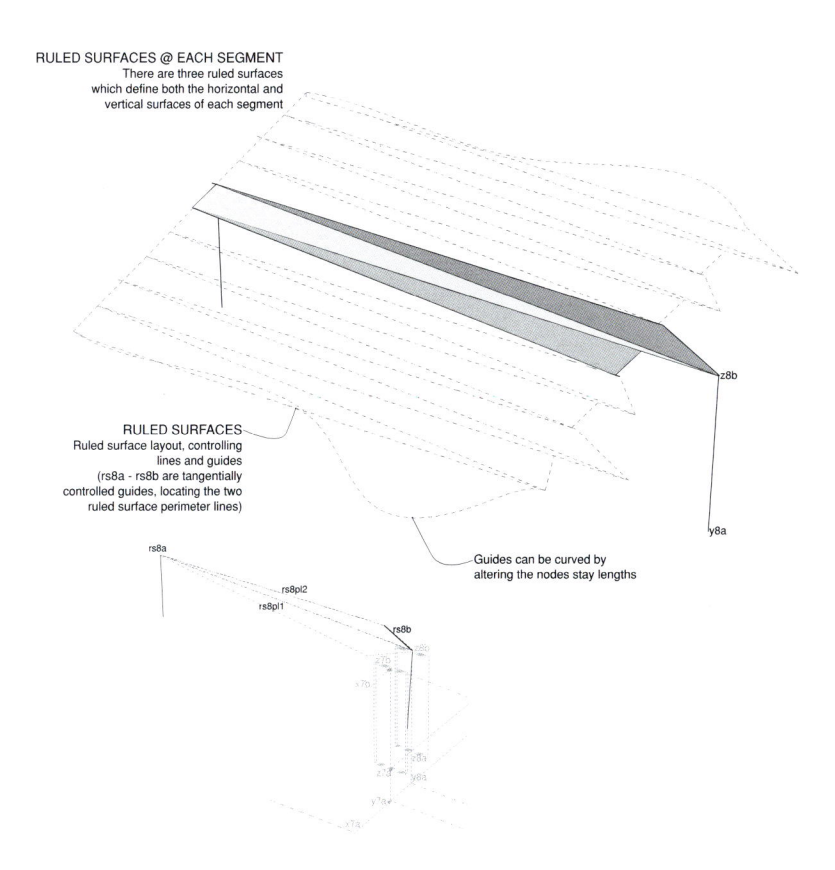

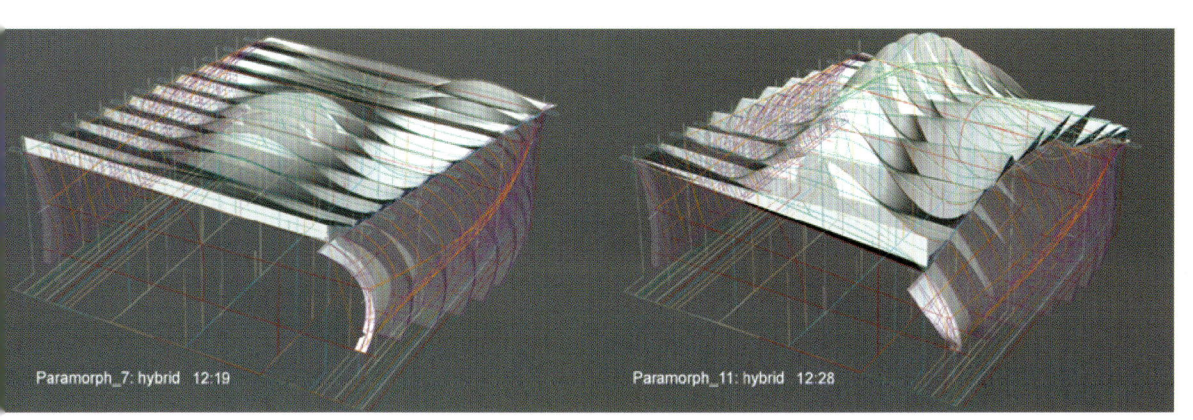

Fig. 10

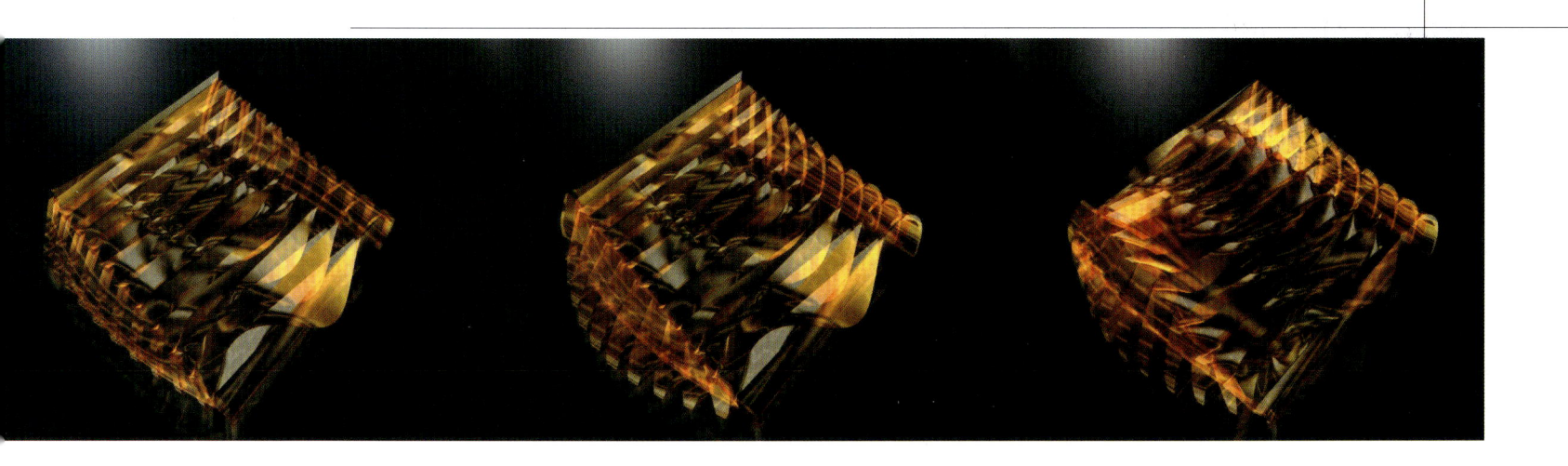

84

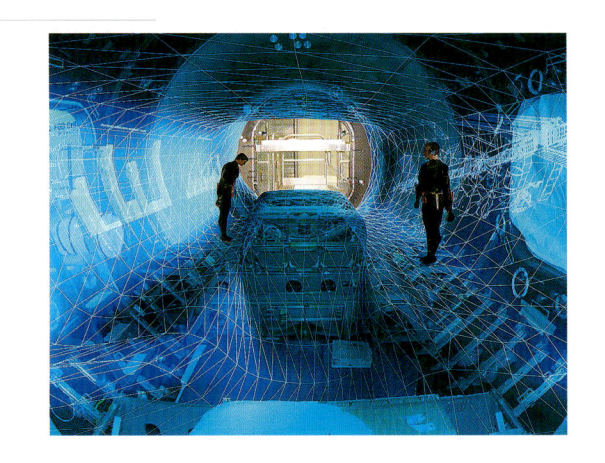

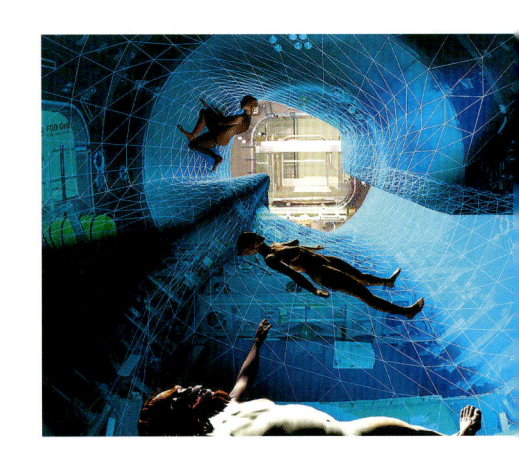

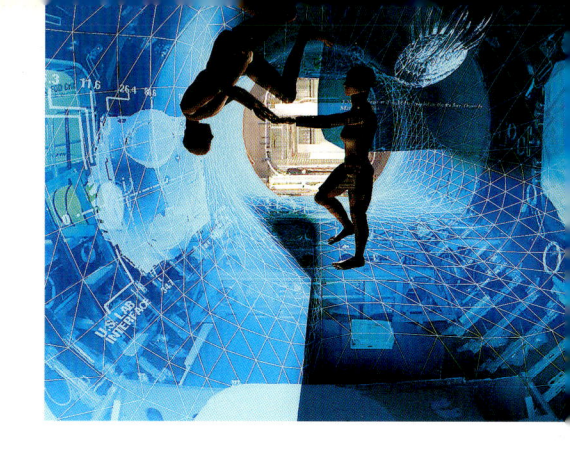

KAS OOSTERHUIS
SPACE STATION MODULE
1998

Here Kas Oosterhuis presents two futuristic projects which, while concepts at the moment, could soon become reality. Both schemes – for a space station and a port – are characterised by their adaptive and communicative skins, made possible by space frames constructed from computer-controlled pneumatic bars.

Active innerskin

For our conceptual exercise, the external shape and function of the Space Station Module are assumed to exist already. This study concentrates exclusively on the interior skin. Though the concept for this active interior skin appears at first sight futuristic and not yet realisable, the contrary is true. All the methods needed to realise it are known; they merely need to be adjusted and targetted to this specific configuration and synthesis of different engineering techniques.

It is possible to imagine (and thus possible to realise) the interior skin as a flexible membrane whose shape can be actively adjusted by the astronauts. A high-resolution spaceframe is inserted in between the inner and outer skins. The individual components of this are cylindrical pneumatic bars and the length of each is adjustable. Each change is calculated in real time by a computer programme, which sends fresh data to the pneumatic cylinders, ordering them to adjust their lengths within seconds. The active data-driven structure works like a bundle of muscles, which contracts and relaxes in reponse to co-ordinated instructions from the brain.

The interior skin is embedded with innumerable LED and LCD panels. The seperate panels work together to form a large overall image or text. The astronauts can build a text-environment or an image-cave according to their needs. This could be an environment in which a group of people could work on a three-dimensional model, or where they could analyse data from scientific experiments, the facts and figures being projected through the LCD panels.

These images, merged into the interior skin, could also represent a leisure-time environment, the skin moulding into the countershape of the desired activity. Real-time images of the family at home, comforting scenes from nature, or projections from webcams displaying panoramic views as seen from the Space Station could be displayed through these virtual windows.

In essence, this concept for an active and adaptive skin offers the astronaut a full communicative environment. Space travellers can communicate both with the scientific staff at the command centre on earth, or with their own private environment at home. The skin adapts to host any conceiveable type of contact, enfolding the wishes of the user.

Active structures

An active structure responds to a programme. It is not a static structure, which is calculated to resist the strongest possible forces. The active structure is a device like a muscle that relaxes when external or internal forces are modest, and tightens when the forces are fierce.

86

KAS OOSTERHUIS
TRANS_PORTS 2001

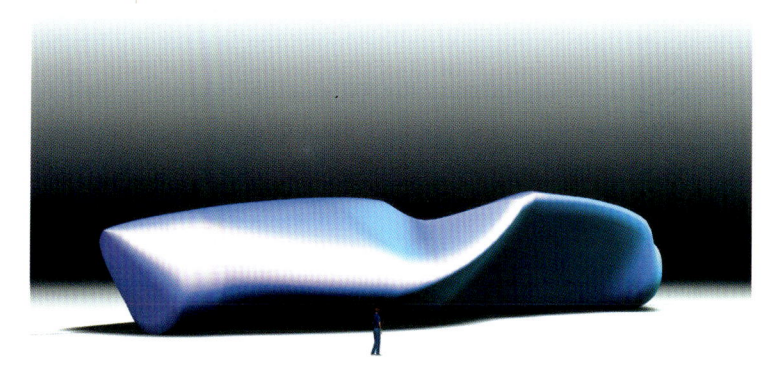

Real-Time Evolution Game
In the trans_PORTs 2001 concept, the external forces come from the Internet. Browsers of the website are the players in the Real-Time Evolution Game; local structures in various major harbours are the performers. These active structures are connected both to each other and to their virtual parent structure through the Internet. Real-time changes to light, sound, configuration and interior atmosphere may be tele-operated through manipulations of the virtual structure at the website.

Virtual Windows
Remote-controlled cameras are placed at crucial points in the harbour and on navigating vessels. These pulse their images on-line to the data-projectors in the interior and exterior of local pavilions. In this way, the pavilions contain a set of virtual windows onto a variety of real-time global maritime activities. Through sensors and LCD panels, the local public can activate the remote cameras and enter websites. The virtual windows shape and fold themselves according to the changes in the physical shape of the pavilions.

Pneumatic Muscles
The pavilions can adjust their shapes both to local circumstances in the associated harbour cities and to data received from the Real-Time Evolution Game. A possibility to achieve this is to build a spaceframe completely composed of adjustable pneumatic bars, working together like the separate filaments in a muscular bundle. All bars are individually controlled by comprehensive structural engineering software. This programme analyses in real time the proposed changes in shape, and caculates in real time the new dimensions of the pneumatic bars.

Flexible Skin
Both the inner skin and the outer skin must follow the changes in physical shape of the pavilion. The waterproof skins must be flexible in two directions at the same time. A new type of membrane must be developed to meet these demands. Primary reasearch focuses on the concept of a three-dimensional moulded rubber sheet. Smaller sheets of rubber would be vulcanised together to form one continuous skin.

Connected cells
The pavilions in the participating harbour cities are connected to each other through the website and through remote cameras. The view seen by a camera inside one of the pavilions is projected inside all the others and is merged in the virtual pavilion on the Internet. The network of physical pavilions in the harbour cities and the virtual pavilion on the internet becomes one big organism with a number of connected cells. In this way, the public experiences the complex of physical and virtual structures as a coherent entity.

88

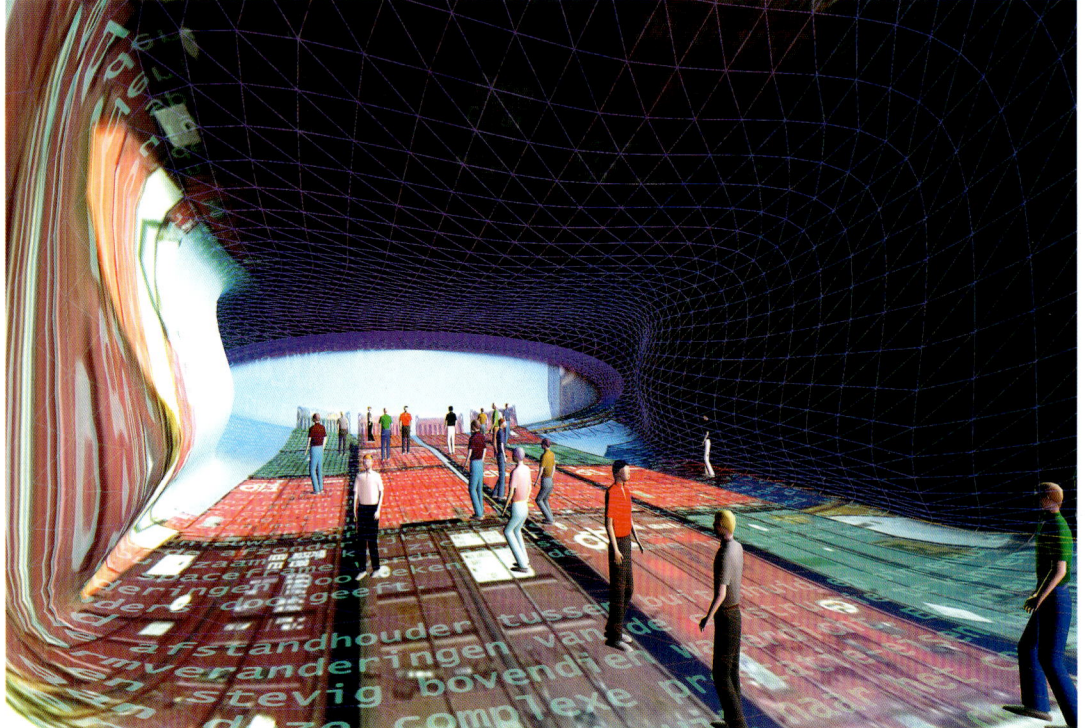

89

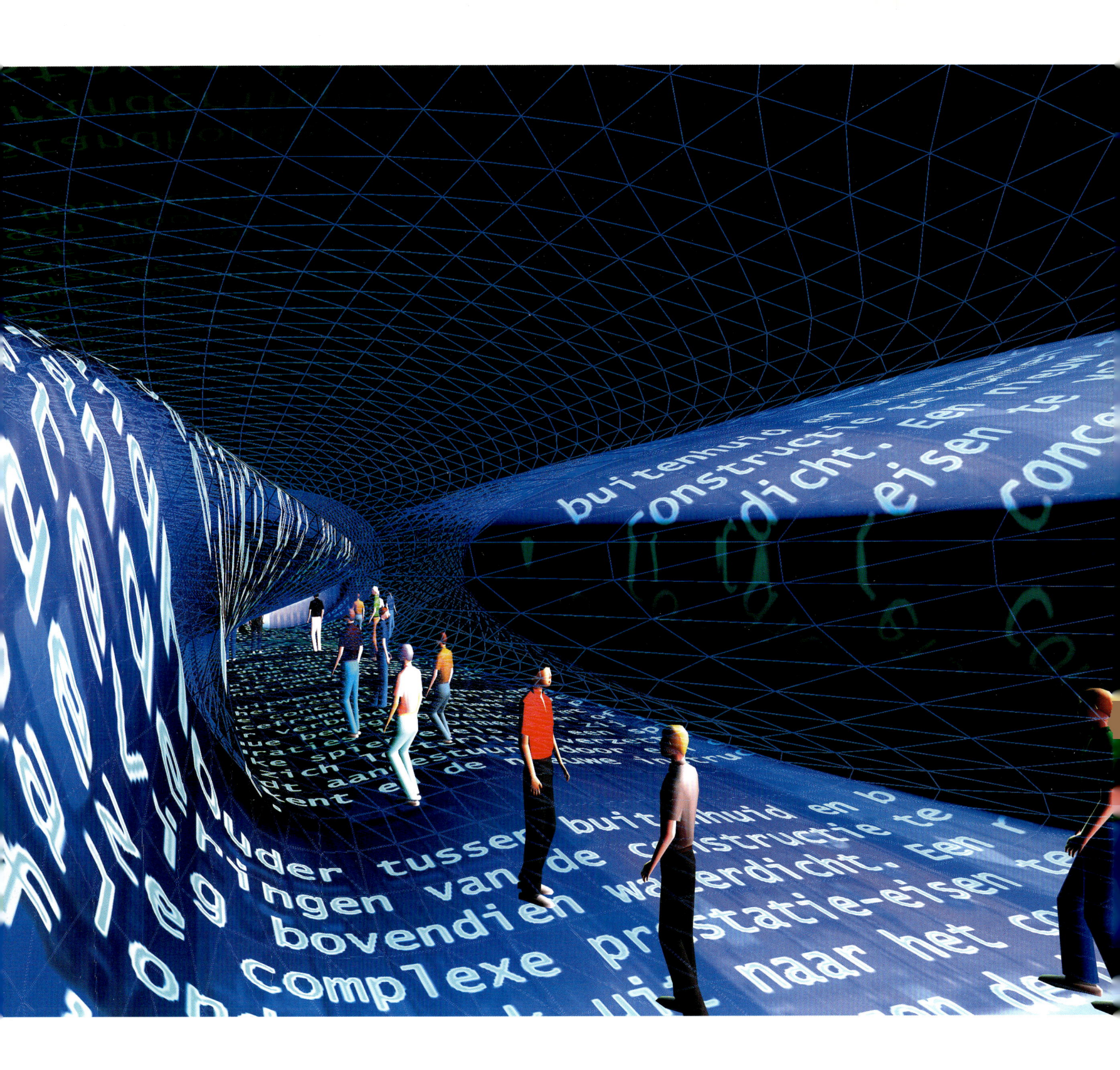

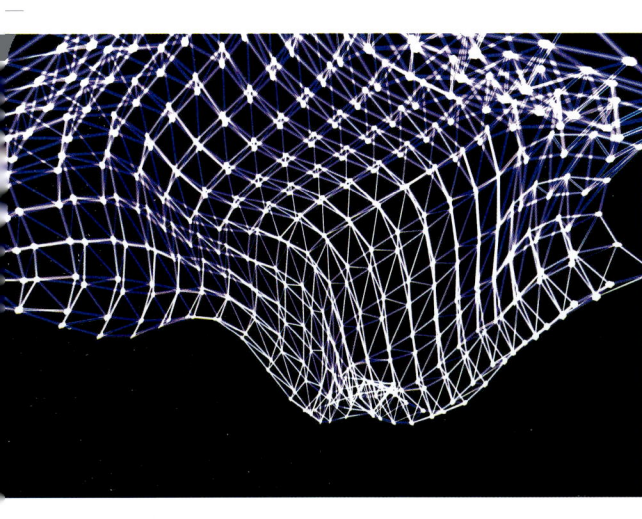

FRANK STELLA

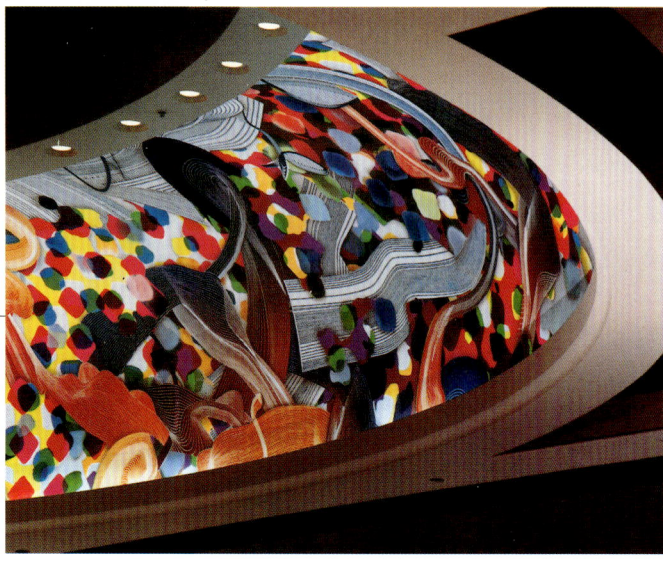

Princess of Wales Theatre Project, *Toronto, Canada, 1992-93*
ABOVE: Outdoor rear wall mural; LEFT: Detail, Dome proscenium mural; RIGHT: Orchestra level mural

All images featured in this photo essay are © ARS, NY and DACS, London 1999. Photos by Steven Sloman.

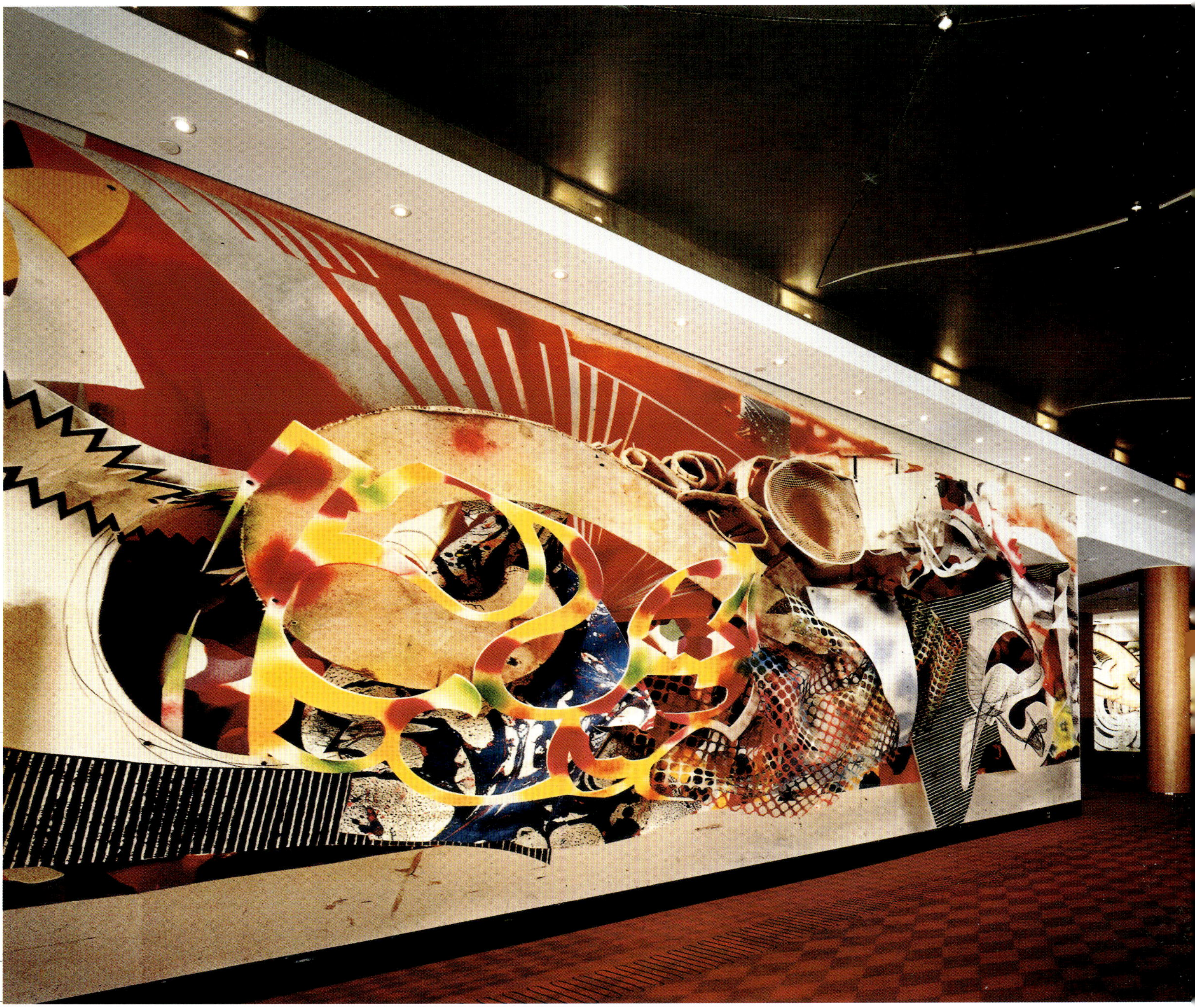

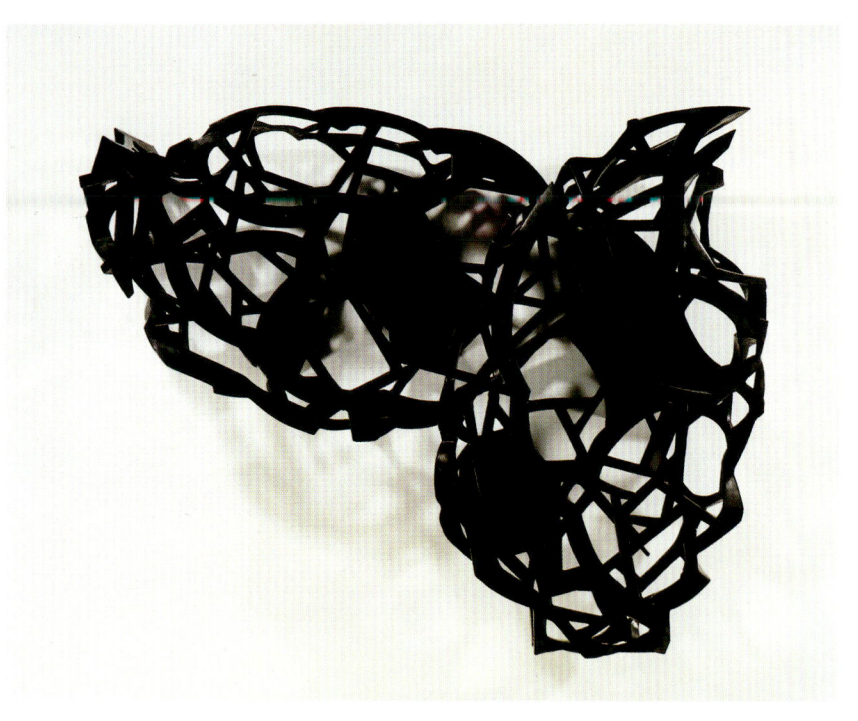

Childress, Cot, Stella, The Leaves, *1993. Structural cage version*

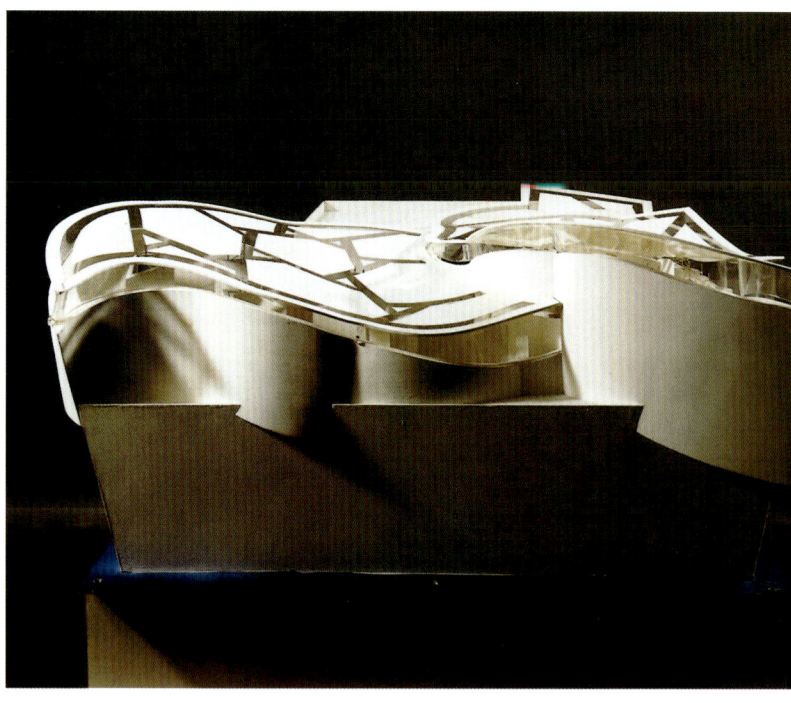

Childress, Stella, The Leaves, *1992 Model, version 2.*
ABOVE: *View 1,* BELOW LEFT: *View 2;* BELOW RIGHT: *View 3.*

92

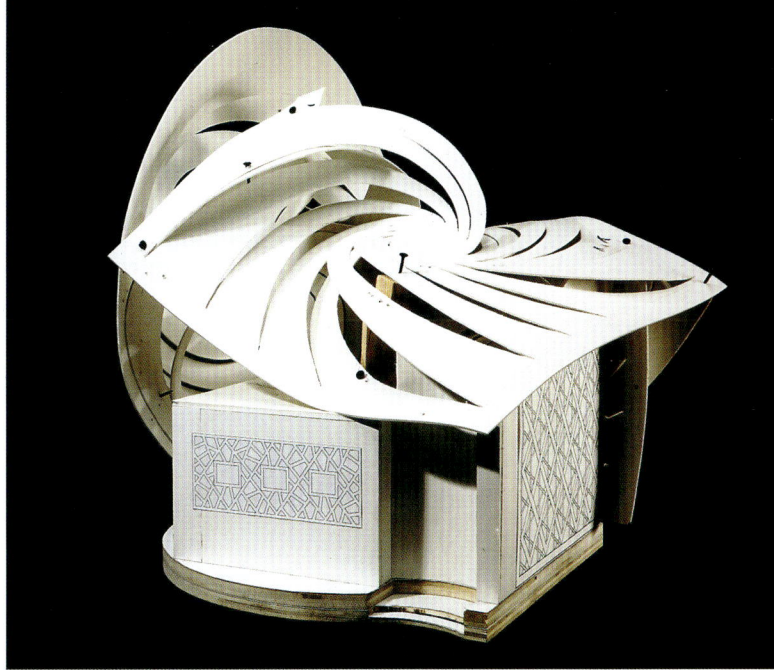

Childress, Stella, The Gate House, *1994. Paper model, views 1 and 4.*

Kunsthalle and Garden, *Dresden, 1992. Stainless steel version of model made by: Arbeitegemeinschaft - Kunsthalle Dresden, Frank Stella, Earl Childress, Robert Kahn & Associates, Nageli & Vallebuona Architekten. View 2.*

BIOGRAPHIES

STEPHEN PERRELLA <haptic@columbia.edu> is an architect and editor at Columbia University School of Architecture, Planning and Preservation. He is the graphic designer and editor of the GSAP's newspaper Newsline and managing editor of Columbia Documents of Architecture and Theory. Since 1991 he has been investigating the relationship between architecture and information. He has taught architecture at various universities in the USA and has lectured internationally. He is also president of Hypersurface Systems, Inc, a design firm created to explore broader architectural interfaces for electronic technology. Website: www.columbia.edu/~sp43/hypersurface.html

REBECCA CARPENTER, who lives in London, received a Master of Architecture from Columbia University GSAP in 1996. She is the recipient of numerous awards from the school including the AIA medal and the Lucille M Lowenfish Memorial Prize.

BRIAN MASSUMI teaches in the English Department of the State University of New York, Albany and is the author of *A User's Guide to Capitalism and Schizophrenia: Deviations from Deleuze and Guattari* and *First and Last Emperors: The Absolute State and the Body of the Despot* (with Kenneth Dean). He is the editor of *The Politics of Everyday Fear*, and co-editor of the University of Minnesota Press book series 'Theory Out of Bounds'. His translations from the French include Gilles Deleuze and Felix Guattari's *A Thousand Plateaus*. His work in progress on sensation, virtuality, and modes of cultural expression is forthcoming from Harvard University Press.

PIA EDNIE BROWN <pia@iii.rmit.edu.au> is a lecturer at the School of Architecture and Design at the Royal Melbourne Institute of Technology (RMIT). She is currently undertaking a doctorate at RMIT jointly through the School of Architecture and Design and the R&D body, the Interactive Information Institute. Her research aims to negotiate the potential for digital technology to assist in implementing the expansion of architectural design processes beyond the privileging of vision.

GIOVANNA BORRADORI is an Ass. Professor of Philosophy at Vassar College. Author of *The American Philosopher* and the editor of *Recoding Metaphysics: the New Italian Philosophy*, she concentrates on Hegel, Nietzsche, Bergsom, Heidegger, French poststructuralism, and the philosophy of architecture.

MARCOS NOVAK <marcos@aud.ucla.edu> is a 'transarchitect', artist, and theorist investigating the emerging tectonics of technologically-augmented space. He is the leading proponent of virtual environments as autonomous and fully architectural spaces and of the Internet as an unprecedented, non-local, transurban, public domain. His work seeks to combine non-Euclidean conceptions of space with aspects of algorithmic emergence and morphogenesis. He lectures worldwide and is Visiting Associate Professor of Architecture at UCLA (CA). Information on Marcos Novak can be found at: www.aud.ucla.edu/~marcos/

BERNARD CACHE conducted strategic studies for companies like Philips, Canal Plus and France Telecom as a senior consultant in image telecommunications and digital television. He has written articles on communication economics and policy in Libération. As an architect, he developed Objectile software and in 1996 he founded the Objectile company, together with Patrick Beaucé and Jean-Louis Jammot. Since September 1998, Bernard Cache is Associate Professor at the Faculty of Architecture, Landscape and Design at the University of Toronto.

DECOI ARCHITECTS, established in 1991 and based in Paris and London, is a design atelier committed to stimulating new developments in architecture. Their work inquires as to the liberating potentials of current technological developments, which extend to new modes of creativity and entirely new working practices. The members of Decoi lecture and teach widely, which gives insight into a rapidly-changing scene, but their central mandate is to operate as an efficient and skillful architectural practice building sophisticated architectural projects.

HARESH LALVANI is a tenured Professor at Pratt Institute's School of Architecture, New York, where he has taught since 1970. He is known for his original contributions in architectural and basic morphology, especially in areas of higher-dimensional, non-periodic and transformational space structures. He is currently working with Milgo-Bufkin, New York, on sheet metal structures using innovative metal-forming techniques.

KAS OOSTERHUIS/NOX studied architecture at the Technical University in Delft. Director of the multidisciplinary practice Oosterhuisassociates where architects, artists and programmers join forces, Kas Osterhuisis is the co-founder of the Attila Foundation (1994) which pursues the electronic fusion of art and architecture. Recent works can be viewed on http://www.oosterhuis.nl

FRANK STELLA's early work addressed the formal aspects of modernism, focusing his attention on a picture's surface and structure. As a sculptor, he had made massive metal objects for Chicago, Luxembourg and Tokyo. As an architect, he had completed extensive scenographic decorations for the princess of Wales Theater in Toronto and designed buildings in Europe for the cities of Groningen and Dresden.

MARK BURRY occupies the Chair of Architecture and Building at Deakin University in Melbourne, Australia. He is a practising architect with an interest in realising 'difficult buildings' without compromising design intent. Since 1979 he has been Consultant Architect to the foundation who commissioned Antoni Gaudí to design the Sagrada Família Church in Barcelona in 1882. Burry's role has included unravelling the mysteries of Gaudï's use of second order geometry (ruled surfaces) for the nave design.

GREG SEIGWORTH teaches cultural theory and media production courses in the Department of Communication and Theatre at Millersville University of Pennsylvania, USA. He is currently co-editing a special issue of the journal Cultural Studies devoted to the work of Deleuze and Guattari.

CHARLIE WATSON currently works as a director of commercials and music videos out of Rhythm and Hues, a production company based in Los Angeles. He has also directed through the production companies Limelight, the End, and RSA for such clients as Coca-Cola, Nike and Budweiser. His body of work also includes documentaries and short subject films. He won a 1999 Clio Award in Film Animation for Mazda "Cool World".

TERRY ROSENBERG <ATRR@aol.com> is an artist whose Generatrix sculpture has concentrated on the scoring and folding of flat surfaces into curved space. The work explores the integration of dimensions through motion, most recently with paintings and drawings related to dance. His work has been exhibited internationally and is included in several museum and private collections.

ARCHITECTURAL DESIGN
SUBSCRIPTION RATES

SIX DOUBLE ISSUES A YEAR

Architectural Design continues to publish a lively and wide-ranging selection of cutting-edge architectural projects. Frequently in the forefront of theoretical developments in the architectural field, *AD* engenders an awareness of philosophy in art and architecture whilst always maintaining a pluralist approach. The treatment of the divergent subjects examined over the years has had a profound impact on architectural debate, making *AD* an invaluable record of architectural thinking, criticism and building.

ARCHITECTURAL DESIGN SUBSCRIPTION RATES

	UK	OUTSIDE UK
Institutional rate	£ 135.00	US$ 225.00
Personal rate	£ 90.00	US$ 145.00
Airmail prices on application		

PRICES REFLECT RATES FOR A 1999 SUBSCRIPTION AND ARE SUBJECT TO CHANGE WITHOUT NOTICE

Back numbers are available. For more information see over.

FORTHCOMING ISSUES

VOL 69 11/12 1999 ....Millennium Architecture
VOL 70 1 2000 .... Architecture & Film II

Brings together the best sacred and secular schemes for the Millennium celebrations.

Recognises film as a major frame of reference for contemporary architecture.

VOL 70 2 2000 ....Space Architecture
VOL 70 3 2000 ....Digital Processes in Architecture

Please complete and return this form with your payment (to be made payable to John Wiley & Sons Ltd) or credit card authority direct to:

OUTSIDE UK Subscriptions (US$)
John Wiley & Sons, Inc
Journals Administration Department
605 Third Avenue
New York, NY 10158, USA
Tel: 212 850 6645; Fax: 212 850 6021
Cable Jonwile; Telex: 12-7463
E-mail: subinfo@jwiley.com

UK Subscriptions (£)
John Wiley & Sons Ltd
Journals Administration Department
1 Oldlands Way, Bognor Regis
West Sussex, PO22 9SA, UK
Tel: 01243 843272; Fax: 01243 843232
E-mail: cs-journals@wiley.co.uk

ACADEMY EDITIONS
A division of John Wiley & Sons
4th Floor, International House, Ealing Broadway Centre, London W5 5DB
Tel: 0181 3263800; Fax: 0181 3263801

ARCHITECTURAL DESIGN

☐ I wish to subscribe to *Architectural Design* at the institutional rate
☐ I wish to subscribe to *Architectural Design* at the personal rate

Starting date: from issue 1/2 1999

.... **Payment enclosed by Cheque/ Money Order/ Drafts**
Value/Currency £/US$..
.... **Please charge** £/US$....................................**to my credit card**

Account no:
Expiry date:

Card: Visa/Amex/Mastercard/Eurocard (*delete as applicable*)

Cardholder's signature..
Cardholder's name..
Address..
....**Post/Zip Code:**......................................

Recipient's name..
Address..
....**Post/Zip Code:**......................................

Please indicate your job title
☐ Architect
☐ Landscape Architect
☐ Architectural Technician/Assistant
☐ Surveyor
☐ Building Services Engineer
☐ Town Planner
☐ Interior Designer
☐ Designer
☐ Building Contractor
☐ Property Developer
☐ Student (*state college/university below*)
☐ Other (*state below*)

Please indicate your organisation
☐ Private practice
☐ Local authority
☐ Public/Government department
☐ Contractor
☐ Industrial/Commercial company
☐ Research establishment
☐ College/University (*state below*)
☐ Other (*state below*)

ARCHITECTURAL DESIGN

☐ I wish to subscribe to *Architectural Design* at the institutional rate
☐ I wish to subscribe to *Architectural Design* at the personal rate

Starting date: from issue 1/2 1999

.... **Payment enclosed by Cheque/ Money Order/ Drafts**
Value/Currency £/US$..
.... **Please charge** £/US$....................................**to my credit card**

Account no:
Expiry date:

Card: Visa/Amex/Mastercard/Eurocard (*delete as applicable*)

Cardholder's signature..
Cardholder's name..
Address..
....**Post/Zip Code:**......................................

Recipient's name..
Address..
....**Post/Zip Code:**......................................

Please indicate your job title
☐ Architect
☐ Landscape Architect
☐ Architectural Technician/Assistant
☐ Surveyor
☐ Building Services Engineer
☐ Town Planner
☐ Interior Designer
☐ Designer
☐ Building Contractor
☐ Property Developer
☐ Student (*state college/university below*)
☐ Other (*state below*)

Please indicate your organisation
☐ Private practice
☐ Local authority
☐ Public/Government department
☐ Contractor
☐ Industrial/Commercial company
☐ Research establishment
☐ College/University (*state below*)
☐ Other (*state below*)

ARCHITECTURAL DESIGN

☐ I wish to subscribe to *Architectural Design* at the institutional rate
☐ I wish to subscribe to *Architectural Design* at the personal rate

Starting date: from issue 1/2 1999

.... **Payment enclosed by Cheque/ Money Order/ Drafts**
Value/Currency £/US$..
.... **Please charge** £/US$....................................**to my credit card**

Account no:
Expiry date:

Card: Visa/Amex/Mastercard/Eurocard (*delete as applicable*)

Cardholder's signature..
Cardholder's name..
Address..
....**Post/Zip Code:**......................................

Recipient's name..
Address..
....**Post/Zip Code:**......................................

Please indicate your job title
☐ Architect
☐ Landscape Architect
☐ Architectural Technician/Assistant
☐ Surveyor
☐ Building Services Engineer
☐ Town Planner
☐ Interior Designer
☐ Designer
☐ Building Contractor
☐ Property Developer
☐ Student (*state college/university below*)
☐ Other (*state below*)

Please indicate your organisation
☐ Private practice
☐ Local authority
☐ Public/Government department
☐ Contractor
☐ Industrial/Commercial company
☐ Research establishment
☐ College/University (*state below*)
☐ Other (*state below*)

BACK NUMBERS

PLEASE CROSS THOSE BACK NUMBERS THAT YOU ARE INTERESTED IN

74	77	81	109	112	117	118	120	123	124	125	126
127	128	129	130	131	132	133	134	135	136	137	138
139											

I am interested in the above marked back numbers. Please quote me a special price for back numbers of this magazine.

Name: _____
Address: _____

Post/Zip code: _____

ACADEMY EDITIONS
A division of John Wiley & Sons
4th Floor, International House, Ealing Broadway Centre, London W5 5DB
Tel: 0181 3263800; Fax: 0181 3263801

PLEASE CROSS THOSE BACK NUMBERS THAT YOU ARE INTERESTED IN

74	77	81	109	112	117	118	120	123	124	125	126
127	128	129	130	131	132	133	134	135	136	137	138
139											

I am interested in the above marked back numbers. Please quote me a special price for back numbers of this magazine.

Name: _____
Address: _____

Post/Zip code: _____

ACADEMY EDITIONS
A division of John Wiley & Sons
4th Floor, International House, Ealing Broadway Centre, London W5 5DB
Tel: 0181 3263800; Fax: 0181 3263801

PLEASE CROSS THOSE BACK NUMBERS THAT YOU ARE INTERESTED IN

74	77	81	109	112	117	118	120	123	124	125	126
127	128	129	130	131	132	133	134	135	136	137	138
139											

I am interested in the above marked back numbers. Please quote me a special price for back numbers of this magazine.

Name: _____
Address: _____

Post/Zip code: _____

ACADEMY EDITIONS
A division of John Wiley & Sons
4th Floor, International House, Ealing Broadway Centre, London W5 5DB
Tel: 0181 3263800; Fax: 0181 3263801

AD 139 MINIMAL ARCHITECTURE
AD 138 SCI-FI ARCHITECTURE
AD 137 DES-RES ARCHITECTURE
AD 136 ARCHITECTS IN CYBERSPACE II
AD 135 EPHEMERAL/PORTABLE ARCHITECTURE
AD 134 THE EVERYDAY AND ARCHITECTURE
AD 133 HYPERSURFACE ARCHITECTURE
AD 132 TRACING ARCHITECTURE
AD 131 CONSUMING ARCHITECTURE
AD 130 CONTEMPORARY MUSEUMS
AD 129 NEW SCIENCE = NEW ARCHITECTURE?
AD 128 FRONTIERS
AD 127 ARCHITECTURE AFTER GEOMETRY
AD 126 LIGHT IN ARCHITECTURE
AD 125 ARCHITECTURE OF ECOLOGY
AD 124 ARCHITECTURE AND ANTHROPOLOGY
AD 123 INTEGRATING ARCHITECTURE
AD 120 COLOUR IN ARCHITECTURE
AD 118 ARCHITECTS IN CYBERSPACE
AD 117 TENSILE STRUCTURES
AD 112 ARCHITECTURE AND FILM
AD 109 ARCHITECTURE OF TRANSPORTATION
AD 81 RECONSTRUCTION/DECONSTRUCTION
AD 77 DECONSTRUCTION II
AD 74 CONTEMPORARY ARCHITECTURE

BEYOND EXPRESSION?

The Relationship Between Architecture and Drama

For many years, the technical difficulties inherent in showing buildings on stage has steered theatre clear of architecture as a subject matter. Two very different productions, however, which are currently touring internationally to great critical acclaim, have reversed that trend. Theatre writer and editor **Howard Watson** looks at how Richard Greenburg's 'Three Days of Rain' and Robert Lepage's 'Geometry of Miracles' have placed architecture at centre stage.

There should be a natural relationship between theatre and architecture. After all, a production often relies on architecture to give it a framework, traditionally setting out the relationship between the action and the audience through a proscenium arch. However, most mainstream theatre practitioners tend to battle against the buildings they use rather than incorporate them into the production. The audience is meant to be sucked into a different world, to believe that it is sitting within an extension of a drawing room, despite its wobbly walls, the chalk markings on the floor and the fact that it is usually several hundred feet away. It is easy to see theatre as a mask of space, and the buildings themselves are at odds with the required illusion.

Not only does theatre struggle to address its surroundings, it also has difficulty in addressing architecture as a subject. There have been countless plays about the work of composers, artists and writers, but it is hard to recall many on architecture and design. Now two plays with the subject of architecture at their core have come along at once, both making a tremendous impact on the international stage.

American writer Richard Greenburg's *Three Days of Rain* has been around for a couple of years, but 1999 will be remembered as the year in which it made its mark. Simultaneous productions in Chicago and London both enjoyed sell-out runs at prestigious theatres, and the London production was so successful it has returned for a four-month run this autumn. In the meantime, Robert Lepage and his company Ex Machina are conducting a massive world tour with *Geometry of Miracles*, which is currently in the United States, having already visited much of Europe.

There are good reasons why theatre shows should steer away from architecture as a subject. It is easy to represent music by playing it, painting by showing it, words by saying them. There are obvious practical difficulties, however, in showing a building on stage. The joy of theatre is that it can make characters seem literally three-dimensional while giving the viewer the ability to control their own perspective of the production. Its drawback is that it can only give one dimension to the inanimate. A camera can take you across the contours of a building and give you some idea of the way its planes shift as you walk around it. There is little point in showing a flat painting of a building, a physical section to scale, or a model, as these devices can provide nothing but a memory of the reality of that building. This trial of logic has led both Greenburg and Lepage, with dramatically different approaches, away from actually attempting to show buildings. Strangely, they both say something rather similar about architecture.

Lepage is the more naturally inclined of the two to give an expressionistic idea of buildings. It is fitting to call his brand of theatre 'the choreography of space', a term that could obviously apply to architecture, while Greenburg is more of a wordsmith. *Three Days of Rain* is wholly a work of fiction: Greenburg's buildings are imaginary and don't necessarily need to be represented in the play. By contrast, Lepage, who is famous for the scale of his ambition, has decided to tell us something dramatic about

Frank Lloyd Wright; *Geometry of Miracles* would be a somewhat impotent theatrical experience if he didn't attempt to show us the buildings.

There are many creative links between Robert Lepage and Frank Lloyd Wright. The theatre works that have earned Lepage respect as one of the greatest directors of the post-war period have a unique quality, born to some degree out of his attempts to demonstrate an otherwise weak national cultural identity as a French Canadian. He also creates connections between apparently disparate things. While Wright could make sense of linking the American prairies and Japanese design, *Geometry of Miracles* thrives on a symmetry between the work of Wright and the Armenian spiritualist and mathematician Georgei Gurdjieff. If anyone's theatre productions can be described as organic, it is those of Lepage. He shares Wright's paradoxical method of working, leaning on technological innovation while emphasising the natural world. His *A Midsummer Night's Dream* for London's National Theatre saw the Athenians careering after each other in a rain-soaked mud bath rather than the anticipated mystical forest. Audience members were made to feel very much part of this chaotic realism as mud and water sprayed across the front rows. Like both Wright and Gurdjieff, Lepage has his own fellowship of followers, now based in his new multi-disciplinary centre, a playground of radical invention in Quebec. His approach is democratic: all his work is co-created with Ex Machina and many of the actors are credited as co-writers. He constantly emphasises that while they are each individual, they work as a collective.

With his fondness for connections, one would have thought that Lepage might have opted to draw on Wright's relationship with his mentor, Louis Sullivan, and their work together on Chicago's Auditorium Theatre. His own interest in the architect began when he was studying in Chicago and became fascinated by Wright's Oak Park projects, which brought about the split with Sullivan. However, *Geometry of Miracles* focuses on the last 30 years of Wright's life, in which he was reborn as a great 20th-century architect, creating the Johnson Wax Administration Building (1936-9), Falling Water (1936) and the Guggenheim Museum (1943). Lepage describes the play as being 'at the intersection of two basic avenues – materialism and spirituality'. He demonstrates that creativity itself lies at this intersection and is born out of the ability to be both conformist and individual. Olgivanna, Wright's third wife, had been a follower of Gurdjieff in Europe and started to influence the Taliesin fellowship with his ideas. The guru believed in a geometrical link between mathematics and dance, and this appealed to Wright: conformity would release the individual spirit. Lepage plays on this and we can see the link between the creation of buildings and the performance of these geometric dances. In truth, not all the members of the Fellowship were as enamoured by the influence of Gurdjieff's teaching; Curtis Besinger, for one, left because of it.

Lepage shied away from showing the buildings that were created during this dynamic period. He is all too aware that back projections could not have created the desired theatrical impression. They would not have conveyed the whirl of the creative process. This refusal to show the actual buildings leads to a series of *coups de théâtre* that show his virtuosity. Wright's drawing board is the central item on the stage throughout most of the production, adapted to form a table, a bed, a car and many other forms, reminding us at all times that creativity is the engine behind most of the events. Early in the play, temptation comes in the form of the Devil who claims that Wright cannot create a three-dimensional image from a single unbroken line. In triumph, Wright draws a spiral. Later, the Devil turns the spiral upside down, and there, miraculously, we have the Guggenheim. (That the Devil had a hand in its design reflects the opinion of the building's early detractors.) Later, a three-dimensional image of the museum is created by a man, a chair and a twirling rope. When Herbert F Johnson comes to dinner to ask Wright to design his new administration building, the Fellowship members push their glasses together and put their plates on top of them. In a matter of seconds, we have a pretty accurate model of the interior of the building. The effect is stunningly theatrical.

Three Days of Rain is a beautifully scripted, far more traditional form of realist theatre, which has little use for dazzling imagery. It is a mind game that relies on the trick of time. The two architectural partners of Walker Janeway, a fictional company whom we are told designed many of the most famous buildings of the last 30 years, have both passed away. Their three grown-up children are in turn a drinker, a confused stammering loner, and an actor who revels in superficial roles. The fact that their fathers were architects holds great dramatic weight: they lack the success and creativity of their fathers. Now, they have to deal with the architects' ultimate legacy, Janeway House. The three believe that Walker was the real inspiration behind the house and this is why Janeway has chosen to leave the house to Walker's son. The house is never shown, but the drawing board takes on huge significance in the second half of the play. The essence of the architects, their success or failure as people, is to be displayed on the drawing board. The creation of the house is essential in the children's understanding of their relationships with each other and their forebears. When the play steps back into the previous generation, we begin to see that everything the children assume to be true is wrong, that the house is a legacy of the previous generation, but not in the way they think.

Legacy also has a huge part to play in *Geometry of Miracles* Wright wishes to be remembered as a 20th-century architect – part of the new America. He also wants the members of his Fellowship to stay true to his ideas: those who do not conform cannot stay. He is disgusted when one of them goes to work for Le Corbusier. He wants his architecture to live on for generations, to establish itself in the buildings of others. The play closes when two of his most disenfranchised followers are left to spread his ashes in the desert. On their journey, they stop off at a nightclub. When they join the whole cast in a dance in which their individual poses start to mirror Gurdjieff's geometric movements, they show an acceptance of Wright's theories.

Both writers have side-stepped the fact that their central theme cannot be expressed in actuality. While Lepage is extremely adept at conveying an idea of the buildings, both writers wisely concentrate on the creation of architecture and its legacy. There is a significant irony in this. In both cases, the design process in some way mirrors the rudiments of theatre: it too is a balancing act between geometry and spirituality. One feels that they are aware of the contrasting, intangible nature of theatre. You see it and then it is gone: the script alone will never tell exactly the same story, and the flats and props aren't enough to set the scene. While theatre has no physical legacy, buildings remain as a testament to creativity. Both writers have managed to capture something essential about the process of architecture and make it theatrical. We are unlikely to see *Mies van der Rohe: The Musical* in the near future, but in the meantime, these two plays demonstrate a rewarding union between architecture and theatre.

The two productions are touring during autumn 1999 and early 2000. Geometry of Miracles *can be seen at the following: Brooklyn Academy of Music, New York (30 November–5 December 1999); Sydney Festival, Sydney (18–29 January 2000); Perth (14–19 February 2000); Adelaide (22–26 February 2000); Hong Kong (29 February–4 March 2000).* Three Days of Rain *will be at the Donmar Warehouse, London (9 November–22 January).*

OPPOSITE AND ABOVE: Robert Lepage and Ex Machina's *Geometry of Miracles* at the Royal National Theatre, London, 1999

100

Organic Ablutions

Like some fantastic snow sculpture, Kevin van Braak's icicle-white bathroom gains its overall visual impact from its highly expressive and exaggerated forms: the washbasin is the receptacle for a massive globular stalactite, and the bath appears like a winter lily straight out of a Georgia O'Keefe painting. When asked about his main influences, Van Braak cites a disparate, yet wholly coherent, lineage of expressionist designers – NOX, MVRDV, Luigi Colani, Ross Lovegrove, Mark Newsom, Eero Saarinen and Antoni Gaudí. (At one sweep, he logically embraces Art Nouveau, decadent late modernism and the curved surfaces of imagined cyberspace.)

Though the stylised mass of its fittings are the bathroom's most distinctive features, they were not the driving force behind the design. Van Braak's main intention for the project was 'to evoke an intense overall experience', and in doing so to create 'a quiet place far away from our hasty society'. It is through the removal of all expected configurations and elements that the experience of using the bathroom is intensified. For this reason, the objects in it appear to be growing out of the floor, the wall and the ceiling. Everything is white and has no corners or seams. Lighting forms a single encircling line, within and flush with the wall. The lack of definition and orientation points, and the overpowering whiteness, all combine to produce a misty, dreamlike atmosphere.

The emphasis on experience gives the bathroom's door a special significance. A slit rubber seal, it symbolically divides the busy reality of the 21st-century world from Van Braak's slow organic space, where time is taken out for ablutions in the purity of a dazzlingly white room.

Bathrooms have tended to remain prosaic territory: a standardised world of glazed and steel fitments. In the 1:1 model for his graduation show, Kevin van Braak, a student of three-dimensional design at the College of Higher Education for the Arts in Arnhem, has exploded sanitised washroom conventions with a highly sensuous and sculptural design.

PRACTICE PROFILE

ABA

Helen Castle takes a look at the London-based firm ABA, headed by Alison Brooks, which after only three years in independent practice has made its mark with the interior of the chic new hotel, Atoll Helgoland, in Germany, and by winning a number of prizes in international competitions.

So often, specialisation or experience in one field brings fresh perceptions to new or wider fields. This is very much the case with Alison Brooks, who until 1996 was a partner at Ron Arad Associates, working on large-scale, often commercial, interiors. While at Arad's, in the early 1990s she experimented with ideas about how form, structure and programme could be malleable, plastic and interchangeable. This resulted in some very successful schemes.

In 1994, she jointly received with Ron Arad the Architectural Record Prize for Interiors for their radically freeform Tel Aviv Opera. Brooks was also the design partner in charge of the extension of the highly popular Belgo Noord in North London, and of the entire Belgo Centraal, a 300-seat restaurant in London's West End. She went on to produce a concept design for the Adidas Sports

TOP: Sketch of Airscape, Europan 5, 1998; LEFT: Alison Brooks; BELOW: Extension to Belgo Noord, Alison Brooks at Ron Arad Associates.

Alison Brooks **resumé**

1981–8 Studied Architecture at the University of Waterloo School of Architecture, Canada and worked in several renowned practices in Toronto, including AJ Diamond & Partners

1989 Moved to London and joined Ron Arad Associates

1991 Partnership in Ron Arad Associates

1993 Exhibited in 'Visions for Vauxhall', Royal Institute of British Architects, London, and 'Continental Drift' organised by the Canada-UK Architecture Group at the RIBA

1994 Received Architectural Record Prize for Interiors of the Tel Aviv Opera jointly with Ron Arad

1996 Founded Alison Brooks Architects in North London

1998 Received second prize for *Daily Mail* Ideal Home Competition, Concept House '99

Selected to participate in the first Architecture Roadshow for urban design exhibited in Hammersmith Town Hall, London

1999 Received third prize for *Building Design*/British Steel Young Architect of the Year

Received joint first prize for Liverpool Rope Walks 'Street Life' Street Furniture Competition

Selected as RIBA Architect Adviser for Hackney Town Hall Square Competition

---

Cafés, the first of which has been built in Toulon, France. Brooks's time with Arad, however, nurtured a desire to branch off. She wanted to develop her own architectural approach and to apply it to a wider variety of projects, addressing social and political issues, particularly housing and urban design.

Brooks's most notable work is her highly coloured and ingenious interior for the Atoll Helgoland (1997-9). This is a hotel built on a German island in the North Sea, and is part of a canny scheme by a Hamburg restaurateur and industrialist to restore Helgoland to its turn-of-the-century status as a luxury health spa. Brook's responsibility for Atoll encompassed its overall concept and the design of all of its 40 rooms, the foyer, bar, bistro, café, restaurant, conference rooms, health club, gym and pool, including details and furniture. By May 1999, the attention already received by the hotel in the international press – it was rumoured that both *Vogue* and *Elle* were planning to make it the site of fashion shoots – suggested that the shrewd gamble its owner had taken had paid off.

Though the hotel does not deal with the sort of urban issues on which Brooks has set her sights, it has proved fertile, in her own words, as a 'testing ground for performing space'. With its various facilities, it has allowed her to work on a public scale in a private space. It has also given her countless opportunities to exercise her innate ingenuity and playfulness. Two huge cones with viewing windows, for instance, pierce the floor of the foyer so that guests can see the swimmers in the pool below. She also took the project as an opportunity to reinvent the vocabulary of the hotel room. The conventional dark entrance and windowless bathroom are subverted – the bathroom has a glass wall and a cylindrical shower. She has also exploded the stereotypical composition of double bed with reading lamps on either side by designing a bed with headboards that light up. Most radically, she has completely eliminated any 'hotel furniture' from the Atoll's rooms by providing seating, a television stand, suitcase rack, chaise longue and multipurpose work surface in a single modular wall unit. Thus, through the use of a 7.5-metre-long carbon-fibre cantilever, she substitutes freestanding pieces with interior architecture.

While working on the hotel, Brooks was also putting together competition entries for housing. The most publicised of these is her prize-winning design for the 1999 Concept House, the *Daily Mail* Ideal Home Competition for a terraced house. Her solution, the FUL (Future Urban Life) House, is a critique of the typical Victorian terrace: it breaks with all the physical and psychological restrictions of the conventional parallel party-wall plan. Her main preoccupation was to satisfy her programme, a 'FUL' scenario, in which the social needs of future city-dwellers were fully accommodated. The scheme is able to house a variety of familial equations – up to five people in three different types of household. This was so much the focus

FROM ABOVE:
Alison Brooks with Ron Arad Associates, Tel Aviv Opera, 1994; Airscape, 1998.

PRACTICE PROFILE

that the curved walls, which emerged as Brooks's signature among the many competing entries, were in fact the last feature to surface in the design.

In Airscape (1998), her Europan 5 scheme for urban design and housing at Haarlemermeer in The Netherlands, she created a more audacious and far-reaching solution. She overcame the limitations of an isolated narrow site, and the high-building density implied by the brief, by suggesting that houses were built on stilts in 'airspace' to free up the ground for an open public park.

It was Brooks's 1998 Urban DNA (diverse neutral accommodation), a competition for the Urban Splash site at Britannia Basin in Manchester, however, that proved her ability to work within the confines of a stringent, low-cost programme.

One of Brooks's greatest strengths is her ability to see the full implications of a scheme within its urban setting. This emerged most strongly in her design for the 1998 Architecture Foundation's Roadshow, in which she expanded the brief from the renovation of a derelict urban square to encompass the broader problem of noise and pollution from an adjacent motorway. The result was Soundscape, a 500-metre-long earthwork forming a double-sided wave that becomes an acoustic barrier between the motorway and the square, making the transformation and rehabilitation of the square possible. The square becomes a transformable park, sculpted into a series of 'negative cones', creating areas for children, and directing sound upwards away from neighbouring houses.

In all her projects, Brooks is intent on pursuing a position between the sensory and the intellectual, the physical and the political. Her enquiring intellect constantly pushes the boundaries of the programme or brief. It is this ability to challenge parameters and conventions in new ways that makes her such a successful competition entrant. Her solution, nevertheless, is always injected with the sensual – an acute awareness of form and colour, which she has transferred from the more conspicuously sensual world of commercial interiors. The further removed she is from this world, the more effective it becomes, as in her winning design for the Liverpool Rope Walks Competition, in which she transforms the ordinary public bench into a wave-like form that seems to beckon weary bodies.

ABA recent works

Atoll Helgoland
Germany, 1999

The name Atoll and the concept of the hotel, devised by Alison Brooks, originated with a manmade atoll, a circular diving platform owned by the Hamburg industrialist who commissioned the scheme. Variations on the atoll's circular form are an insistent theme throughout the interior, as is an abstracted interpretation of a sea world – jellyfish-like forms and floating translucencies recur. Though the hotel building was designed by NPS Architecten Hamburg to comply with rigorous building regulations – the 1960s 'democratic' architecture of Helgoland has been designated a national heritage site – once Brooks's interior design proposals were accepted, NPS invited Brooks to design the entire southeast corner of the hotel in which the bistro is accommodated.

List of Works

1996 Marsham Street Urban Design Competition, London

1997 Beer & Schnapps Glass Design, 'Liquid Gold' for Ritzehhoff, Germany

1997–8 Private Residences, London

1997 Spraytower Harburg; office loft proposal, Hamburg

1997 Atoll Helgoland Hotel Concept for hotel interior, furniture and bistro building in Helgoland, Germany (completed 1999)

1998 Island House, Georgian Bay, Canada

1998 Foundation Roadshow

1998 Britannia Row Studios, warehouse conversion for firm's offices in Islington, London

1998 Concept House '98, prototype terraced housing for future urban life

1998 Europan 5, urban design and housing competition, Harlemermeer, Netherlands

1998 Britannia Basin, urban prototype housing competition, Manchester

1999 Armiga Residence, house and landscape transformation, London

1999 Liverpool Rope Walks 'Street Life' Street Furniture Competition

1999 Private Residence, town house, London

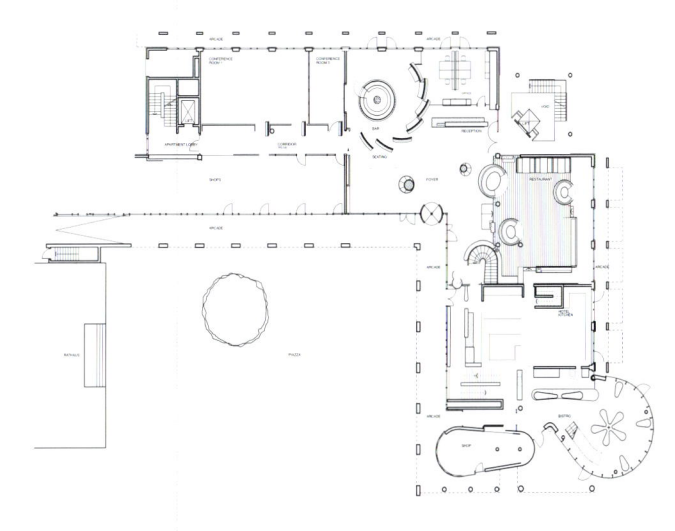

PRACTICE PROFILE

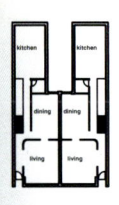

FUL House
Concept House 1999, The *Daily Mail* Ideal Home Competition
By presenting a villa image to the street that is redolent of Ernö Goldfinger's 1930s houses in Willow Road in Hampstead, Brooks aligns herself with a modern tradition of terrace design. She, however, excels her modernist predecessors in her critique of the Victorian terrace both in her loosening of the spatial boundaries – by curving the walls the houses' width is varied from the standard 5 metres to a full 7.5 metres – and in her formation of a flexible, climate-responsive social habitat for a fluctuating family unit.

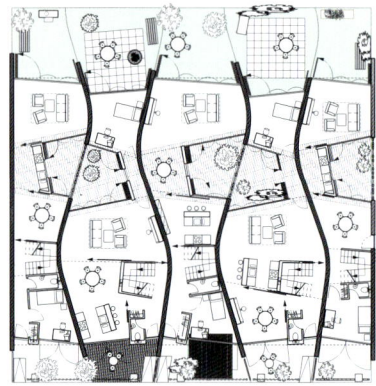

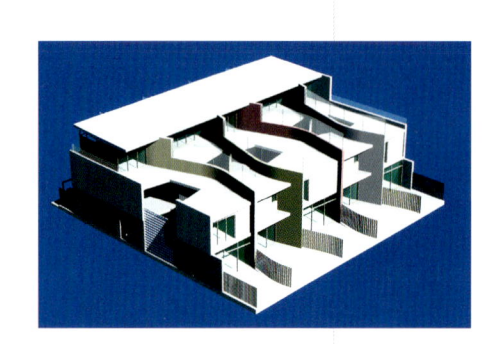

ground floor plan

Urban DNA
Britannia Basin Competition, Manchester, 1999
Like human DNA (here an acronym for diverse neutral accommodation), this housing scheme provides the basic conditions for life but the manner in which it is inhabited is very much up to the individual. Brooks responded to the brief for low-cost living spaces on a brown-field site by proposing two five-storey blocks of 84 units that would allow the greatest flexibility for occupants. The structural system of the buildings would have the potential to allow an owner to occupy an entire floor plate of open-plan space. Most flats are double height in order to accommodate the largest variety of internal arrangements, prefabricated using a mezzanine 'kit'. From the outside, the facades are rearticulated as two-storey strips colourencoded in a field of glazing. Within, partition walls are exposed self-colour block work. Bathroom and kitchen kits aside, there are no internal finishes provided, maximising the occupiers' input and minimising initial building costs.

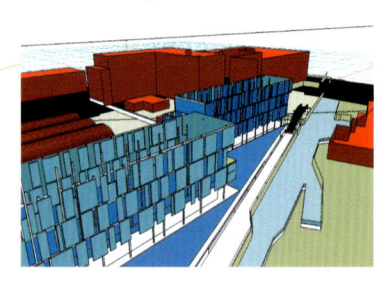

Shaping a Generation

While Paul Rudolph was considered one of America's leading architects and educators for much of his life, he fell from critical favour in the late 1970s. Tony Monk's monograph, published two years after Rudolph's death, seeks to restore him to his rightful place in American architecture.

At the peak of his career, Philip Johnson described Paul Rudolph as 'so off by himself and so successful'; while Serge Chermayeff regarded him as one of the most talented spatial conceptualisers of his generation. By the onset of Postmodernism in the late 1970s, however, Rudolph's practice was suffering from its association with outmoded Late Modernism and its favoured building material, concrete – with all its emerging technical flaws. It was a demise from which Rudolph never fully recovered.

Now, two years after his death, an important new book by Tony Monk, *The Art and Architecture of Paul Rudolph*, re-evaluates Rudolph's work as both teacher and designer. In doing so, it reasserts his place as one of the century's leading architectural educators and as a key figure in the progression of modern American architecture. Here, we look at how Rudolph influenced a whole generation of internationally renowned architects.

When Paul Rudolph was appointed Head of Architecture at Yale in 1958, he was only 39 years old. He had graduated from Harvard's Master class a mere eight years earlier, having spent a period in the Navy during the War. He had also completed a handful of elegant houses in Florida, the Mary Cooper Jewett Arts Center at Wellesley College and the Senior High School at Sarasota. Despite his relative lack of experience, he was to make Yale the leading architecture school in America. For many of his students, such as Lord Norman Foster, whose foreword prefaces Monk's monograph, Rudolph was the main reason to study at Yale. By the early 1960s his reputation for giving ruthless crits and hard work had become legendary. He was reputed to have produced all the designs for his own house, including the production drawings, in a single weekend. At the same time, he had become a revered practising architect. Between 1958 and 1964, he executed perhaps his best known work, the Art and Architecture Building at Yale, which housed his own department. This meant that he was able to offer his students the unique opportunity of working on real projects: Douglas Roberts, a Master's graduate, recounts making drawings in the summer of 1964 for Rudolph's Government Service Center in Boston, Crawford Manor Housing and Tuskegee Institute.

Unlike his own teacher at Harvard, Walter Gropius, who was preoccupied with architectural principles, Rudolph was not interested in theory. He was a pragmatic educator who placed a strong emphasis on graphic studio work. As Robert AM Stern – another Rudolph graduate – states, he had a 'brilliant sense of architectural composition and a passion for formal invention'. This, he taught to his students one-to-one while working at their drawing boards and by submitting their designs to juries of prominent visiting architects.

For it was not only Rudolph's own tutoring that put the Yale School of Architecture on the ascendancy. In his capacity as Head of the School, he attracted renowned architects of many different nationalities who made it the centre of lively architectural debate. He invited many illustrious names, not only to lecture the students, but also to teach them for six weeks or a full term. They included Craig Ellwood, Philip Johnson, Pierre Koenig, Frei Otto, Peter Smithson, James Stirling, Colin St John Wilson and Robert Venturi.

Healy Beach Cottage, Sarasota, Florida, 1948–50

As Jacquelin Robertson states in Mark Girouard's biography of Stirling, who was invited to Yale for two sessions by Rudolph in the 1960s, Rudolph 'brought really interesting visitors into the School, and they came from very very different places. The entire life of the School was twenty-four hours, and it was all about architecture.'

This all-consuming architectural environment was to have a far-reaching and lasting impact on the school's graduates. Those who passed through Yale, in Rudolph's time alone, were to include Allen Cunningham, Eldred Evans, Norman Foster, Su and Richard Rogers, Robert AM Stern and Stanley Tigerman. Monk, also a student at Yale, attributes Rudolph's success to his emphasis on the visual and spatial qualities of design and the issues at hand rather than the expounding of a single theory. He writes: 'Perhaps it was because of this climate of enquiry that so many of the graduates who had been selected to join Rudolph's Masters programme from different cultures around the world, and who brought their own convictions and qualities to the course, have subsequently made significant contributions to modern architecture in their ensuing careers.'

Tony Monk, The Art and Architecture of Paul Rudolph *is published by Wiley-Academy, priced £29.95.*

The Art and Architecture Building at Yale, 1958–64

Private lives, public lives

Miles Glendinning reviews the 1999 Booker nominated novel Our Fathers *by Andrew O'Hagan, which places the broken lives of three generations of Scottish men amidst the drive for the construction, and then destruction, of the tower block. While an effective device for exploring the cycle of life and the boundaries of public and private, Glendinning questions whether the reality of modern mass housing is more one of continuity than rupture.*

It seemed to that [the tower block] had a strangely reflective skin: it stood against the past, like a great finger it had seemed to beckon the future, and yet it was riddled from the start with old troubles ... I always knew I would one day want to write a novel set here.

Andrew O'Hagan

In *Our Fathers*, the tower block forms a medium through which the relatively slow and impersonal forces of change in the built environment are directly related to the more urgent yet rapidly fluctuating personal experiences of individuals, as they build up throughout the successive generations of families. *Our Fathers* is about the relationship, over time, between the 'public' and the 'private'. Of all elements of the present-day built environment, it is in blocks of collective housing that this relationship is most obviously seen at work. Their external monumentality and public dignity, contrasts with modern cultural expectations that the 'homes' they contain will be places of internalised privacy. On the one hand, there are the grand, totalising ideals and ideologies suggested by the public face; on the other, there is the life built up by the people behind, a life made up of emotional, subjective and unstructured forces.

The book focuses on the experience of three Scottish men; the narrator, Jamie Bawn, an expatriate who has taken refuge from his troubled childhood by moving away to England; his once violently tyrannical but now reformed father, Robert; and Jamie's grandfather, Hugh, a former high-rise council housing 'crusader' of the 1960s, now himself living in a decaying tower block and facing corruption investigations. Hugh's terminal illness brings Jamie back to Scotland, and provides the catharsis which forces the grandson to grasp the loose ends in his own past and present, and reach some kind of resolution and reconciliation.

This cyclical story of individual and family struggle, with its suggestions of renewal springing from disillusionment and decline, is powerfully and emotively told in *Our Fathers*. What specifically concerns this review, however, is the relationship between this personal story and the story of the city and its buildings. For this is not a tale which keeps the public and private separate or autonomous. Rather, the drama of the public is systematically used to enhance the story of the private. The novelistic impact of the family vicissitudes is increased by their entanglement with the public story of utopian rise and fall: would Hugh Bawn's decline seem so poignant if it did not coincide with the decay of 'his, multi-storey flats?

In its dramatised confrontations of private and public lives, the book relies heavily on the grand old English/British architectural tradition which, ever since Pugin's *Contrasts*, has discussed urban change in terms of violent clashes between sensationalised formulae, each one claiming to totally reject its predecessor; rejections which, however, usually conceal a high degree of actual continuity. The reaction against Modernist social housing between the late 1960s and the early 1990s was a textbook example of this polemical process. It was accentuated not only by the inherent tension between public and private in collective housing, but by an outside factor: the way in which social housing in Britain, almost uniquely in Western Europe, was directly built by the municipal state and thus became a focus of direct party-political competition and propaganda. The vast majority of public housing, which had been absorbed unobtrusively and unglamorously into the everyday urban environment, was ignored in the denunciations of 'sink estates' and 'terror towers' until the time arrived, in the late 1990s, for a fresh 180-degree turn, towards our present cult of 'chic towers', 'Asian bigness' and 'urban density' In these highly simplified adversarial formulae, there is no room for the individual experiences and diversity of the dwellers themselves, who are assumed to do no more than live out the architectural ideologies, good or bad.

The newly fashionable status of tower blocks in London is not reflected in *Our Fathers*, whose picture of Scottish high flats is still stranded in the Alice Coleman world of broken lifts and smashed windows. And more generally, an adversarial and somewhat theatrical approach has shaped the presentation not just of the blocks, but of the entire external world of the book, which is subtly dramatised in order to provide a suitable counterpart to the private tensions of the Bawn family members. O'Hagan portrays Scottish urban society from the 1950s to the 1990s through the filter of 'Clydesideism'. This is the well-worn literary and journalistic ideology of hard-bitten working-class deprivation and community-in-adversity, which originated in the Depression in books such as *No Mean City*, and reached its height of popularity in the 1980s, when its gritty urban realism was for a time trumpeted as an opposition force to 'English Thatcherism'.

The municipal socialist struggle for mass housing provision, which provides the historical foundation for O'Hagan's theme of failed utopianism, is adjusted and, in some respects, coarsened in *Our Fathers*, to conform to the demands of Clydesideism. This shift is clearest in the central character of Hugh Bawn, which is based on an important historical figure from the era of Scottish mass housing production: David Gibson. Gibson was the convener of Glasgow Corporation's housing committee in the early 1960s and the mastermind of the city's massed building of tower blocks to rehouse its slum-dwellers. In reality, he was a rather complex figure, who drove his 'crusade' through the world of municipal politics not with guile or intimidation but with an ascetic force of conviction stemming from the ethos of secularised

TOP: Ladywell multi-storey housing; BELOW: David Gibson (far right) one of the Housing Committee Delegation visiting Duke Street Prison, 1959. Gibson was the model for Andrew O'Hagan's Hugh Bawn.

Presbyterianism and Sunday-School Socialism. The real Gibson, a quiet, almost monk-like figure who only drank tea and hardly ever even raised his voice, would have been horrified at the bullying loutishness of Hugh Bawn, with his constant swearing, his outbursts of anti-English bigotry and mawkish self-pity, and, of course, his corruption and bribe-taking.

In some ways, *Our Fathers* seems to have put the cart before the horse, by starting from a polemically defined 'dystopia', the 'high-rise slum', and using that as the public peg on which to hang the private lives of the Bawns _ trying to build up 'real lives' around a mirage. Dramatised in this way, the architectural seems neatly to embrace the personal. But what if the everyday reality of modern mass housing was one of continuity rather than rupture, and the built environment issues, even exaggerated ones like the tower block question, made only a limited and unclear impact on private lives? After all, the fundamental drive of 20th-century urban housing in Scotland and Britain – the provision of self-contained dwellings – was carried on almost independently of architectural and political fluctuations, and under conditions of relative stability.

This undramatic continuity in the reality of 20th-century 'dwelling' in Britain is emphasised by comparison with another book of 1999, a work not of fiction but of history, which deals with one of the few significant revolts against the self-contained home, and in a country where the reality of dwelling was frequently one of extreme trauma. Victor Buchli's *An Archaeology of Socialism* (Berg, 1999) is an account of the conception and subsequent vicissitudes of Moisei Ginzburg's pioneering Constructivist Narkomfin Collective House in Moscow (1928-30). Conceived by post-revolutionary reformists as a showcase of Bolshevik communal living and a repudiation of petit-bourgeois self-containment, its principle of 'externalisation' of domestic life was successively rejected under Stalin, reasserted under Khrushchev, and finally broken down under *perestroika* and post-Soviet capitalism - leaving the block itself in a dilapidated and degraded condition. Buchli meticulously correlates the public life of the Narkomfin complex with the ad-hoc attempts of the inhabitants to get on with their personal lives, or even just to survive at all, under these violently fluctuating regimes, and their frighteningly arbitrary irruptions into domestic existence. For example, in a set of plans of the blocks helpfully provided at the end of the book, several of the flats are shaded. These, it transpires, denote communal apartments, shared by several families, which were 'purged' in the 1930s: that is, some households were removed and executed without warning, and replaced by the families of secret police officials.

What 'domestic life' could have meant under those conditions can scarcely be imagined today. By comparison with that overwhelming reality, the 'tower block hell' of Glasgow council housing seems as compelling as an episode from a soap opera. Of course, the Westminster system has traditionally sought to maintain public interest in the consensual and the unremarkable by making them seem contentious and dangerous. But polemic is a very blunt instrument, and easily becomes repetitious and tedious. Perhaps, with the ending of the monolithic political power of the Westminster parliament, the time has also come to put behind us, in Scotland and England, the endless and empty clashing of utopian visions of architecture.

Miles Glendinning is co-author with Stefan Muthesius of *Tower Block*, Yale University Press (London), 1994. He works for the RCAHMS in Edinburgh, specialising in Scottish housing. Andrew O'Hagan's *Our Fathers* is published by Faber and Faber (London) priced £16.99.

REVIEWS

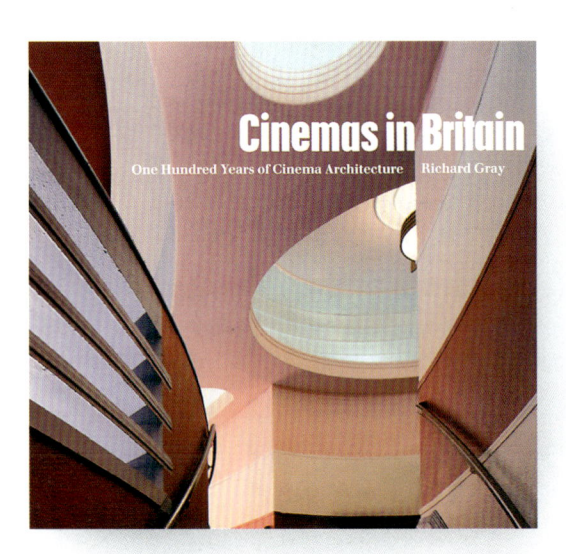

From fairground booth to art house
Edwin Heathcote

Cinemas in Britain: One Hundred Years of Cinema Architecture by Richard Gray, Lund Humphries (London), 1996, 144 pp, b/w photos (11 colour), HB £29.95

Along with garages and airports, the cinema is an invention of the 20th century. Films were first shown as entertainment in fairground booths, but as a market was spotted theatres were equipped to show films. The exuberance and escapism of the fairground was transferred into cinema buildings. Cinemas have, until very recently, been regarded as no more than a disposable buildings; it is only in the last few years, that their importance has begun to be realised as they are recognised for being accurate barometers of popular taste.

Richard Gray's book is a recognition of the increasing importance attached to cinema architecture in Britain. Packed with fascinating and often bizarre cinemas, it demonstrates the fantastic effect the movies must have had on the lives of ordinary people. Today, the attraction of the cinema is little more than the big screen and a big sound. From the 1920s to the 1950s cinemas were dream palaces, fantastic adventures in architecture. It is this lost exoticism which is so striking; sham theatricals make these auditoriums magical palaces. It also, however, accounts for their exclusion from histories of modern architecture by modernists who abhorred them. It was only in 1969 that Dennis Sharp began to address this gap with *The Picture Palace*, and Gray's book eloquently takes off where Sharp left off. Often veering towards train-spotterish detail, it endearingly expresses the author's enthusiasm for the subject. The decision to focus on British cinemas does mean that they are shown in isolation when they owe so much to developments in the USA and Germany. This imbalance is addressed in two short chapters, so that the British buildings are not seen entirely in a vacuum, yet there are a still a lack of European designs. There are also few modern buildings. Though many modern cinemas are characterised by an incompetent and careless commercialism, this does not make them less important. The renewed interest in art-house cinemas and new cinema buildings, also, could herald a renaissance of cinema architecture that the author has omitted. It would, however, be nice to think that people inspired by this book will begin to demand a higher standard from their new cinema buildings, or alternatively, stop the old picture houses being bulldozed.

Edwin Heathcote is a contributor to Architecture and Film II, Architectural Design, January 2000 issue

Begin the Begun
Bob Fear takes a look at two new publications on the market that might make good introductions for the architecturally uninitiated.

Icons of Architecture: The 20th Century, edited by Sabine Thiel-Siling, Prestel (Munich), 1998, 192pp, 307 colour and 215 b/w illustrations, HB £19.95; Architecture: A Crash Course by Hilary French, Simon & Schuster (London), 1998, 144 pp, HB £9.99.

An anniversary or the advent of a new decade invariably sees the market awash with retrospectives desperately trying to be the first to encapsulate the past few years' events and achievements into one easily categorisable soundbite. Any reference to the 20th century on a book cover rapidly sets off my already well-rung millennium alarm bells. It does, however, have the advantage for the architectural novice of neatly packaging whole periods of building history in single volumes. Most keen beginner's appetites would be whetted by either a quick reference pocket guide or some voluminous, chronological journey through the 20th century charting the rise and fall of various movements, placing each architect's work in its social and historical context. The decision to structure *Icons of Architecture: The 20th Century* around individual works or 'icons', however, has tended to isolate single buildings rather than introduce the reader to a wider concept of architecture and its history. At a cover price of just under £20, *Icons of Architecture*, with all its colour illustrations, can be regarded as good value. Yet it is not able to quite deliver all what it has set out to do – to cover the century's major architectural achievements both visually and through brief essays. It is let down by both its style and production.

Architecture: A Crash Course serves as a better essential tool for beginners - by never implying that its intention is beyond its means. It charts different movements chronologically through history. Each decade is characterised by the dominance of a particular architectural style and its leading architects are profiled. This allows the reader to read from cover to cover as a 'brief history of architecture' or as a handy, though not detailed, reference book to be dipped into at will. Certainly if you are hoping to find beautiful, quality photographs of Gaudi's Sagrada Familia or the Chrysler Building then you will be left feeling undernourished. This edition is compiled very much for the unitiated with listings of useful nuggets of information (such as excellent biographical bullet points for each featured architect).

Guiding us through
Ahmet Kaynak

France: Contemporary Art and Architecture Handbook by Sidra Stich, art • SITES (San Francisco), 1999, 284pp, b/w, USA $19.95; Architecture Guide. Spain 1920–2000 with introductory essay by Ignasi de Solà-Morales, edited by Raúl Rispa, Tanais Ediciones (Spain), 1997, 400pp, b/w.

A guide for both architectural enthusiasts and coffee-lovers alike, Art•SITES' France is the inaugural book in a series of geographically based guides published by its author Sidra Stich, an art historian, in San Francisco.

France opens with a useful introduction that gives a brief history of the French and various ways that they commission art and architecture. The guide is structured very much with the foreign tourist in mind and is organised by sections that take the reader on excursions in Paris, day trips from the capital and excursions to the provinces.

Easy to use, each topic is preceded by a map which shows and numbers the buildings/galleries in any given area, with useful transport links and main streets. The entry for each building is accompanied by helpful information, which includes nearby coffee shops and other places of interest, as well as phone numbers and opening hours.

This 'zooming' in guide allows for the fact that you might be in the mood for browsing, and once having chosen your destination, that you might take a few moments to enjoy the surrounding area and its recommended watering holes.

In contrast *Architecture Guide. Spain 1920–2000* is drawn from an inventory of Spanish architectural heritage by the Spanish Directorate of General Housing, Architecture and Urban Planning. The entries have been compiled by a committee of experts, giving it the character of a thorough reference book rather than a friendly informal guide.

It opens with a 'guide to the guide' that sets out the approaches used to compile the 767 buildings, works of art and engineering works listed. The preface is written by Ignasi de Solá-Morales, who poses three ways of interpreting Spanish 20th-century architecture. His main thesis is that Spain has historically been at the periphery of world culture, and thus has been a great absorber and reinterpreter of creative ideas. He shows, however, that since the 70s this tendency or 'asymmetric position has been reversed'. This premise is further supplemented and followed up by a comparative chronology, which lists events in Spain on the right-hand page against events in the rest of the world on the left-hand page. Some of the events listed, such as the death of James Dean, the arrest of Al Capone and the publishing of Lolita, appear curiously incongruous placed against contemporary events in Spain.

The guide is divided into the 18 districts of Spain with each entry appearing under its respective town. Statistics are given with each town's description: geographical size, position, climate, population and GDP. The enormity and all-inclusiveness of the subject matter means that images and descriptions of individual buildings are minimal. The lists of biographical data, works, place names, architects and works make it a useful resource, but also a guide for the anorak rather than the dawdling traveller.

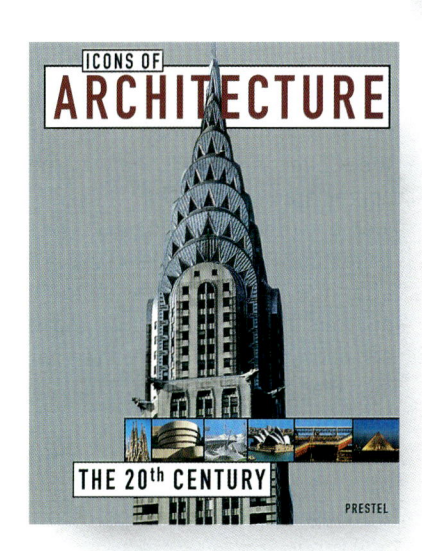

SITE LINES

Circular Thoughts

Yael Padan, an Israeli architect practising in Jerusalem, looks at Zvi Hecker's Spiral Apartment House in Ramat Gan, Israel, designed in collaboration with Shmuel Gruberman, ten years after it was first built.

Viewed for the first time, the Spiral is an astonishing building. From a partly barren hillside emerges a sequence of eight floors, each rotated by 22.5 degrees, creating a succession of stepped terraces surrounding a central void. The building overlooks an urban pattern of streets lined with apartment blocks of about four to six storeys, mostly dating from the 1950s onwards. This cityscape is largely a representation of the Modernist urban vision of orderly utilitarian machines for living, that make the Spiral's uniqueness all the more obvious. Built between 1985 and 1989, the Spiral is a well known and much appreciated building, for which Zvi Hecker was awarded the prestigious Rechter Architectural Prize in January 1999. Ten years after its completion, a revisit to the Spiral still raises questions about the dullness and anonymity of so many apartment buildings that play such an important role in our urban life.

Architecture, wrote Bachelard, opens up different perspectives for a phenomenology of the imagination. The process of experiencing architecture is both conceptual and sensory. Of this process, Frankl wrote, 'once we have reinterpreted the optical image into a conception of space enclosed by mass, we read its from the spatial form. We thus grasp its spiritual import, its content, its meaning.' The Spiral is an object to be explored, as well as an enclosure, a theatrical setting for human activities. Perception of the Spiral occurs in motion, for this architectural promenade is an experience of the moving body. At the building's edge, numerous ring-shaped flights of stairs are linked to the apartments by semi-open corridors and ramps. A walk up or down these flights of stairs, each different in size and shape, gives an insight into the very meaning of The choreography of rotation performed by the body, the changing views of building and city presented by this movement, and the mind's interest in deciphering this promenade's code create a constant dialogue between the enclosed subject and the building. This dialogue is reinforced by the tension between the diversity of intuitive impressions offered by the building and the strict geometric precision of the plan. Hecker here suggests an experimental alternative to the critique of modern architecture, termed 'prosaic construction' by Perez-Gomez. He criticises architecture for being alienated from its symbolic and cultural values in favour of a necessarily rational structure. It has therefore lost its role as one of the fine arts, and became a mere technological process or superficial decoration. The act of reconciliation is defined by Perez-Gomez as a poetic mission involving personal expression on the architect's part, to be interpreted in the realm of intuitive perception. Hecker's Spiral's promenade, which originated in the architect's mind, is invested with meaning by the stroller's feet, permitting space to evoke memories in a process of de-compressing time. For space, in Bachelard's words, contains compressed time: that is what space is for.

The Spiral's exactness and rationality of plan is lost when examining the elevations, which offer a playful world of fantasy and humour, charged with local mythologies and symbols. Beginning with the site, the very act of placing a building on the bare natural hillside rather than in a dense urban grid invokes the notion of pioneering, itself an ethos in Israeli culture. Palm leaves and sabra cactuses, both symbols of locality, have been inserted into the exposed concrete ceilings of the corridors, together with pieces of mirror, stones and pigments. Patterns of irregular stone cladding, often used in Israel as cheap building and paving material, were applied to the external plastered wall, emphasising windows and stairs. Pieces of corrugated metal clad the balconies, suggesting in their directionality the importance of the horizontal aspect within this leaping structure: the individual dwelling, with its semi-open entrance deck, leading into the private personal world.

The building's rough detailing and especially its spiral shape, in theory endless, suggest that it remains 'unfinished', leaving space for its dwellers to form their own daily experiences within it. The application of various materials invested with local connotations of basic shelter create what Vattimo has called 'recognizableness', the use of ornamentation which responds to needs that are symbolic rather than immediate and vital. The resulting structure responds to his two 'primary conditions' of architecture: an enrootedness in a place, and an explicit awareness of multiplicity, which are the conditions of Israeli society. Within this society different communities with diverse cultural traditions have made it clear that there can no longer exist a single privileged point of view. A search for distinctive cultural expression and recognition, as well as for shared values, challenges the dominant narratives of unity and localisation. The Spiral is an effort at projecting an architectural awareness of these conditions, creating an opportunity for Vattimo's notion of indefinite, or poetic, dwelling.

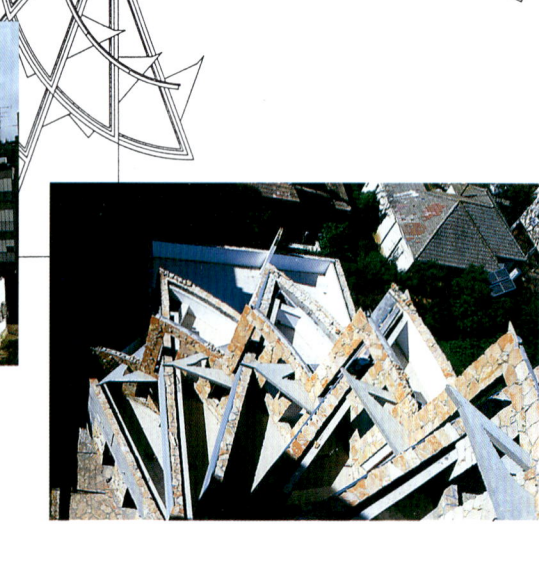